THE CONJURED SPIRIT

Portrait of Swift as a young man, by an unknown artist

THE
CONJURED SPIRIT
SWIFT

A Study in the Relationship of
SWIFT, STELLA, and VANESSA

By

Evelyn Hardy

GREENWOOD PRESS, PUBLISHERS
WESTPORT, CONNECTICUT

The Library of Congress has catalogued this publication as follows:

Library of Congress Cataloging in Publication Data

Hardy, Evelyn, 1902–
   The conjured spirit, Swift.

   Reprint of the 1949 ed.
   Bibliography: p.
   1. Swift, Jonathan, 1667–1745. 2. Vanhomrigh,
Esther, 1690–1723. 3. Johnson, Esther, 1681–1728.
I. Title.
PR3726.H28 1973   828'.5'09 [B]   70-136933
ISBN 0-8371-5405-7

Originally published in 1949
by The Hogarth Press, London

Reprinted with the permission
of Evelyn Hardy

First Greenwood Reprinting 1973

Library of Congress Catalogue Card Number 70-136933

ISBN 0-8371-5405-7

Printed in the United States of America

Contents

ERRATA

Page 7, quote line 3: *Insert* comma after people
                                For command *read* commend
              line 4: *For* or *read* nor
Page 11, line 21: *Delete* had
Page 52, line 2 from bottom: *For* Lucas *read* William (Wil'm)
Page 74, line 19: *Delete* one great, making the generations
   one less
Page 86, line 3: *For* Dunlevin *read* Dunlavin
Page 217, line 4 from bottom: *For* Lady *read* Alyse
             line 3 from bottom: *For* wainscoats *read*
                  wainscots
Page 257, line 20: *For* Lady *read* Alyse
Page 261, second column, line 24: *For* ands *read* and
                    line 4 from bottom: *For* Lady
                    read Alyse
Page 266, second column, line 9: For Lucas read William
   (Wil'm)

                  line 18 from bottom: *For*
                 Winchelsea *read* Winchilsea

List of Plates

Acknowledgments

I wish to thank the following individuals and publishers for their courteous and generous assistance:

Mr. Martin Freeman for allowing me to quote without stint from his edition of the letters of Swift and Vanessa taken from the originals:

Mr. Harold Williams and the Clarendon Press for copious use of the former's edition of *The Journal to Stella*, and *The Poems of Swift*:

Mr. John Hayward and the Nonesuch Press for permission to quote from their edition of the selected prose and verse of Swift:

Dr. David Nichol Smith for letting me use an excerpt from one of Swift's letters to Ford:

Messrs. George Bell and Sons for allowing me to quote extensively from both the *Prose Works of Swift* and Swift's *Correspondence*:

and the following authors and publishers for permission for smaller and less conspicuous quotations:

Professor Mario Rossi and Mr. Joseph Hone; The Clarendon Press, the Oxford University Press, and the University Press; Cambridge; Messrs. Constable, John Murray, George Harrap, George Routledge, George Allen and Unwin, and Ernest Benn:

and finally, the staff of the London Library for their unfailing patience, good humour and courtesy.

With regard to the Portraits, I wish to thank the Board of Governors and Guardians of the National Gallery of Ireland, as well as of St. Patrick's Hospital, Dublin, and Mr. C. Villiers Briscoe, of Bellinter House, for allowing me to make use of the portraits in their possession. I should also like to thank Mr. C. K. Adams of the National Portrait Gallery for his courteous attention, and Dr. Francis Bourke for his kindness in obtaining a negative of the Bellinter Swift.

I am likewise indebted to the Trustees of the British Museum, to the Countess Mountbatten, Sir Shane Leslie and the Directors of both the Oxford University Press and the University of Pennsylvania Press for permission to reproduce facsimiles of the handwritings of Swift, Vanessa, and Stella, made from the originals.

NOTE

The following surnames in the footnotes indicate the following sources, which are fully given in the first use:

Williams: *The Journal to Stella*, edited by Harold Williams, Clarendon Press, 1948.

Freeman: *Vanessa and her Correspondence with Jonathan Swift*, edited by A. Martin Freeman, Selwyn & Blount, 1921.

Temple Scott: *The Prose Works of Jonathan Swift*, 12 Vols.: edited by Temple Scott, George Bell & Sons, 1913.

Ball: *The Correspondence of Jonathan Swift*, 6 Vols.: edited by F. Elrington Ball, George Bell & Sons, 1914.

Scott: *The Works of Jonathan Swift*, 19 Vols.: edited by Sir Walter Scott, London, 1883.

Hayward: *Swift (Gulliver's Travels and Selected Writings in Prose and Verse)*, Nonesuch Press, 1934.

NOTE ON THE PORTRAITS

ALTHOUGH the three people about whom this book is written lived in the eighteenth century, the problems concerning the authenticity of their portraits are so numerous and complicated that they might have been born in the Middle Ages. For a full treatment of the subject readers should consult Sir Frederick Falkiner's essay in the twelfth volume of the *Prose Works* (edited by Temple Scott), and the more recent one of Mr. Mangan in the second volume of the *Journal to Stella* (edited by Harold Williams).

The conclusions reached by the experts seem to be that scarcely any of the portraits of Stella and Vanessa are authentic, since all of their pedigrees are either doubtful or missing. Such was the popularity of the portraits formerly, and such the fame of those depicted, that they were many times copied but often wrongly labelled, the name of Vanessa sometimes being given to a portrait of Stella, and vice versa. I feel personally, without conclusive proof, that the portrait of Stella as a young girl, in the National Gallery of Ireland, is authentic and was probably painted either during the last year of her residence at Moor Park before the death of Sir William Temple, or in the year following, before she crossed over to Ireland, ostensibly under the care of Swift, in 1701. At this time she would still have been in touch with Lady Giffard and possibly sometimes at Court with her. In feeling, the portrait resembles a Lely, and since this artist died in 1680, it is probably by one of his pupils. The portrait of her in later life, at present attributed to Jervas, was formerly considered to be by Hogarth. If it is by the former artist it was probably painted at the same time as the portrait of Swift by the same painter. (See below.) Its simplicity and sincerity make it endearing, and preferable to the harder, more sophisticated and better-known portraits, more frequently reproduced. It has, however, a doubtful pedigree.

The portrait of Vanessa was formerly in the collection of Dr. Leeper and is still on the walls of Swift's Hospital, St.

Patrick's, Dublin. It has been suggested that the painting is of Vanessa's sister, Mary.

The authentic portraits of Swift are, of course, far more numerous. But even with his, confusion creeps in. The portrait of him as a young man probably came from Wood-park, the home of Charles Ford, friend of Swift, Stella, and Vanessa, but the artist is unknown. The features and expression give promise of developing into those of the older man as painted by Jervas, Bindon, and others. I have chosen, secondly, the portrait by Jervas, in the National Gallery of Ireland (rather than the Bodleian Jervas, or the Jervas in the National Portrait Gallery), begun in 1709 and finished to the artist's satisfaction in 1710, when Swift was on the threshold of his most active and famous days. I prefer the Dublin Jervas and if it is indeed the portrait painted for the first Earl of Oxford, it is the one which he himself preferred.

"I hope the picture of me in your house is the same which Mr. Jervas drew in Ireland, and carried over, because it is more like me by several years than another he drew in London."[1]

There are, however, many Jervas portraits and many copies of these, and what became of the one which Swift writes about is not clear. But there is every possibility that this very painting may be that one. If so, it must have been painted in 1716, 1717, or 1721, when Charles Jervas was in his native country.

[1] Letter to the 2nd Earl of Oxford, Aug. 14, 1725, Ball, III. pp. 262-3.

'*A person of great honour in Ireland . . . used to say that my mind was like a conjured spirit that would do mischief if I would not give it employment.*'

SWIFT ON HIMSELF

INTRODUCTORY PASSAGE

IN September, 1710, Jonathan Swift, Doctor of Divinity, then forty-three years of age, climbed the stairs of his London lodgings. Weary with seven days' travelling, two of which had been spent in crossing the Irish sea and five in lurching and swaying on the springless seat of a coach which had borne him from Chester, tired out with visiting his circle of the great—a task which had occupied him immediately on arrival, he mounted gladly to his room and bade his servant Patrick—(that 'dog Patrick', that 'rascal Patrick', that 'booby', 'puppy' and 'extravagant whelp')—lay out his clothes for the night, light some candles, and take himself off to bed.

But what did Patrick's master do? *He* did not go to bed. Restless with the lack of exercise to which he was accustomed, he sat down to write a letter, not to the Lord Treasurer, Sydney, Earl of Godolphin, with whom he had business; not to my Lady Giffard, sister of his former patron, whose animosity it were best to dispel; nor to the Duke of Ormonde, whom he planned to visit; but to a woman, left behind in Ireland, whom he loved as much as he dared love any woman.

With ear half-cocked for the voice of the bellman who will carry his letter for him, he dips his quill in the ink (which Patrick with irritating forgetfulness locks up) and writes line after line—a mixture of cold statements, hot emotional outbursts, business details, gossip, tenderness, and studied reserve.

The political world is in a state of ferment, seething like a great cauldron on the point of boiling:

> "Everything is turning upside down; every Whig in great office will, to a man, be infallibly put out; and we shall have such a winter as hath not been seen in England."[1]

A hint of nostalgia creeps in to the letter, a longing for his

[1]*Journal to Stella*, edited by Harold Williams, Clarendon Press, 1948, p. 7.

Irish orchards, his trout stream and willow-walk, from which
in spirit he has not yet had time to detach himself.

"Everybody asks me, how I came to be so long in Ireland, as naturally as if here were my Being; but no soul
offers to make it so; and I protest I shall return to Dublin,
and the Canal at Laracor, with more satisfaction than I
ever did in my life."[1]

With something of the same vituperative hatred which
made his predecessor Donne exclaim "I perfectly do hate this
town," he affirms, "I protest upon my life, I am heartily
weary of this town, and wish I had never stirred."[2]

But before this there is a strange sentence, ominous mark
of disturbing events, and unhappy inner discord:

"I hope you are now peaceably in Presto's[3] lodgings;
but I resolve to turn you out by Christmas."[4]

Why should Stella be in his lodgings and why, upon his
return, should she be turned out? The determination sprang
from more than convention, and the arrogance of the statement indicates the writer's difficulty in making it.

Assurances follow that he will write something every
day to her,

". . . and make it a sort of journal; and when it is full, I
will send it whether MD[5] writes or no: and so that will be
pretty; and I shall always be in conversation with MD,
and MD with Presto."[6]

He writes at ten o'clock, yet so loath is he to let her go, so
anxious to hold the threads tenuously binding them, that on
the very same night, as he is going to bed, he cannot forbear

[1]Williams, p. 7.
[2]Ibid, p. 16.
[3]His nickname, given him by the Italian Duchess of Shrewsbury
and inserted in the *Journal* by a later editor.
[4]Williams, p. 8.
[5]His monogram for Stella, or Stella and Rebecca Dingley.
[6]Williams, p. 8.

to write another dozen lines with which he opens the *Journal* proper.

And, since he did not cross over and return to her by Christmas, for the best part of three years, day in and day out, this man who began to have a finger in governing the nation, who without position, title or recompense became responsible for its welfare, wrote to his Stella, looked in the windows of the coffee-shops for her answers with a heart beating like any schoolboy's, kept them in his pocket fearing to read them for excess of joy, or premonition of disaster, hid them under the sheets at night, and studied them in the morning.

Such absorption, intentness, devotion and perseverance betoken love, yet of loving phrases there are few. His concern for Stella's welfare is confined to admonitions for her physical health—she must take care of her eyes, even if he must do without her letters; she must exercise, always exercise, for she is "naturally a stout walker, and carries herself firm: methinks I see her strut, and step clever over a kennel;"[1] she must ride her pony, "Little Johnson, who must needs be now in good case,"[2] and exchange him if he is not satisfactory: amuse herself with cards, wine, and evening parties with his clerical friends in Dublin, or Trim.

But of major matters between them there is always an evasion. Her name, in the purposely confusing cypher MD, must always be bracketed with that of Rebecca Dingley, her faithful companion, even in loving phrases—"my dearest lives and delights", "little monkies mine", and "impudent little rogues", except on unguarded occasions when emotion breaks through the artificial net—"Farewell, dearest MD, and love Presto, who loves MD infinitely above all earthly things, and who will." She must never question his truthfulness and sincerity, or expect anything definite as to their relationship: she must furnish abundant understanding, never restrain him, criticize him, or irritate him by looking for a show of open affection. For are not the postal censors always on the watch to slip one up and ruin one's reputation, are there not rogues and gossips on both sides of the Channel

[1] and [2] Williams, pp. 408-9.

anxious to trap a man and disgrace his name and cloth? Yet the fear of discovery went deeper than that, for it was a fear of disclosing the very self, naked and vulnerable to the world.

What sort of woman was Stella to endure such treatment? Was she happy in serving a man so selflessly, with such little hope of reward, her worldly reputation perilously balanced, only maintained in equilibrium by stringent artificial measures and by her own strength and simplicity of character? To wear away the flower of her youth in an alien society (for she was English and had left England under Swift's protection some nine years earlier), to look for nothing other than the fortnightly packets with their scant words of endearment, to enjoy the doubtful honour of occupying his house when he was absent, to slip out unremonstrating when he chose to return, to manage his business affairs in his absence and his domestic duties when he was present, was this sufficient? Did she accept the role willingly, or unwillingly? How did it begin—with open delineation of boundaries and territories, or with heart-breaking, silently tactful adjustment on her part to needs which he could not even express but which he filled with exacting rapacity? How did she contrive to make shift with her portion, to concur uncomplainingly in this unnatural relationship? What charm, what cruelty, had Swift exercised to force her to accept this half-life, which imposed a strain that wasted her health and caused her to lead an equivocal, ambiguous, unfulfilled life?

Having made these sacrifices for the man whom she loved, had she not the right to consider herself the sole object of his affections, tenderness, and intimate concern? If, for an instant, a shadow figure too like her own loomed behind her, disturbing her imagined calm, might she not disregard it, refusing to give it life and power by denying its existence?

If, on the other hand, the figure stubbornly remained, standing silent and portentous like one of the tragic, heavily-draped women of a Piero della Francesca, to which should be granted significance? (Like clouds in an evening sky, does each take radiance, outline, form from the same planet, the one only appearing to exceed the other in beauty by contrast, and in importance by the presence of the other?)

Stella may not answer, for she is dead. Nor could she have done so were she alive: nor might Vanessa. For, caught in a tangle of suffering, of baffling action and reaction, they remained captive, not only to the man they loved (whom neither could wholly understand), but to themselves as well, to their own actions, so incongruously isolated yet united, to their natures, so improvidently granted, and to their early experiences so ignorantly handled. The thread which would have led them from the painful maze was never mercifully put into their hands, and the torments and apprehensions which they endured were the reflections of those lying deep in the soul of the man whom they loved. It is only we in posterity who can attempt to unravel the tangled skein, by sifting the evidence of friends and biographers; by studying the words, actions and writings of the three who were so pitifully interlocked; by interpreting the vision which informed, the compulsion which drove them; but above all, by regarding them with a discerning and compassionate eye free from censure, prejudice, and condemnation.

CHAPTER ONE

*The effect of severity on a child is to produce a low-spirited,
moped creature who, however with his unnatural sobriety he
may please silly people who command tame inactive children
because they make no noise or give them any trouble, yet at
last will probably prove as uncomfortable a thing to his
friends as he will be all his life an useless thing to himself.*

JOHN LOCKE

I

THE central core of a man's life, round which contentment
and fortune or misery and misfortune grow, is his attitude
to himself. His actions, although unconsciously motivated,
will be the complement of this attitude. With patience and
understanding a child may be taught to regard himself as
valuable and certain to prosper; or, through ignorance, mal-
treatment, or neglect, as worthless and doomed to fail.

If early encouragement is meagre or lacking, the child
first and then the man, in order to survive is apt to create
artificial encouragement—a false, inflated view of himself to
balance the feelings of hollowness which his poor conception
causes, and an unreal, phantasy world to counteract the bitterness and disillusion consequent upon a knowledge of the
experienced. Thus, in Shakespeare's *Lear*, Edmund, bastard
son of Gloucester, was made to feel ignominious and shameful
from his birth, a cause of reproach to his parents, and consequently to himself. His life out of desperation took a down-
ward course bristling with revenge: no villainy was too hard
for him, no deception too difficult. He plotted to destroy his
brother, involved himself with Goneril and Regan simultaneously, and finally brought about his own destruction.

Running parallel to his attitude to himself is a man's
interpretation of the influences moulding him. Birth, parent-
age, heredity, environment, the accidents of life even if they
be calamitous, may in themselves be less important than the
manner in which he regards them.

Half a century after Swift's death many children in England, victims of the wretched conditions arising from lack of proper wages and social interest, literally starved. William Huntingdon, the Methodist preacher, records that he was one of eleven children whose father received nine shillings a week in summer and seven or eight in winter. The parish did nothing to help them and, he writes:

". . . we seldom knew what it was to have a bellyful of victuals above once in the week. But it often happened that rent or some other debt had to be discharged, and on such occasions no meat could be procured. These barren Sabbaths were mourning days indeed, but to our sorrow they frequently came. Suffering with hunger, cold, and almost nakedness, so embittered my childhood that I often wished, secretly, that I had been a brute, for then I could have filled my belly in the fields."

Such urgent, animal needs Swift never knew, yet he speaks of his early years with such bitterness, and the effects of them upon him were so marked, that he might well have been one of these starvelings who envied the very cattle. His starvation, which was an emotional one was, however, equally stunting.

For the details of his ancestry and childhood we are indebted to a fragment of his own, less than a dozen printed pages in length, which reveals the particular ancestors, their characteristics, and the incidents of their remote lives, which caught and held his fancy. The Swifts, he tells us, came from Yorkshire, and he is instantly attracted to an ancestor "who passed under the name of Cavaliero Swift", a man of wit and humour, "created an Irish peer by King Charles the First, with the title of Viscount Carlingford, but never was in that kingdom."[1]

From the very start Swift apparently feels impelled to vindicate himself in the eyes of the world by superiority and nobility of ancestry. He mentions two other titled collaterals of vague or doubtful relationship, and is at pains later to give

[1]*Anecdotes of the Family of Swift, The Prose Works of Jonathan Swift,* ed. by Temple Scott, Vol. XI, p. 367 ff. G. Bell & Sons, Ltd., London, 1913.

us the facts that his great-grandmother, the "heiress of one Philpott, I suppose a Yorkshire gentleman," bore arms of her own with which those of her husband's were joined. Notice, too, that in the second sentence of the fragment he states with apparent pride that "Cavaliero" Swift never set foot in Ireland. It was a matter of great importance to him in later life, although he denied it earlier, to assert that he belonged to the "ascendency," that is to that group of English colonists who had gone comparatively recently to Ireland and were not to be confused with the "old English," or worse, with the Irish themselves.

Mistress Swift, the heiress, he records, was

> "capricious, ill-natured and passionate . . . and it has been a continual tradition in the family, that she absolutely disinherited her only son Thomas, for no greater crime than that of robbing an orchard when he was a boy."[1]

His mistrust of emotional women, more especially those who robbed their husbands and sons of their liberty, creeps out in repeating this family legend of his great-grandmother, the only woman, excepting his mother, described in any detail. She had, he alleges, "a good deal of the shrew in her countenance."[2]

Thomas, the disinherited "shrew's" son, became Vicar of Goodrich in Herefordshire, a village on a rounded hill above the Wye. Swift takes an obvious pleasure in recounting the incidents of Thomas's life: he seems to identify himself with this ancestor more than with any other, for his grandfather's story is, he hopes, his own—that of the rejected son who lived his life with courage and dignity despite his early misfortune. Another note is surprising in this essay—the romantic, for Swift was a diehard anti-romantic, whom Scott and Thackeray could not fully understand for that very reason ; several times in these anecdotes he allows himself to relate and admire what can only be called romantic details of the lives of his ancestors.

The Reverend Thomas Swift was a zealous royalist,

[1] and [2] op. cit., p. 369.

"distinguished by his courage, as well as his loyalty to King Charles I, and the sufferings he underwent for that prince, more than any person of his condition in England. Some historians of those times relate several particulars of what he acted, and what hardships he underwent for the person and cause of that martyred prince. He was plundered by the Roundheads six and thirty times, some say above fifty. . . . He engaged his small estate, and gathered all the money he could get, quilted it in his waistcoat, got off to a town held for the King; where, being asked by the Governor, who knew him well, what he could do for His Majesty, Mr. Swift said, he would give the King his coat, and stripping it off, presented it to the Governor; who observing it to be worth little, Mr. Swift said, 'Then take my waistcoat'; and he bid the Governor weigh it in his hand, who, ordering it to be unripped, found it lined with three hundred broad pieces of gold, which as it proved a seasonable relief, must be allowed an extraordinary supply from a private clergyman of a small estate, so often plundered, and soon after turned out of his livings in the church.

"At another time, being informed that three hundred horse of the rebel party intended in a week to pass over a certain river, upon an attempt against the Cavaliers, Mr. Swift having a head mechanically turned, he contrived certain pieces of iron with four spikes, whereof one must always be with the point upward; he placed them over-night in the ford, where he received notice that the rebels would pass early the next morning, which they accordingly did, and lost two hundred of their men, who were drowned or trod to death by the falling of their horses, or torn by the spikes".[1]

Thomas Swift was deprived of both his livings and his estate was sequestered. For a time he was imprisoned in Raglan Castle but ultimately lived to "be restored with the Church and his Majesty." It was a great grief to Swift that he was unable to get possession of some papers of his grandfather's which were held by his friend, Lord Treasurer Oxford, but he took care to return to the church at Goodrich a chalice which had been used by his grandfather and to erect in his memory a tomb which lies to this day beneath the high Altar.

[1]op. cit., pp. 371-2.

He also worked on some memoirs of his grandfather intending to enlarge them, and it is obvious that he regarded him with intense admiration, even though he never saw him.

Out of the fighting parson's family of fourteen children only two need concern us—the eldest, Godwin, and the seventh or eighth son, Jonathan, father of the Dean. Godwin, Swift's uncle, a barrister of Gray's Inn at the time of the Restoration, must have had something extraordinarily attractive about him, for he was married four times, three times to women of fortune. His first wife belonged to the Ormonde family and easily persuaded him to display his legal ability in Ireland, where he was ultimately made Attorney General in the Palatinate of Tipperary, by his wife's kinsman the Duke of Ormonde. By diligence and subtlety and through his circumspect marriages he amassed a fortune and it was natural that his brothers, sons of the plundered Vicar, should hope for preferment from him. Five followed him to Ireland, among them Jonathan, father of the Dean, who says that he was respected for his integrity. He was appointed to the stewardship of the King's Inns, Dublin, and brought over with him the girl he had married, Abigail Erick of Leicestershire.[1] Swift now declares that his mother's family were a "most ancient" one, who derived

> "their lineage from Erick the Forester, a great commander, who raised an army to oppose the invasion of William the Conqueror, by whom he was vanquished, but afterward employed to command that prince's forces: and in his old age retired to his house in Leicestershire, where his family has continued ever since, but declining every age, and are now in the condition of very private gentlemen".

Someone has been at pains to prove that Abigail was the daughter of a butcher in Wigston Magna, Leicester,[2] but his descent may have been as illustrious as Swift makes out, and

[1] Denis Johnston in *The Mysterious Origin of Dean Swift*, Dublin Historical Record, Vol. III, No. 4, states that Jonathan, senior, preceded Godwin Swift to Ireland, and that he married Abigail Erick in Dublin in 1664.

[2] *Trans. of the Leicestershire Archæological Society*, V, 26. Rev. W. J. D. Fletcher.

it is known that the poet Herrick sprang from a branch of the family. What is noteworthy is that Swift, with his love of history and warrior-like characteristics, delighted in believing himself descended from this old man of battle who had defied even the Conqueror, who afterwards entrusted "the Forester" with a command.

Jonathan and Abigail had two children, a daughter and a son, but while the girl was hardly more than an infant and the son barely conceived, Jonathan, the elder, died. This threw Swift's mother into great distress, for as Steward of the King's Inns his father had,

"out of his scanty income, been compelled to advance money for commons, but the members of the Inns now refused to refund it. He had died in debt to the Benchers, and his widow was unable to meet the claim. She owed money to the doctors who had attended him; and to the very undertaker who had buried him. He had been taken from her before she was aware that she was again to become a mother. Every week her distress and embarrassment increased. Her health was wretched, her heart was breaking."[1]

In these circumstances, ameliorated by the kindness of Godwin Swift, seven months later Swift was born, on November 30th, 1667. Writing of this catastrophe which preceded his birth, and writing in the third person as if he did not wish it to be known that he was the author of these notes on himself and his family, Swift says of his father's death:

"his death happening so suddenly before he could make a sufficient establishment for his family, his son (not then born) hath often been heard to say, that he felt the consequences of that marriage not only through the whole course of his education, but during the greatest part of his life."[2]

Therein lies the secret of much of Swift's later unhappiness. He looked upon his parents, more especially his father, as

[1]*Swift, A Biographical and Critical Study*, John Churton Collins, Chatto & Windus, London, 1893, p. 19.
[2]Temple Scott, XI, pp. 375-6.

having unintentionally but lamentably provided him with two
great causes for resentment which he nursed throughout life,
first that he had been born outside England, and secondly, a
posthumous, poor, unwanted child.

> *"Malignant Goddess! bane to my repose,*
> *Thou universal cause of all my woes. . . ."*[1]

he wrote when he was twenty-five in a poem dyed in bitterness,
and although here he was addressing the Goddess of Poesy, it
is a predominant tendency of Swift to regard himself as
especially marked out by fate for persecution.

His infancy brought him fresh grievances, for:

"When he was a year old . . . his nurse, who was a woman
of Whitehaven, being under an absolute necessity of seeing
one of her relations, who was then extremely sick, and from
whom she expected a legacy; and being at the same time
extremely fond of the infant, she stole him on shipboard
unknown to his mother and uncle, and carried him with her
to Whitehaven, where he continued for almost three years.
For, when the matter was discovered, his mother sent
orders by all means not to hazard a second voyage, till he
could be better able to bear it. The nurse was so careful of
him, that before he returned he had learned to spell; and
by the time that he was three years old he could read any
chapter in the Bible."[2]

He was obviously both delicate and precocious. When at
length he was returned to his mother in Ireland she crossed
over to Leicester almost at once (where she lived on an
annuity which her husband had purchased for her of £20
a year), leaving the child behind. An arrangement seems to
have been reached, not recorded by Swift in the *Anecdotes*,
whereby his uncle Godwin became financially responsible for
the boy's care and at six years old he was sent to Kilkenny
Grammar School, sometimes called "the Eton of Ireland."

[1]*Occasioned by Sir William Temple's Late Illness and Recovery*, 1693.
The Poems of Jonathan Swift, ed. Harold Williams. Vol. I, p. 51.
Clarendon Press, 1937.
[2]In his MSS. Swift wrote "two" years old, substituted "almost
three" and then decided finally upon "three." The MSS. is in
the University Library, Dublin. Temple Scott, XI, p. 376.

Thus, before he had been perfectly formed in the womb, Swift had lost his father. At little more than a year he was stolen from his mother. When he was returned to her she appeared to desert him, although her motives, past his childish comprehension, were probably excellent. He had lost, in addition to his father, not only a mother but a foster-mother as well, and changed his country twice before he was six years old. After this, virtually an orphan, dependent upon the grudging charity of relations, he grew up confused, resentful and solitary. If the exterior events of this young life were harsh and unpropitious the shock to the hesitantly unfolding emotional life was even more disastrous. Extremely sensitive, inclined to be anxious and melancholy by nature, Swift felt these early disruptions profoundly. They made him apprehensive, suspicious, fearful of committing himself to female care, ignorant of family life, distrustful of his powerful but wavering emotions and therefore of those of others. The fount of love had been dangerously divided and poisoned for him at its source.

Both his subsequent actions and writings bear witness to an emotional disturbance of a severe character having occurred very early in life. It is not sufficient to give the bare facts without interpretation, and what can be more expressive of a man's innermost nature, than his own writings? There are signs in these that Swift regarded himself, almost from his birth, as a superior extraneous being, almost extra-terrestrial. He did not belong to the land of his birth, hardly to his parents. By so short a margin he might never have been conceived, never have been born. He felt cut off from that natural birth-right to which we are all of us entitled, belief in one's self and in one's proper powers, and in a stable world which will support us reliably. The lack of consistent parental affection made him feel that he had been abandoned to toss like flotsam on disturbed and treacherous waters. He belonged to no one, and no land: dispossessed and washed on to alien shores he fled from the difficulties which life presented, always desiring to be somewhere else, somewhere safer and more remote. This haunting restlessness found its ultimate embodiment in the fabulous other-worlds of *Gulliver*: and seems to show itself in Swift's disinclination to remain long in one place unless compelled to, as well as in his occasional irresolution. He leaves Ireland for England and vice versa, without committing himself permanently to either country; abandoning one and accepting the other when the hatred or neglect of the first throws him into the arms of the second. He alternates between his work in the Church, and politics and political writing, as professional relaxations from the tension. He evades Stella in order to court Vanessa, or binds himself more securely to Stella in order to escape Vanessa, being drawn to both of them in turn.

He was robbed so early and so profoundly of self-esteem that he appears to consider himself isolated and exceptional, and straightway, by every unconscious device, sets about making himself so in order to conform to his conception. He exhibits the peculiarities of a polarized ray of light whose vibrations are so modified that it radiates different properties on different sides. At one end he feels riddled with false humility: the core has been eaten away leaving only the hollow husk: he fears persecution, disparagement, denigration. At the other end he is superior to all mankind, whom he despises for their weaknesses. He is harder, more upright, more singular than the finest amongst them and he can do without the little tendernesses, the revolting intimacies, the ridiculous emotional supports on which they lean; can do without love since he has never known any but a treacherous one, can do without loving, since this is only a base imitation of the other. He is extra-social and can do without family ties and even nationality. Only in hating can he forget himself and he turns this hatred into an active, dynamic, conserving force by which he gains a magnificent sense of both destructive and constructive power, which destroys his enemies and establishes him, Jonathan Swift, or those individuals or institutions which he determines to protect. But the price of this relief is a corrosive self-hatred, which turns inward and works towards his own destruction.

It is the building of a character by sheer force, by a man who felt himself so early wounded and neglected that he will allow nothing further either to wound or overlook him; a pitiable attempt which tends to fossilize one while still alive. It is the genesis of the egoist who buries himself deep beneath a shell, at first malleable, which slowly hardens day by day until nothing or no one can touch him. And in this he is not to be blamed, for it is his only chance of survival: if he does not set about this hardening process, life with its deadly power and persistence, like a gigantic wave, will topple him over and submerge him.

II

At some later period in his life Swift discovered that his birth was not even recorded in the parish registers, a fact which was certain to confirm his feeling of not belonging, of having been neglected, and of being exceptional. Unlike the other children of St. Werburgh's parish, which circled his future cathedral, he had no recognized existence.

The alienation from his true self continued at Kilkenny. Of his eight years at school, of his companions, his holidays, his impressions or reflections on this vital period, Swift has nothing to say. It is as if he wished to forget the whole of his childhood which was too bitter for him to recollect. We know that Congreve, his life-long friend, two years his junior, was his contemporary at school, and that Berkeley, another faithful friend of long standing, succeeded him at Kilkenny. Thus the writer of satire, the author of biting comedies, and the metaphysical philosopher were bound together in a curious triumvirate and Berkeley, through no intention or action of his own, was later placed in a difficult and equivocal relationship with Swift half a century later.

An old prospectus of the school states that the boys were allowed to fish and bathe. They were able to do this without leaving the college precincts, and no doubt while at Kilkenny Swift learned his love of swimming which appears in the *Journal to Stella*. The college had been founded by the Ormondes, leaders of Irish Royalism, whose 12th-century castle looms across the gentle Nore and casts its shadow on the meadows.

Late in the 18th century, travellers remarked that the citizens

of Kilkenny exhibited particularly good manners, said to be a
relic of the great Duke's days. But although his Grace, the
"richest subject of any monarch in Europe," kept a court
more magnificent than modern Viceroys, Kilkenny had been
famous long before his birth. With its 13th-century dove-grey
Cathedral, to which the Vatican had sent a Papal Nuncio, its
ruined mediaeval abbeys, its streets of black-and-white
marble quarried outside the town, its ancient inns with their
high-pitched gables and warm, wainscoted interiors, it had
long been a town of influence in Irish history and the seat of
more than one parliament.

Enthusiastic writers, in search of natural beauty which
might rouse them, remarked on the wildness of the surrounding scenery and admired the line of mountains on the horizon.
Some compared the town to Oxford while deploring the lack
of spires and pinnacles. . . . Others were drawn to it because of
its theatre, its delightful walks along the river, its four great
quarterly fairs at which the favourite blue woollen cloth of the
district was much in evidence. They noticed the troops of
women riding into the town on small horses with milk to sell,
the countrymen walking with their greatcoats thrown over
their shoulders, "spaniard-like," the crowds gathered round
the Tholsel waiting to be hired in the reaping season. Bag-
pipes squeaked in the ale-houses by night, and in the Assembly
Rooms the ladies in their fine linen aprons danced with
gallants, booted and spurred.

These are some of the glimpses we get of Kilkenny when
prosperity, brought about by an increase in the woollen and
linen trades, revived by Swift's later endeavours, had doubled
the population and stirred the town into new-bustling life.[1]
But Swift never speaks of Kilkenny or its lovely surroundings.
Nature had no appeal for him. Already shut in the close
circuit of his numbed spirit, unconsciously intent on self-
defence and self-preservation, he ignored the natural beauty
around him.

A single anecdote remains to us from this period in his life:

[1]See Constantia Maxwell, *Country and Town in Ireland under the
Georges*, pp. 229, 245, 248 and 273. Also Rossi and Hone, *Bishop
Berkeley*, pp. 12-13.

"I remember, when I was a little boy, I felt a great fish at the end of my line which I drew up almost on the ground, but it dropped in, and the disappointment vexes me to this very day, and I believe it was the type of all my future disappointments."[1]

Like the actions and events in a dream-world this episode symbolized for Swift both his ambitions and the tantalizing successes which, time and time again, came within his grasp only to finally elude him.

III

He was barely more than a boy when, as a pensioner, he entered Trinity College, Dublin, in April of 1682, at which, academically speaking, he was a failure.   His own later summary of himself at this period was that he was "a dunce."[2] So distant or unpalatable is the memory of his entire scholastic career to him that he lumps his years at Trinity together with those at Kilkenny—nearly fifteen years in all—into a single paragraph, which ends with a sentence wounding to himself.

"After his return to Ireland, he was sent at six years old to the school at Kilkenny, from whence at fourteen he was admitted into the University of Dublin; a pensioner, where by the ill-treatment of his nearest relations, he was so discouraged and sunk in his spirits, that he too much neglected his academic studies; for some parts of which he had no great relish by nature, and turned himself to reading history and poetry; so that, when the time came for taking his degree of bachelor of Arts, although he had lived with great regularity, and due observance of the statutes, he was stopped of his degree for dullness and insufficiency; and at last hardly admitted in a manner, little to his credit, which is called in that college *speciali gratia*. . . . And this discreditable mark, as I am told, stands upon record in their college registry."[3]

[1]Letter to Bolingbroke and Pope, *The Correspondence of Jonathan Swift*, ed. by F. Elrington Ball, G. Bell & Sons, London, 1914, Vol. IV, pp. 76-7.
[2]Laetitia Pilkington's *Memoirs*, ed. by J. Isaacs, p. 58.
[3]Temple Scott, Vol. XI, pp. 376-7.

The parts of his studies distasteful to him were the
syllogistic forms of argumentation upon which the philosophy
of the day, clinging to the roots of old scholasticism, was
based. Swift, as the country people say when expressing their
deepest dislike, could not 'abide' these stultifying, formal
methods of training the mind, although, owing to his sensitive
and retentive memory, he could repeat the very question which
had been disputed when he was a boy far on in his life. He was
too original and too rebellious a thinker to compress his
interest into such a study and to his death rightly despised
those pedantic logicians with their ridiculous names, Smigle-
cius and Burgersdicius. He was attracted by history and
poetry. But the golden granaries of ancient civilizations were
then locked and neglected as if their wealth, which would have
released his native talents, had never been garnered.

It is interesting to note that Swift received his worst marks
for theology. His college reports show a *bene* for his Greek
and Latin, a *male* for the despised philosophy, and a *negligenter*
for his theology. In those days vocational guidance had never
been heard of: Swift plodded through his studies dutifully
enough, with the exception of his revolt against syllogistic
reasoning, without any notion of what he was going to do, or
might become. The emotional starvation which stunted his
inner growth, hampered his powerful, sharply discerning
intellect, preventing him from making the mark he should. He
was like a hobbled animal, unable to exert himself fully, and
his own diagnosis of the cause of his failure—"that he was
discouraged and sunk in his spirits"—was entirely correct.
His very thoughts were chilled and numbed: he needed loving
and warming.

His comrades at Kilkenny had been sons of the small gentry
and local clergy, of attorneys, yeomen and farmers, whose
names smacked of the "new English," with a sprinkling of the
aristocracy. At Trinity they were very much the same. It
would be interesting to compare the achievements of a group
of graduates from the Irish and English Universities at the
close of the 17th century and see what such a comparison
implies, for Trinity had the reputation of maintaining exceptionally high standards. Swift, at the age of sixty, told a

friend that "The youth of this University are instructed with
a much stricter discipline than either in Oxford or Cambridge,"[1] a fact later corroborated by Goldsmith in his *Life
of Parnell*.

But if the University was noted for its academic superiority
it had,

> "even for the reign of Charles the Second, an unenviable
> notoriety for loose manners, and a government official said
> that the college was more a sepulchre than a nursery, for
> the youth of Ireland."[2]

A lad of Swift's fibre, while noticing the profligacy around
him and possibly being drawn into the experience of it at
times, would probably shrink from it, making himself more
unpopular by his rectitude and lack of general participation.
His relations do not seem to have paid much attention to him,
although he must sometimes have enjoyed himself with his
cousins, for Godwin Swift had eighteen children by his four
marriages and one of these cousins, Willoughby, was more
than kind to Jonathan.

Up till the time of taking his degree Swift was exemplary
in his outward conduct, but the discouragement and slight
upon his already unstable self-respect, caused by the grudging
concession of his degree, which publicity branded him as
having received it through the favour of the University heads,
and not by his own merit, made him break out in reckless
defiance of rules and regulations. If no one cared for him he
would not care what became of himself, nor would he regard
the strictures of the University longer since she had behaved
so badly towards him. One of his chief characteristics was
that he could not bear to be under an obligation to anyone or
anything: he felt throttled by "the favour" of the college as
much as by his uncle's charity. He would revenge himself,
not only by wounding others, but, first and foremost, himself.
He began to "haunt the town and tavern," to "neglect lectures
and chapel," to arouse domestic dissensions, and to despise

---

[1]Letter to Earl of Peterborough, Ball, III, p. 309.
[2]F. Elrington Ball, *Swift's Verse*, pp. 4 and 14. See Ormonde
MSS. Historical MSS. Com. N.S., vi, 421.

and insult the junior dean, whose pardon he was forced to beg in public—a ceremony which must have galled Swift to the bone. If he had failed to be notorious for intellectual brilliance he would make a name for himself by being a rebel. It gave him a sense of power and attracted attention. Mad and violent, like Samuel Johnson in the succeeding century, Jonathan thought to fight his way out of his troubles by literature and wit.

In extenuation of his behaviour one must realize that Swift was only eighteen when his degree was granted him, and that the discipline of the College was extraordinarily strict. No student might leave the college at any time without a written ticket or pass, and then for only two hours at a time. Organized recreation was unknown and it was not until the year before he took his degree that a modest bowling-green was made within the walls, and not until ten years afterwards that a fives court was built. University Statutes forbade the playing of any games within the courts or gardens.[1]

> "The only legitimate reason that a student could allege for visiting the city was to go to service at Christ Church, and yet there the seats reserved for him and his companions were exposed to cold and draught and were so situated that to them the sermon was inaudible. No doubt permission was often given on other pretexts, but the parades of the city, the bull and bear-baiting, the processions round the circuit of the walls, all such distractions were wholly forbidden and punished by severe measures."[2]

These defiances of collegiate law—which he probably considered stupidly narrow, unfitted to a young man of his intellect and character—and these punishments, took place during the two years after he had taken his first degree when he was still attached to and domiciled in the College, preparing to take his Master's degree. For as many as seventy weeks he was under censure. His most serious misdemeanour was in

[1]See Stubbs, *History of the University of Dublin to the end of the 18th Century.* Dublin, 1889. pp. 142-5.
[2]*An Epoch in Irish History, Trinity College, Dublin,* 1591-1600. Dr. John Pentland Mahaffy, Ernest Benn, 1903, pp. 190-1.

helping to compose a scurrilous harangue which marked out some of the principal members of the Trinity Common Room for disrespect. This heroic poem, or tripos, which bears some resemblance to Swift's mature work in its use of doggerel Latin and indecent humour, was delivered by another student who narrowly escaped expulsion. In many of the charges for contumacy and insubordination the name of Swift's cousin, Thomas, occurs to confuse us as to whether all of the charges relate to Jonathan or must be divided between them. But in this case the firebrand is most certainly Jonathan, for his cousin never exhibited any real ability in writing and in

> "reading the *Tripos* we feel under the poor jokes some strong stream of hatred, of uncouth anarchism, which goes deeper than the superficial and pert fun. . . . There is the will and capacity to wound, and above all a directness in the insolence, a mercilessness in the savage laughter. . . ."[1]

Here we have the young man who was to make his name as a writer of dangerous and biting satire tentatively testing himself. He lacked the courage to acknowledge his part in its composition, or to deliver the poem, but he gained, one presumes, immense satisfaction by unloading some of his hatred of the college authorities, in guying individuals—always his method of revenge—and in skating so close to danger.

Meanwhile, to add to the precariousness of his position at the University, his uncle Godwin, upon whom his residence there depended, began to fall ill. His fortunes had dwindled, partly owing to the number of his progeny and partly to the fact that he had been speculating in "iron manufactories." In the following year he fell into a lethargy in which he remained for the five years preceding his death. For these misfortunes Swift appears to have had little, if any, pity. They were causes for increased apprehension, resentment and revilement. When someone asked him in later years if it was true that he was indebted to his uncle Godwin for his education, Swift retorted: "He gave me the education of a dog!"—

[1] *Swift, or The Egoist*, by Rossi & Hone, Victor Gollancz, 1934, p. 58.

"Then," rejoined the intrepid enquirer, "you have not the gratitude of a dog."[1]

He accepted gifts from Godwin's son, Willoughby, with greater alacrity. This cousin, settled in an English factory at Lisbon, sent home to Jonathan a gift which, both in kind and manner of delivery, rivalled those of one of his own fantastically imagined isles. For one day, gazing dejectedly from his college window, reflecting on his penniless state and enforced dependence on the charity of relations, Swift spied a sailor staring about him and looking more lost in academic surroundings than Swift himself would have done cast up on the shores of Coriantia. His imagination, always fertile, instantly drew the cause of the sailor's advent upon himself and, in a wildly felicitous conjecture he dared to think that the man might be looking for *his* bare quarters, that out of all those windows it was *his* towards which the sailor waveringly directed his gaze, that it might be *he*, Jonathan, whom he was seeking. He hailed him, heard him frame the astounding words that he was looking for one with such a name. Quaking with delightful yet fearful anticipation, Swift led the sailor to his room, where he set down the satchel he was carrying, declaring it was full of gold, a gift from his cousin Willoughby. The sailor then completed the fairy-tale episode by refusing to take any share of the gift.[2] Jonathan stuffed his pockets and rushed into the town.

These early years of poverty and dependence showed him that if he wished for independence more than any other state he must learn the art of economy, so that instead of spending his cousin's gift he is said to have hoarded most of it and from that time forward he "became a better economist." This fear of penury, further indication of his insecurity, remained with him throughout life, and we see him in his London lodgings enjoying a fire in his room with almost furtive indulgence, filling in his grate with bricks to narrow the

[1]*Life of Swift*, in *Works of Jonathan Swift*, by Sir Walter Scott, Vol. I, London, 1883, p. 11, footnote. Anecdote based on Delany's *Observations*.

[2]*Essay upon the Life, Writings and Character of Dr. Swift*, by Deane Swift, 1755.

chimney-throat, and picking off the half-burnt coals like any thrifty housewife.[1]

But the most terrifying legacy of these years was the bent which his mind had already taken, which led him further and further from natural affection, the normal outlet for his strong emotions; and branded him with a secret fear so terrible that he dared whisper it to no one, a fear that he, like his good, his despised uncle Godwin, would be cursed with madness.[2] Already, in his own eyes, he was marked out from the more stupid but more healthy members of the flock, and like some wild animal, not savage by nature but forced to become so by the cruel implacability of Fate, must roam the mountain fastnesses, only daring to feed stealthily for fear of coercion and subjection. For to Swift submission was subjection.

Which was it to be, desertion or possession? Which was the greater evil? Should he fly mankind and be none of it, or, drawn by the urgent insistent demands of his warm and sensitive nature, mingle with it, while secretly fearing it?

IV

Swift left Trinity without taking his Master's degree, which would very likely not have been granted him in any case owing to his "frolics." His uncle's financial embarrassments were a secondary cause for his departure, the primary was the national catastrophe—which Swift tersely calls "the troubles" —a name echoed in our own day. James the Second was about to fly from Whitehall, and the revolution of 1688 which threatened to exterminate the English protestants in Ireland was brewing. Some hid themselves in castles and dungeons, some, preferring the hazards of flight to imprisonment and possible massacre, fled to the ports. Among these was the young Swift who fled, out of sheer panic, to the one being and

[1]See the *Journal to Stella*.
[2]Recent investigations suggest that Swift's father may have suffered from a severe nervous breakdown or deteriorated mentally just before his death. This would explain the gibe of his cousin Thomas that madness was a subject with which Swift was acquainted.

the one sanctuary he could envisage, his mother and her cottage in Leicestershire.

At least he would be on English soil, might shake off the dust of that despised country where he had been so wretched. That other, that promised land, was for him always more desirable than the one in which he found himself and this culminating experience taught him, as he thought, to hate and fear the land of his accidental birth more profoundly than ever. Some embarked in packets and larger vessels, others in open boats of doubtful sea-worthiness; many were drowned. No matter, he must attempt the crossing, for the danger behind was greater than that before. For the second time in his life he crossed over to England and made his way on foot southwards to Leicester. He was twenty-one years old.

Abigail Swift was a woman of "easy and contented spirit."[1] What a lovely eulogy!—and what perverse fortune denied this most blessed of all gifts to her only son? It comes from Godwin Swift's grandson, confusingly named Deane Swift, who says that:

> "She was a woman greatly beloved and esteemed by all the family of the Swifts. Her conversation was so exactly polite, cheerful and agreeable, even to the young and sprightly, that some of the family who paid her a visit nearly fifty years ago at Leicester speak of her to this day with the greatest affection. . . . She was of a generous and hospitable nature . . . very exacting in all the duties of religion . . . a very early riser, always dressed for the whole day at about six o'clock in the morning in a mantua and petticoat, which, according to the fashion of those times, she constantly wore. . . . Her chief amusements were needlework and reading."

He adds that "she was equally fond of both of her children, notwithstanding some disagreement that subsisted between them." Jonathan cannot have been the easiest of brothers although years later he aided Jane after her unfortunate marriage with Fenton, a bankrupt currier of Bride Street, Dublin.

[1] Deane Swift, pp. 22-4.

Mrs. Swift cheerfully subsisted on her annuity of twenty pounds augmented by the gifts which her husband's relations, "particularly nephews," showered on her. One would like to hear more of these nephews and to know whether the Lisbon cousin was as generous to her as he had been to Jonathan. These gifts, she said,

> "sufficiently made up for the scantiness of her circumstances, insomuch that she declared in her latter days . . . that she was rich and happy and abounded in everything."[1]

When her son came to her in Leicester he was virtually a stranger. It must have required tact as well as loving-kindness on Abigail's part to adjust herself to this moody, lonely, rebellious young man whom, as far as we know, she had last seen when he was between three and six years old. He remained with her for about seven months, revolving vague plans for the future and amusing himself by philandering with country beauties. His mother became alarmed at his apparent attachment to one, Betty Jones, who eventually married an innkeeper, and to whose daughter Swift was also kind many years later when she was in trouble. Mrs. Swift seems to have feared that he would marry early and impecuniously, and, remembering her own life of constant and precise economy, tried to dissuade him. But she need not have worried. The seeds of aversion which narrowed Jonathan's life, excluding intimacy, happiness and fruition, were already sown.

Three years later he wrote to a friend, who had questioned him about this particular flirtation. (And why is it that so many of Swift's biographers have invented preposterous theories about him, and gone to great pains to prove them, when the simplest and best authority is *Swift on himself*, both consciously and unconsciously revealing his weaknesses and difficulties?) In this letter he distinctly says that he has always suffered from an over-activity of the brain which he eases by writing, and by conversing—"whether it be love, or common conversation, it is all alike." This emphasis on "conversation" in its larger sense is important as we shall see later, when Stella has a suitor, and after her death.

[1]op. cit.

"I shall speak plainly to you," he writes, "that the very ordinary observations I made with going half a mile beyond the University, have taught me experience enough not to think of marriage till I settle my fortune in the world, which I am sure will not be in some years; *and even then myself I am so hard to please that I suppose I shall put it off to the other world.* . . .

"*There is something in me which must be employed, and when I am alone turns all, for want of practice, into speculation and thought*; insomuch that in these seven weeks I have been here, I have writ, and burnt and writ again, upon almost all manner of subjects, more than perhaps any man in England. And this is it which a person of great honour in Ireland (one who was pleased to stoop so low as to look into my mind), used to tell me, that my mind was like a conjured spirit, that would do mischief if I would not give it employment. It is this humour that makes me so busy when I am in company, to turn all that way; and since it commonly end(s) in talk, whether it be love, or common conversation, it is all alike. This is so common, that I could remember twenty women in my life, to whom I behaved myself just the same way; and I profess without any other design than that of entertaining myself when I am very idle, or when something goes amiss in my affairs. This I have always done as a man of the world, when I had no design for any thing grave in it, and what I thought at worst a harmless impertinence. But, whenever I begin to take sober resolutions, or as now, to think of entering into the Church, I never found it would be hard to put off this kind of folly at the porch."[1]

The causes for most young men ruining themselves by early and imprudent marriages, he suggests, are threefold. Being "raw and ignorant" they "believe every silk petticoat hides an angel"; secondly, many, instead of enduring the torments of unfulfilled love, entail a misery on themselves and posterity by an over-acting modesty: thirdly, others, "inclined to frolics have married and rid themselves, out of a maggot."

As for himself, his "own cold temper and unconfined humour" is the greatest "hindrance" to any kind of folly. "Besides that I am naturally temperate, and never engaged in

[1] Letter to Rev. Kendall, Feb. 11, 1691. Ball, I, pp. 3-6 (Italics mine).

the contrary . . . I hope my carriage will be so as my friends need not be ashamed of the name" . . . he adds, declaring that he does not give a fig for "the obloquy of a parcel of very wretched fools," for above all things he values his "own entertainment."[1]

This early letter is the key to the inner chamber of Swift's mind and heart, to his mental and amorous complexities. It is the confession of one who tried to be honest about himself, who knew his disposition and difficulties better than those around him who were inclined to misinterpret and condemn his behaviour; who stated his case frankly, without shame, without appreciation of the fact that there might be anything questionable, thoughtless, or cruel in his treatment of others. It thereby reveals his salient characteristics at a stroke—his sincerity, arrogance, diffidence, and blindness. His search for truth and objectivity was clouded by the more powerful, unrecognized, emotional drive to escape at all costs, and by those deep-seated revulsions which biased his judgment. His arrogance was the counterpart of his feeling of worthlessness rooted in discouragement, and his blindness the hard, defensive, impenetrable shell in which he had encased himself.

It is the letter of an ill man, forced by early anguish and predicament to consider himself first, and only himself. As long as he might relieve the tension of an over-active mind— an absolute necessity if fear, disgust and a stringent moral sense drove him to perpetual celibacy—other actors in the drama remained insignificant: *they did not count.* Mere foils or buffers for his needs, *their* emotions and aspirations might be involved, *their* hearts perplexed, tormented, and abandoned, but Swift was either wholly unaware of it, or incapable of facing himself as so heartless and mean a spirit.

Thus, quite early, his character had set, moulded by the bitter experiences of youth and childhood, so that before leaving the University he prided himself on his knowledge of the ways of the world (as he saw them), and on his wisdom in refraining from submission to them. His determination not to be involved in perpetual penury, while sound and based on an unpleasant intimacy with that state, was partly an excuse for

[1]op. cit., p. 6.

his fear of the loss of liberty which he envisaged if he were to marry; so that when he says "I am so hard to please that I suppose I shall put it off to the other world" he is speaking subtler truth, prophesying his own isolation.

For him, women were no more than an outlet for his cerebral activity: he needed them to assuage the irritability and restlessness of a mind ever ready to turn inward, to vex, and to work against its owner. Denied physical relief he dissipated his disturbing mental energy in this licit but questionable fashion and the game, begun as a conscious diversion, settled into a habit from which he was unable to extricate himself since the unconscious forces at work became too strong for him to control.

Another aspect of Swift's relations with women was his need for their admiration. "I am," he writes many years later, *"a desponder in my nature,"*[1] that is, one who looks darkly on projects, on himself, and humanity in general. If we look more deeply into the word's derivations we find the added meaning "to give up or to resign,"—one's words, one's hopes, one's promises. From this fundamental disbelief in himself he needed to be weaned by encouragement. Swift thought to find it in a false encouragement, in the flattery and admiration which men, but more especially women, gave him, or which he demanded from them. What better way could be found to distract oneself than to experiment with one's power, first on a village girl, who took his intentions seriously, and finally on the highest ladies of the land? His self-esteem was inflated, his vanity gratified, his restlessness appeased, and the sense of tremendous power which he felt lurking within him, undiscovered fully as yet, was tested. But the remedy was superficial and the antidote insufficient to counteract the poison which permeated his system.

A batch of letters from Betty Jones (or another "Eliza"), turned up ten years later and Swift, either out of embarrassment or indifference, bade his friend the Reverend John Winder burn them.[2] Once again, vanity, or a kind of embalmed

[1]*A Proposal for giving Badges to the Beggars in all the Parishes of Dublin*, 1737, Scott, Vol. VII.
[2]Ball, Vol. I, p. 29.

affection which no longer had any vital meaning for him, had made him keep them. He became more discreet as he grew older, for none of Varina's, Stella's, or Vanessa's letters to him have come down to us through his agency. He took care to destroy them all.

But in 1689 his philandering was cut short, since he obtained entrance to the home of Sir William Temple at Sheen, in Surrey. Sir William's father had been on terms of intimacy with Godwin Swift in Dublin, and the affection in which Temple held the Swifts is indicated by his kindness to the younger and less fortunate generation of that family, for not only Jonathan, but Jonathan's sister, Jane, and his cousin, Thomas, became members of Temple's household, the last as Chaplain.

CHAPTER TWO

True fortitude I take to be the quiet possession of a man's
self, and an undisturbed doing his duty, whatever evil besets,
or danger lies in his way. This . . . so few attain to.
Dangers attack us in other places than the field of battle,
and though death be the king of terrors, yet pain, disgrace,
and poverty have frightful looks, able to discompose most
men on whom they seem ready to seize.

JOHN LOCKE

I

LIFE, as Swift had been acquainted with it hitherto in Ireland or Leicestershire, was in sharp contrast with that at Sheen. Where previously he had known poverty, and associated with those of less gifted intellect than his own, now he moved in affluent surroundings and cultured society and was in touch with minds of exceptional quality.

The household at Sheen was large and consisted of many persons in addition to Sir William and Lady Temple, better known to us as Dorothy Osborne, the writer of grave yet lively love letters. There was Sir William's sister, Martha, Lady Giffard, a woman of unusual talents and somewhat domineering temperament. Twenty-six years earlier, a fortnight after her marriage, her husband had died, and since that day she had lived with her brother (to whom she was devoted with more than sisterly affection) and his wife, whose talents rivalled Lady Giffard's and who excelled her in sweetness of nature. There was Sir William's French daughter-in-law, Mistress John Temple, and her two little girls, as well as her mother, old Madame Duplessis Rambouillet. There were their ladies-in-waiting, who were often friends and confidantes, and the children of these ladies, chief amongst these Mrs. Johnson and her daughter, Hester. There was Sir William's chaplain, his agent, servants, and gardeners. To Swift, accustomed to the homelessness of life at Kilkenny or Trinity, or to the solitary companionship of his mother in

her cottage in Leicestershire, the Temple household, with its
multiplicity and ramifications of relationships, occupations and
interests, must have seemed more like a mediaeval village
than a home.

He had, at first, no fixed employment. His chief duty was
to be useful, to read to Sir William and to write his letters.
It was well for him that he had no more exacting work at the
start, for in addition to adjusting himself to the normal temper
of his new surroundings he must also have been affected by the
sorrow which infected the entire household. Two months
before Swift's arrival, John Temple, Sir William's promising
son, his heir and the last of his nine children, had taken his
life. Filling his pockets with stones and sculling out into the
fast-receding, tidal waters below London Bridge he had
lowered himself from a boat, relinquished his hold, and been
carried under. Only a short time before he had been appointed
Secretary of State for War, but the treachery of a confidential
agent whom he had employed and recommended to the King,
unbalanced a mind delicately poised and too sensitive to
stomach the knavery of mankind.

If, as Sir Walter Scott puts it, Sir William's patronage
seemed at first "to be unattended either by confidence or
affection,"[1] is this surprising? Lady Giffard describes her
brother as

> "wounded to the heart by grief . . . till recovered by
> reason, and philosophy, and that perfect resignation to
> Almighty God which he thought was so absolute *a part of
> our duty.*"[2]

Swift ill-resembled his polished and talented son, and months
must pass before Temple might face his loss with equanimity.
Slowly, and with faltering mind, he set himself to study certain metaphysical and moral problems which had concerned
him many years ago, when, as an ardent young man separated
from the girl whom he loved, he had withdrawn into the quiet

[1]Vol. I, p. 22.
[2]*Life and Character of Sir William Temple*—in G. C. Moore Smith's
Early Essays and Romances of Sir William Temple, Clarendon Press,
1930, p. 28.

of his chamber in Paris or Brussels. He revised his early writings.

He considered the fourth Virgilian *Georgic* and the last *Eclogue* which he had translated for his young wife when he had been nothing more than a country squire in Carlow and he had, with all sincerity, identified himself with *Gallus* singing to the Arcadian swains:

> "*Would it had pleased the gods I had been born*
> *Just one of you, and taught to wind a horn,*
> *Or wield a hook, or prune a branching vine*
> *And known no other love but, Phillis, thine. . . .*"

He turned over his imitations of Horace, his early essays and romances; were they worth printing? Slowly, the shocked mind steadied itself. From putting his letters and memoirs into order he advanced to fresh writing; and as the years succeeded, the young man from Ireland, quick to criticize and appreciate, to read and to study—sometimes as much as eight hours a day—assisted the older. The essays on *Gardening*, on *Heroic Virtue*, on *Poetry*, on the *Cure of Gout by the Moxa* were published, and more ambitious works, such as the essay on *Ancient and Modern Learning*, which raised tremendous controversy. The limpid phrases, interspersed with a gallicism caught from the author's intimate knowledge of French, or with native English idiom, flowed more and more freely, and the young Secretary, who "wrote, re-wrote and discarded" work of his own, studied and learned to admire the prose which Chesterfield, Johnson, and Lamb later commended.

But the transition was slow. Temple did not commit his interests at once to Swift, since the latter was unfit to handle them and Swift, cautious and mistrustful, failed to give his heart to Temple. Literary collaboration was necessarily deferred until the old and the young might draw more closely together without constraint, selfconsciousness or effort.

The distance between Sir William and Swift was immeasurable. It lay between them like a river which could neither be forded nor bridged. It seems to have both angered and irked Swift, who could not accept it, for he began by admiring Temple, whose reputation he envied, and then by despising him for his superiority, until the worth of the older man won him over. But the weight of Temple's experience, like broad running waters, was there and must be acknowledged by Swift if he entered the older man's landscape.

When Swift came to him at the age of twenty-two, Sir William was sixty-one years old. Behind him lay a life closepacked with romantic adventure, solitary study, diplomatic mission and confidential trust. Born in London, he had spent his youth at Penshurst, like Sir Philip Sydney, to whom his grandfather had been secretary. Without taking his degree he left Cambridge to travel on the Continent where, by diligent study he acquired an exceptional knowledge of languages. For a time, after his marriage to Dorothy Osborne, whom he never ceased to love from the day that he first caught sight of her courageously taking the blame for an impulsive act of her brother's, he lived with his father, Sir John Temple, Master of the Rolls, in Ireland. In 1660 he sat in the Convention Parliament at Dublin, and in the following year he returned to England as a commissioner from the Irish parliament, eventually attaching himself to the Secretary of State, Lord Arlington. When the disastrous war with the Netherlands began Temple was sent to negotiate with that wily old fox, Van Ghalen, Prince-Bishop of Munster. He became envoy at the Vice-regal court at Brussels, cultivating friendly relations with Spain, and upon Louis XIV marching an army into Flanders and threatening the Spanish Netherlands, Temple got permission to go to Breda, where peace between England and the United Provinces was concluded. In the following year he negotiated the Triple Alliance of England, Holland and Sweden with skill and celerity, and on this negotiation his chief fame rests. His efforts for the rehabilitation of the balance of power in Europe were better appreciated some twenty years later when both time and experience had approved his policy. The Commercial Treaty with the Dutch of 1668 was also Temple's work and when, as Ambassador at the Hague, he remained on good terms with the oligarchic de Witt and the quasi-monarchical Prince of Orange at one and the same time, he gave proof of his extraordinary ability for tactful, yet sincere, diplomacy. The discreditable war with the Netherlands, and the reversal of all that he had worked for, disheartened him and he retired to his estate at Sheen, from which Charles the Second, unwilling to lose so able an arbitrator, recalled him to assist in the drawing up of the Treaty of Westminster. He was offered the embassy to Spain but refused because of his father's declining health, preferring to accept a renewal of the embassy to the Hague. Three time the Secretaryship of State was offered him and three times Temple, unable to pay the fee demanded or unwilling to meddle with faction and intrigue, declined it. In 1679 he advocated and effected a revival of a Privy Council, but when the King broke faith by dismissing Parliament, without the consent of the Council, Temple again retired to Sheen and ceased to be publicly influential.

The marriage arranged through his and Lady Temple's mediation between Princess Mary and William of Orange was another proof of Temple's love of peaceful settlements, and although, after coming to the English throne, William failed to persuade Temple to accept the Chief Secretaryship he continued to consult him constantly and intimately.

For more than a score of years Temple had been personally concerned with international relationships and

"in all that is praiseworthy he had a principal hand. His record as a public servant was blameless, which is the more remarkable since he served the State in an unprincipled age and in circumstances peculiarly open to corruption."[1]

He stands apart from the other political characters of his day by reason of his engaging frankness and his meditative qualities. There is about him, even in retrospect, something aloof and perpending, something magically persuasive, and if Swift is still alive for us by reason of the terrible force which emanates from his very grave, Temple remains attractive because of his philosophical detachment. By his honesty, by his impartiality in religion and politics, by his lack of personal ambition—for he would rather have remained obscure and rustic, cultivating his foreign fruits and improving his lands, writing, translating, enjoying the companionship of his wife

[1] *Dictionary of National Biography*, W. P. Courtney.

and family, from whom he was so often separated—he threaded his way unscathed through the maze of Court and continental intrigue.

II

Slowly, Temple won Swift's heart, but the conquest was partial and temporary because the two men had not the same fundamental values, and because Swift, whose tendency was to reject kindness and interest when it did not bring the particular rewards he sought, later turned against Temple, before finally capitulating.

In 1691-3 Jonathan tried his wings as a poet in a series of hollow and frigid odes after the manner of Cowley, whom he had admired from adolescence. "Cousin, you will never be a poet," declared Dryden, and the verdict cut the young aspirant to the quick. He never forgave his kinsman, pursuing him with invective and satire. Yet the poetic fire which appears to be absent from Swift's verse is in reality latent, yet so repressed that it scarcely dares rear its head.[1] This agrees with his character, for he *had* a streak of the romantic and poetic in him which crept out now and then when it plucked up courage and fancied that no one was there to laugh at it. Perhaps it is best revealed in the *Journal to Stella* in which the lines about Laracor, and the almost verbal endearments to his "impudent little rogue," give it room to breathe.

Two of these early poems are addressed to Temple. In the first, an Ode, upon which he worked over a long period of time (1689-91), he contrasts his merits with those of Sir William:—

> *"Shall I believe a Spirit so divine*
> *Was cast in the same Mould with mine?*
> *Why then does Nature so unjustly share*
> *Among her Elder sons the whole Estate?*
> *And all her Jewels and her Plate.*
> *Poor we, Cadets of Heav'n, not worth her Care,*
> *Take up at best with Lumber and the Leavings of a Fate."*[2]—

[1]See *Life of Swift*, by Sir Henry Craik, Vol. II, 1882, p. 262.
[2]*Ode to Sir William Temple*, 1692. *Poems*, Vol. I, p. 32.

and excuses his apparent impertinence in addressing so august a being as his employer, by explaining that he cannot help but express himself in verse. The praise of Temple is almost fulsome but does not necessarily ring untrue, for in his early days at Sheen and Moor Park Swift felt uneasy and inferior.

The second poem, caused by thoughts arising during a severe illness of Sir William's when the household was once more steeped in sorrow, was written in 1693.[1] In it Swift attempts to describe Lady Temple, whom he praises for her devotion and intellectual gifts. These were always more attractive to Swift than physical charms, since he trusted them more.

> "*Sprung from a better world, and chosen then*
> *The best companion for the best of men;*
> *As some fair pile, yet spar'd by zeal and rage,*
> *Lives pious witness of a better age,*
> *So men may see what once was womankind,*
> *In the fair shrine of Dorothea's mind.*"

Again the lines, although formal and ill-expressed as in the case of those written to Sir William, are indicative of a genuine emotion which moved Swift at this time. Whether he brought these poems as tributes of esteem and affection to Temple or whether he let them come indirectly to him, which is a method more in keeping with his character, does not matter. What is significant is that, for once, this mistrustful, hesitant, repressed young man who had never known a father's loving approval and who had never dared to love, began to be moved belatedly by these primary emotions.

If only we might hear more of Lady Temple, author of those enchanting love-letters to Sir William during the long years of their courtship—letters for the first time in English literature ungilded by a thick lacquer of decorous, ceremonious language in which we eavesdrop on informal, personal matters. Her father, Royalist Sir Peter, Governor of Guernsey, had defended Cornet Castle and defied every attempt to dislodge him with a tenacity and loyalty rivalling that of the

---

[1]*Occasioned by Sir William Temple's late Illness and Recovery*, 1693. *Poems*, Vol. I, p. 52.

Reverend Thomas Swift, which must have endeared him to
Jonathan, who loved a fighting spirit. Her mother, counted as a
wise woman, had warned her as a girl that "she had lived to
see that 'tis impossible to think people worse than they are,
and so will you!" Here was something cynical which Swift
was to echo a century later when he wrote to a friend of the
"ungrateful task of reflecting on the baseness of mankind
which I knew sufficiently before."[1] There was something
inherent in the characters of both Swift and Lady Temple
which was strangely akin. The girl who had been apt to fall
silent in company, sitting dreaming over the fire, listening to
the goose-girls singing on the green, or walking by the
"small river" till she was "lost with thinking," had always
suffered from a tendency towards that lowness of spirits which
Swift dreaded so much—commonly called "the spleen."

Could Swift, nascent master of English satire, be near her
and not appreciate her gift for mockery and sharp wit, and
could she, with her exquisite powers of observation and
criticism, be his hostess and not sense in the awkward, morose,
hypersensitive youth a temperament very like her own? "I
confess that I have a humour that will not suffer me to expose
myself to others' scorn," she had written to Temple. Sensitive, moody, taciturn, she dreaded mocking eyes and tongues,
the censure of a world which she silently ridiculed. Only her
sense of humour saved her—a long, dull sermon set her
inwardly shaking; the pomposity of a suitor (and she had
many, including a son of the Protector, and her cousin the
future Earl of Denby), nearly made her laugh in his face;
ceremony, display, or the pride of people in their birth, seemed
to her nonsensical. She even mocked her lover, whom her
brother labelled "the proudest, most imperious, insulting,
ill-natured man that ever was."

Furthermore, she had suffered from an inveterate dislike
of marriage. Sir William's courtship had been forced to
survive the meddlesome interference of her Royalist family,
the tyranny of hot-tempered brothers, the schemes of relations
to marry her off to old Sir Justinian Isham, distressing years of

[1]Letter to Knightley Chetwode, April 19th, 1726. Ball, Vol.
III, p. 305.

separation crowned by her catching the small-pox—and lastly her obstinate prejudices. She tried to rationalize her fears by citing examples of failure after failure. If people but knew each other before marriage there would be an end of it. That despicable emotion—passion—carries us away from reason, causes us to become brutish and tyrannical and, when unwisely indulged in, makes us "the talk of footmen and boys in the street." In this last sentiment Swift perfectly agreed with her, although perhaps he was ignorant of the fact that she had ever held it.

Sir William had wisely rebutted her, admonished her with robust, temperate argument. He trusted where she distrusted, countered her sensitivities with a slight hardness, firmly overcame her scruples, and swept her away into his rising tide of diplomatic life. There was no longer time for meditation or hesitation, for she had to follow his fortunes in Ireland and Brussels, to reign as mistress over the great house shining with plate at the Hague, remain behind in London to negotiate his arrears of salary, appear unafraid when her yacht was fired on in one of the channel crossings. There was scarcely time for sorrow. She bore seven children and lost them, "almost in their cradles"; the favourite, Diana, died at fourteen, and ten years later John killed himself.

"Mild Dorothea, peaceful, wise and great"—writes Swift in his laudatory poem. Is this what life had fined her down to? As Virginia Woolf says, "We do not know that silent lady. . . . The light falls upon a ghost."[1]

Yet if Swift never mentions her elsewhere and if they never grew intimate enough to appreciate each other's similarities, it is after all not surprising. Lady Temple was forty years his senior, her son's unnatural end had profoundly shaken her. (Amongst her papers after her death were found John Temple's apology for his action and neatly pinned to it, in his mother's handwriting, the words, "Child's paper he writ, before he killed himself.") She was accustomed to courts and their despised ceremonies, to the confidences of queens and princesses. A certain undefined and perfectly accepted barrier

[1]*Dorothy Osborne, The Common Reader*, Second Series, The Hogarth Press, London, 1935.

separated her and Swift. She was much occupied in caring for her husband when he was ill or in managing the large, unwieldy household with its complex and wearisome duties. As she sat at the head of the great table, surrounded by the other ladies and the ladies-in-waiting, she might glance across at Sir William's table—for the men still dined separately—and bow to his secretary who sat with some of the privileged upper servants, below the salt. She might pass him in the yew walks or find him brooding in the grotto studded with imported shells, might chance upon him in Sir William's library or in the long corridors, but his work lay with her husband and it was, as she would have wished, *his* influence which affected Swift.

III

When Swift had been with Temple less than a year he returned to Ireland, carrying in his pocket a recommendation to Sir Robert Southwell, Secretary of State, from Sir William. The document was in the nature of a character, such as one gives to a discarded or dissatisfied servant: it set out Swift's knowledge and accomplishments and suggested that a clerkship, a fellowship in Trinity College, or a position as agent to Southwell might be desirable for him. With a tinge of ironic amusement we read that he was "honest and diligent," that he "wrote a good hand," had kept Sir William's accounts, that he knew Latin, Greek and some French. The recommendation is proof of Temple's goodwill but evidently he had not yet measured the younger man's capacities or Swift himself, struggling to digest the intricacies and refinements of a new world, had not yet revealed them.

The immediate and apparent reason for Swift's return to Ireland was the condition of his health. About this time he began to suffer from a malady whose evil effects plagued him for the rest of his life and it was at Sheen that he experienced the first sharp and terrifying attack. Swift believed the illness to be due to a "surfeit of stone fruit" which he had eaten in Temple's garden, since the symptoms were sickness, giddiness, and a recurrent deafness with a horrid booming in

the ears. As time went on and the malady reappeared he
compared notes on his seizures with his friends, copied out
prescriptions likely to relieve him, amongst them that of the
celebrated Dr. Radcliffe based on the efficacy of sack-whey,
sage, rosemary, syrup of cowslip, and a cap of powered spices,
laid between quilted silk, to be sewn "within side his wigg."
The physicians whom he consulted, ignorant of the true causes
of his attacks, recommended a return to his native air, the
drinking of steel water, and the pouring of hot oil down the
ears, as possible remedies.

The disease has now been diagnosed as *labyrinthine vertigo,*
a malady of the inner ear connected with the stomach. The
ignorance of the physicians and their inability to prevent
attacks, or allay his discomfort, convinced the patient that he
had been singled out to suffer from some unique disability,
beyond understanding or cure, to which ultimately he must
succumb. The intermittent seizures, which attacked him
without warning and for no apparent reason, gave him the
feeling of being unsafe with himself, and emphasized the
tenuity of his connections with his fellow-beings. His life at
these times became a kind of living death, life was suspended
and resurrection prayed for. The physical malady symbolized
for him what he already suspected, that life was dangerous
and treacherous, an incomprehensible burden which he was
unfitted to carry.

Swift's attitude to the disease was probably more harmful
than the disease itself, and the fears which it aroused in him
out of all proportion to its seriousness. At the back of his
mind the remembrance of his uncle Godwin in his closing years,
a hulk of a body no longer activated by a lively spirit, seems
to have lain. The image haunted him, so much so that he used
it allegorically when writing of totally different matters.[1]

> "*For when the animating Mind is fled,*
>
> . . . .
>
> . . . .
>
> *The Body, tho' Gigantick, lyes all Cold and Dead.*"

It is the fear which dogs men of morbid but exceptional

[1] *Ode to the Athenian Society. Poems,* Vol. I, p. 25.

intellect, who rate their faculties of reasoning high, who trust
their wits and doubt their more subtle, unconscious processes,
who alternately whip and neglect their powers of spiritual
response. It is the fear which made Donne write two months
before he died:

> "I am afraid that death will play with me so long, as he
> will forget to kill me, and suffer me to live in a languishing
> and useless age, a life that is rather a forgetting that I am
> dead, than of living"—

and Swift exclaim to Young of the *Night Thoughts:*

> "*I shall be like that tree, I shall die at the top.*"[1]

His tenacious will to live and the hypochondriacal fears
which beset him tossed him about relentlessly like an inanimate
shuttlecock. The one drove him to violent exercise and a
healthy routine of life, the other to perpetual self-watchfulness
and ministrations based on perpetual fear. He felt the constant need to drive himself to the limits of endurance and
yet, almost at the same time, to husband his resources lest
they run out too profligately. While at Moor Park he
punctuated his studies by running up and down a hill which
lay behind the house every two hours, noting with pride his
time of performance as if he were jockey and racehorse in one.
"I row," he remarked in later years, "after health like a
waterman, and ride after it like a postboy, and find little
success."[2] When first he visited his mother in Leicestershire
he walked by long stages from the north, partly because of the
prick of penury and partly because he enjoyed it. His sense
of comradeship with the lower classes was increased and his
ironic fancy tickled by watching the antics of wagoners,
hostlers, chambermaids, grooms, postboys, pedlars and pack-
men. But behind the journey on foot stalked the phantom of
ill-health which might waylay him like an insubstantial high-
wayman. From Moor Park to London he walked the distance
of thirty-eight miles rejoicing in his triumph. His constant

[1] *The Life of the Rev. Dr. Jonathan Swift*, by Thomas Sheridan,
1st edition, p. 280.
[2] Swift to Archbishop King, 1721. Ball, III, p. 103.

injunctions to Stella in the *Journal,* to Vanessa and to his
friends in letters, to exercise, ride, and walk are a reminder
of the desperate uneasiness which sat like an incubus on his
heart, mixed with a real perception of the inertness of his
fellow citizens who ate and drank far too much, avoided fresh
air from a belief in the dangers of "damps and vapours", and
hugged their fires in idleness.

Yet how much to be pitied he is, this gaunt and giant
figure, striding over the Surrey heaths, riding from London to
Chester, sculling like a waterman on the Thames, or bathing
perilously in some Chelsea reach with his manservant, Patrick,
fending off the boatmen. For there is never a word of enjoy-
ment, either imaginative or physical, in all this purposeful
expense of energy, no mention of the delights to be gained
from a contemplation of the landscape or from the meditations
aroused by it, and no sense of physical well-being. It remains a
violent yet sterile shadow-play between opposing forces, by
which Swift alternately convinces himself of his consummate
strength and escapes from the fears of illness which pursue
him with demoniac fury.

Years later he wrote to Pope, "I could have leapt over the
moon at your age"[1], but the leap would have been one of a
creature bewitched, turning his head over his shoulder and
casting fearful eyes at the lengthening shadows.

IV

His stay in Ireland was not prolonged. In three months
he was back at Moor Park, Temple's second estate to which he
had returned at the end of 1689 with his "desolate family."[2]
Among the many relations and retainers of this sprawling
household were two who were to become inextricably en-
twined in Jonathan's life, Rebecca Dingley, a cousin of Sir
William's, and little Hester Johnson.[3] Hester, or Stella as

[1]Ball, V, pp. 1-5.
[2]Lady Giffard, *Life of Sir William Temple.*
[3]Although she signs her will and letters *Esther* Johnson her
baptismal record, as well as her monument, bears the name *Hester.*
See Ball III, p. 79, Note 1.

she came to be publicly known long after Swift wrote her the *Journal*, was then a sprite of eight years old. She was the daughter of a merchant, now dead, and a woman of "acute and penetrating talents,"[1] who waited upon Lady Giffard, attending her at Court and other functions. Thus Stella from an early age ran about the great halls and gardens, and climbed into the hearts of everyone, even the saturnine young secretary.

There is tragic irony in the fact that in order to learn about Stella at this age we have to go direct to Swift's melancholy tribute to her, begun on the night of her death, when the Dean sat broken-hearted remembering her part in his life, turning away from the windows when the torches of the grave-diggers flared up as ghastly interruptions.

"I knew her," he writes, "from six years old."[2] (This is an error, for he distinctly says in the previous sentence that she "was born at Richmond in Surrey on the thirteenth day of March, 1681," and Swift did not join Temple until 1689. But let the inaccuracy stand: it is of little moment.) He continues,

". . . and had some share in her education, by directing what books she should read, and perpetually instructing her in the principles of honour and virtue; from which she never swerved in any one action or moment of her life."

Throughout her life he taught her. The only extant examples of her writing come from her mature hand some thirty or more years beyond this time. In these you have the key to their relationship—the exacting master and the ardent pupil, eager to learn and prone to love, for the handwriting resembles Swift's own, although it lacks the assured ease of his and retains instead a childish undeveloped character. Even his friends chaffed him about the similarity when they saw her letters propped in the coffee-house windows and asked him if he wrote to himself.[3] And although Swift praises Stella's

[1] Scott, Vol. I, p. 49.
[2] *On the Death of Mrs. Johnson.* (A Character of Stella). *Swift,* Nonesuch Edition, edited by John Hayward, 1934, p. 725.
[3] Williams, p. 183.

mental accomplishments, her learning and her extraordinary appreciation of history, philosophy, medicine, the nature of government, and various religions, yet we find him instructing her in words and their meanings, and rallying her on her poor spelling a dozen years later.

Swift's masterful and imperious nature inclined to make him regard any woman as ignorant and inferior, in need of improvement and education. With Swift, to teach was to make love. It was a permissible avenue of approach. He must annexe a woman and mould her as Pygmalion did. He was shortly to demand of another woman, in a withering letter of challenge and dismissal, whether she could "comply with his desires and way of living" and "be ready to engage in those methods I shall direct for the improvement of your mind. . . . Can you bend your love and esteem and indifference to others the same way as I do mine?" in other words, adopt his very affections irrespective of her own inclinations. His women, if he was to love them, must first submit to being students and then become slaves, extensions of himself, who offered no opposition.

Yet the need which Swift felt to instruct his women was not entirely an expression of the imperious side of his nature. It was an appreciation of the lamentable state into which the education both of boys and girls had fallen. He saw the boys in great houses pampered when they were small, taught from the nursery that they were to inherit great estates and therefore had no need to "mind their books", to study anything so dead as the classics or so arid as mathematics. Accomplishments were all that a gentleman needed, and inefficient tutors and French dancing-masters might readily give them these.

But the mischief attending the education of girls was greater. Up to the time of the Reformation their instruction had lain entirely in the hands of the Church: the Dissolution obliterated swiftly and finally all organized education for them. They remained at the mercy of intermittent, casual instruction and continued so for three succeeding centuries. The daughters of the royal house and of great scholars were taught the classics and even learnt Hebrew, but the loss of the "she-schools", or convents, meant that the great mass of women of the middle and lower classes, as well as a portion of the aristocracy, were cut off from learning.[1]

Stella was born midway between the three barren centuries, a century-and-a-half after the Dissolution, in an age which grew increasingly lethargic, intent upon material ease, delighting in artificiality. She was likely to feel the full force of these enervating influences, to suffer, even in comparative isolation, from the lack of dominant spiritual guidance which, for the first time since the coming of Christianity these islands were experiencing: to realize albeit remotely the inertia of moral feeling, the quenching of enthusiasm, the hardening of conventionality.

A woman's role was to be negative, passive, obedient. To be genteelly idle was the height of her ambition, until, as the first Marquis of Halifax declared, a man was like to find his home at the mercy of "an empty, airy thing who sails up and down the house to no purpose and looks as if she came thither only to make a visit."[2] Since women were apt to be regarded as useful and successful only if they married, the inference that education might be dispensed with easily followed. A suspicion that to cultivate their intelligence might be harmful to their mental and physical health as well as to the serenity of their men-folk, crept in. Swift asserts that it was the common opinion that books on any other subjects than devotion or domesticity might turn their brains.[3] A display of learning was both unnatural and embarrassing and Pope's admirer, Lady Mary Wortley Montagu, studied her Latin surreptitiously and advised other women to conceal any knowledge they might have with as much intentness as they would a physical deformity.

Thus according to Defoe girls learnt how to "stitch and to sew, or to make baubles . . . how to read and perhaps to

---

[1]See: *Women in English Life*. 2 volumes, Georgiana Hill, London, 1896; and *The Education of Girls and Women*, Christina Bremner, London, 1897.

[2]*Advice to a Daughter*, 1700. Edited by Sir Walter Raleigh. Oxford University Press, 1912, p. 1.

[3]*Of the Education of Ladies*, Temple Scott, Vol. XI, p. 62.

write their names, and that is the height of their education."[1]
But Swift went even further than this—he stated that not one
young gentlewoman in a thousand was taught to read or spell.[2]
The result was that the two sexes had few interests in common.
Travellers from the continent, quick to appreciate novel and
strange elements in another country, remarked that in England
men and women did not talk together. How could they when
they seldom met except at occasional meals, for the men preferred the coffee-house, club or tavern, and looked down on
domesticity as a bourgeois failing.

Yet ironically, men reproached women for the ignorance
and superficiality which they themselves had encouraged.
Here and there a voice rose to call out against such a contradiction.

"I dare be bold to admit young maidens to learn, seeing
my country gives me leave and her custom stands for me.
Their natural towardness should make us see them well
brought up,"

declared Richard Mulcaster, Master of the Merchant Taylors'
School, before Swift was born. And when Stella was maturing,
Mary Astell, a fearless woman whom Swift ridiculed as a
blue-stocking, spoke out:

"A man ought no more to value himself upon being
wiser than a woman, if he owe his advantage to a better
education, than he ought to boast of his courage for beating
a man when his hands were bound." [3]

Involved in the vexing and depressing business of bank-
ruptcy Defoe found time to agree with her:

"I have often thought it one of the most barbarous
customs in the world, considering us as a civilised and a
Christian country, that we deny the advantages of learning
to women. We reproach the sex every day with folly and
impertinence while I am confident, had they the advantages

---

[1] *The Education of Women,* 1697.
[2] *Of the Education of Ladies,* Temple Scott, Vol. XI, p. 62.
[3] *A Serious Proposal to the Ladies for the Advancement of Their True
and Greatest Interest.* 1694.

of education equal to us, they would be guilty of less than ourselves."[1]

He advocates that "they should be taught all sorts of breeding suitable to their genius and quality":—music, dancing, and languages, "all the graces of speech": for, he writes, "I would venture the infamy of giving a woman more tongues than one." They should also be taught to read history,

> "and so to read as to make them understand the world and be able to know and judge of things when they hear of them. . . . A woman that is well bred and well taught, furnished with the additional accomplishments of knowledge and behaviour is a creature without comparison. . . . The man that has such a one to his portion has nothing to do but rejoice in her and be thankful."[2]

Swift's bias against the sex would not permit him to call women

> "the finest and most delicate part of God's creation. . . . His darling creatures . . . all softness, sweetness, peace, love, wit and delight,"

but he agreed with Defoe's fundamental conclusions. The solitary, neglected child of wealthy parents, left to amuse himself by playing span-counter with the little blackamoor, moved Swift to compassion,[3] and a daughter relegated to the care of an English or French governess, "generally the worst that can be gotten for money,"[4] stirred him to argue on her behalf at the dinner table, to draft notes for a dissertation, and to make that most dangerous of all experiments—a personal test of his theories with two women whom he held dear.

V

Little by little Swift began to make himself felt as a vital force at Moor Park. Sir William was often ill with the gout,

---

[1] *The Education of Women.* 1697.
[2] Ibid.
[3] *Essay on Modern Education*, Temple Scott, Vol. XI, p. 49.
[4] *Of the Education of Ladies*, Temple Scott, Vol. XI, p. 61.

unable to write with ease of mind, unable to perform his office as host (with ease of body), even to his friend King William whom he had assisted to the throne. He tested Swift's reliability and found that it bore the strain which he put upon it, if not with grace, at least with staunchness. He trusted him to take up the cudgels for him in one of those absurdly pompous, pedagogical battles, survivals of the old religious polemics of Elizabeth's time, concerning the merits of ancient and modern learning, a controversy transplanted by Temple from France to England. Swift's contribution was the mock heroic *Battle of the Books*. Temple even entrusted King William to him and together they paced the long, terraced avenues. William, pleased with the young man's rugged honesty, and mistaking his powerful frame and fierce blue eyes for those of a potential military leader, offered him a troop of horse. In more intimate moments he instructed him how to cut and eat asparagus after the Dutch fashion, a lesson which went so much to his head that years later, in his usual imperious fashion, he ordered his old friend and ally, Printer and Alderman Faulkner, to eat up the stalks "as King William did" before he might have a second helping.

Upon another occasion when the Earl of Portland visited Moor Park, on behalf of the Sovereign, to discuss the Triennial Bill for which the King had a hearty aversion, Temple, arguing in the Bill's favour, buttressed his opinions with examples from English history which Swift had drawn up for him, and used Swift as his intermediary over the same matter in the Palace at Kensington on a second occasion. The Bill was ultimately thrown out in the House of Commons, and Swift acidly remarked that, having fancied he might be successful in fostering it and having failed, it "helped to cure him of vanity!"[1] At least it discouraged an already discouraged nature but Swift, like all of us, continued to hope against hope that his merits might be recognized and his services rewarded.

He began to share his own work with Temple. His powers of observation were mated with an appalling, gross sincerity, that of the satirist who exposes and flays that which he abhors

[1] Temple Scott, Vol. XI, p. 378.

from a sense of injured susceptibility as well as from an urge
to moralize or rectify. The satire burst out like molten lava
from the sides of a crater in a scathing denunciation of
theological pedantry—*A Tale of a Tub*, which was circulated
privately, remaining unpublished for another eight years.
Looking back as an old man upon this, his earliest prose work
of significance, Swift exclaimed: "Good God, what a genius
I had when I wrote that book!"[1] (Even Samuel Johnson, who
doubted its authorship, commended the rich "swarm of
thoughts, so much of nature and vigorous life.") Like Donne's
so-called *Satire on Religion* it was a dangerous work and produced suspicions of his orthodoxy when it appeared. It lost
him the Bishopric which he coveted, for Anne, receiving him
graciously at first and then taking fright at the terrible,
denunciatory power of Swift, consistently refused his advancement; but it earned him the title of master of satire and marked
him out as a great intellect.

The discontent, the restlessness, the alternating moods of
overweening pride and gnawing humiliation which character-
ized both actions and writings, culminated in his determination
to leave Temple and enter the Church. His wishes in this
matter depended upon the inclination of his master and the
King, for in a letter to his uncle, William Swift, who obtained
testimonials for him from Dublin, he mentions both Temple's
apparent reluctance to lose or advance him, and the King's
prohibition that he is not to take orders until he gives him a
prebendary.[2] However, in 1692, Swift went up to Oxford and
received his Master's degree at Hart Hall. Like his cousin
Dryden, he found the courteous reception granted him at this
university gratifying after the censure and grudging honours
bestowed upon him by his own.

Like all men of conscience he disliked admitting the fact
that he was willing to enter the Church merely to earn a
living, and his scruples reflect both his indecision over which
profession to adopt, and his doubts of his own spirituality.
For a time he considered earning his living by writing, as
Dryden had done, but his muse was recalcitrant. His longings

[1]Scott, I, p. 81.
[2]Letter to William Swift, Nov. 29, 1692. Ball, I, pp. 8-10.

for independence chafed and enraged him constantly, so that although he lingered on a further two years at Moor Park, he forced Sir William, unwilling to part with an active and talented secretary, to find him other openings. Temple, who like his father before him was Master of the Rolls in Ireland, offered Swift the chance of working in that office. The latter rejected the offer, worth £120 a year, and considered that such a suggestion relieved him of his scruples of entering the Church purely for maintenance. They parted in displeasure, Swift smarting under the sense of being undervalued and unassisted, and Temple under that of having his efforts too haughtily received. But Temple retained the master hand, for the bishops to whom Swift applied upon arrival in Ireland required testimonials of his character and behaviour while resident with Sir William. Swift, with characteristic obstinacy, refused to apply for them and for the best part of half a year champed his bit in silence. When at last he wrote, the letter of entreaty cost him dear. To admit his failings was at all times difficult for him and more than that, dangerous, for it placed him in the power of his imagined adversary. With somewhat hollow phrasing he expresses repentance for past "weaknesses, follies and oversights,"[1] and solicits Temple's recommendation. Temple showed his magnanimity by forwarding the testimonial at once, together with a further recommendation to the Lord Deputy of Ireland, and within three weeks Swift was ordained deacon, and within three months, priest. He was granted the small prebend of Kilroot, in the diocese of Connor, and retired to take up the life of a remote country clergyman, cut off from association with any but the most poor and ignorant for the greater part of his time. Accustomed as he now was to the verdure of Moor Park and its cultured society, Swift found the dreary shores of Belfast Lough intolerable. The Scotch Presbyterians brought out his most insulting and stubborn detestation, and excepting for meteoric visits into society provided by Lord and Lady Donegal, a society in which he must still have been somewhat ill at ease, he had little to distract him from an assiduous round of clerical duties.

[1] Ball, Vol. I, pp. 13-14.

One of the many legends still attached to his name relates to his days at Kilroot, for Swift, with his eccentricities, moods, and violent reactions, his quick wit and singular appearance, is the stuff around which legend gathers. The stories about him, although often inaccurate and distorted, have their basis of fact and plausibility. Here, in the solitude of his sea-washed parish, the "mad parson," despairing of gathering together a congregation, is said to have gone down to the shore and "skipped" stones into the sea and when sufficient idlers came to watch him, he swept them up and carried them off to the church.[1]

Even the parsonage which stood near the ruined church was insignificant. Its shape, which verged on the cylindrical, had earned it the absurd name of "the Egg."[2] From its dim interior Swift, often made prisoner by incessant rain, noted with irritation the minutiae of his immediate setting—the fowls with drooping wings huddled beneath the broad-leaved vine, the martins silent under the eaves. Again he turned the hour glass; again counted the raindrops hanging from the inner ledge of reeded thatch, wagering which would fall last. It was a scene conducive to melancholy introspection. In vain he attempted to appreciate the quiet which, in attacks of his illness, he had fancied would suit him; to adapt himself with grace to provincial society; to discipline himself with the routine of his duties; to count the blessings of his new-found clerical life. But, as always, that which he had renounced had for him more attractions than that which confronted him.

It was an experiment doomed to failure. He needed to be amongst men and things, not cloistered out of, but actively engaged in, the world, the noise and bustle of which called him. He felt himself wasted and wasting in a dripping wilderness.

VI

One means of diverting himself was to ride into Belfast to see his old friend and chamber-fellow at Trinity, Lucas Waring, whose sister Jane acted as hostess for him. Jonathan

[1] Sir Henry Craik, Vol. I, p. 51.
[2] Ball, Vol. I, p. 29.

promptly fell in love. Outwardly he worshipped the girl who bore the same name as his own sister; inwardly, without being aware of it, he approached her suspiciously and with venom in his heart. Not content with "plain Jane" he must deify her and give her a name exclusively his own. Dorothy had not been good enough for Lady Temple, she must be "Dorinda," and so, playing upon her surname and classicizing as best he might, he called her "Varina."

His passion reached a climax towards the end of April, 1696, for suddenly Sir William recalled him to Moor Park, tempting him with the offer of advancement. He used the offer as a lever with which to coerce Varina into agreement and decision, declaring that he would sail in a fortnight and demanding her submission before his departure. The letter to Varina, one of an extant pair worlds apart in feeling yet expressive of the twin-sides of Swift's ill-balanced nature, is extremely interesting. It shows us that as a young man—not yet thirty—he was capable of passion, was not ashamed of avowing it, even on paper, and that he not only contemplated matrimony but appeared to ardently desire it.

"Impatience is the most inseparable quality of a lover," he begins, and continues with the statement that "a violent desire is little better than a distemper, and therefore men are not to blame in looking for a cure." He upbraids the lady for seeming to trifle with him and bursts out with the charge that

"By Heaven, Varina, you are more experienced, and have less virgin innocence than I! Would not your conduct make one think you were hugely skilled in all the little politic methods of intrigue?"[1]

He lays his heart and his meagre fortune at her feet, assures her that he will in no way hinder her in her pursuits, or choice of life, while he is still earning a right to possess her, and offers to forego his chances of worldly advancement in England "for her sake."

Varina temporized, and for pausing to doubt she has been called a coquette. She may have loved Swift, or have been

[1]Letter, April 29th, 1696. Ball, Vol. I, pp. 15-20.

seriously attracted by him, for the affair continued intermittently for a further four years; but Swift was a baffling and
somewhat terrifying lover with his peremptory commands
and ultimata, his thrusts and sallies. The state of tension in
which he lived, which sought to relieve itself by these violent
means, may well have caused Varina to hesitate and to consider seriously whether such a partner was fitted to her, or
whether happiness lay in store for either, should she agree to
such a union. For the same letter in which Swift so hastily
woos her contains seeds of doubt and difficulty, revealing the
negative sides of his nature which grew in strength as his life
lengthened, and like ice in the white-light days of January
insidiously closed over the warm springs of affection beneath.

"Why was I so foolish to put my hopes and fears into
the power or management of another? Liberty is doubtless
the most valuable blessing of life; yet we are fond to fling
it away on those who have been these five thousand years
using us ill. Philosophy advises us to keep our desires and
prospects of happiness as much as we can in our own
breasts, and independent of anything without. He that
sends them abroad is likely to have as little quiet as a
merchant whose stock depends upon winds, and waves, and
pirates, or upon the words and faith of creditors, every
whit as dangerous and inconstant as the other."[1]

The search for false freedom had begun, for Swift regarded
submission as a humiliating and vulgar form of capitulation.
He could not see that submission to a law higher than reason,
larger than his own self-determined one, might be infinitely
greater and more rewarding. Any such simple yielding, or
committing of himself to another, grew to seem fearfully
dangerous, and Shakespeare's men gathering samphire along
the fierce-falling cliffs gazed with less dread at the distant
shore than Swift at imagined surrender.

Still, he made one last bid before the ice, in a few years'
time, closed finally over.

"Love," he writes to Varina, "with the gall of too much
discretion, is a thousand times worse than with none at

[1] op. cit. pp. 15-20.

all. . . . To resist the violence of our inclinations in the beginning, is a strain of self-denial that may have some pretences to set up for a virtue; . . . but 'tis as possble to err in the excess of piety as of love."[1]

A fortnight elapsed without Varina capitulating and Swift, who could not endure indecision and vacillation in others any more than he could bear their rejection, escaped from his predicament by flight. He gave away his Irish prebend, for no explicit reason other than that of benefiting a friend, and involved himself once more with Temple.

When Swift returned to Ireland in 1699 his fortunes had improved. Varina ventured to approach him with more assurance. Poverty would be one deterrent less to a partnership threatened with insecurity and possibly with hostility, for surely those words describing her sex were pregnant with hatred—"those who have been these five thousand years using us ill." Nor was she very strong, she might easily embarrass his pocket and aggravate his temper; but now that he had a better living, she might perhaps propose their union with safety.

Swift's retort was irrational and abusive: he upbraids her for the company she keeps; "dwindling away her life and health in such a sink, and among such family conversation."[2] (Varina was the daughter of an Archdeacon and this description of her home and family was inexcusable). He tactlessly inquires whether her health has improved, and reminds her that neither is her fortune large nor her beauty exceptional. He stresses the need for "cleanliness" in her person and "competency" in the management of their joint affairs, if she is to please him. In other words,

"Swift's plan was to offer to fulfil" the marriage engagement "on conditions so insulting that no one with a grain of self-respect could accept. . . . When anyone tried to enforce claims no longer congenial to his feelings, the appeal to the galling obligation stung him into ferocity,

[1]op. cit., pp. 15-20.
[2]Letter of May 4th, 1700, Dublin. Ball, Vol. I, pp. 31-5.

and brought out the most brutal side of his imperious nature."[1]

Yet there was sound commonsense in much that Swift had to say. He felt it essential to point out, however bluntly, the chief demands of his egocentric nature: mixed with his savagery was a certain ruggedly honest plea for the recognition of the sort of man that he was, for without this basic acceptance, no happiness could be possible. Yes, he *was* imperious, he needed a woman who would "comply with his desires and way of living," one who would submit to being taught by him, in order that they might enjoy common study, common diversion, and not be bored with one another's company in remote country fastnesses. Could she bear with him in his ill-natured passages and be indifferent to his moods—moods of black temper, of melancholia, of hatred for her as Woman, threatening his masculinity, of hatred for a world which had so early betrayed him?

It was both a challenge and an ultimatum, even a declaration of war. His doubt of Varina's ability to fulfil his conditions was so painfully obvious that she did not take up the gauntlet but shrank away into injured obscurity. It is significant that in this, his second and final recorded letter, he no longer addresses her as Varina: she has reverted to her status of mortal. Before, he had raised her above femininity, out of the sordid human, even bestial, sphere; now he reduced her to her proper place, that of a creature whom he both despised and shunned for her very frailties.

VII

It will be noticed that, in his second letter to Varina, Swift stresses cleanliness as his primary requisite in a wife. Why this unnatural emphasis on an attribute generally taken for granted? Unless one understands the part that cleanliness played in Swift's mind one cannot estimate his difficulties in approaching women. It is the characteristic for which he

[1] Sir Leslie Stephen's *Swift*—English Men of Letters Series, Macmillan, London, 1889, p. 52.

praises Stella and Vanessa[1] to their faces: he urges a young lady about to be married to attend to her person rather than to her clothes.[2]

Our forbears were generally not so cleanly as we are: the amenities for hygiene as we know them did not exist. Swift was in advance of his day in the care of his person,[3] yet there is a more than ordinary preoccupation with the subject and there is something unnatural in his insistence upon both tidiness and cleanliness in those around him. One of his *Resolutions* which he made as a young man was:

"Not to neglect decency, or cleanliness, for fear of falling into nastiness". . . .

and late in life, in his last great work, he speaks of Gulliver, his own creation, as surprising the inhabitants because he did not stink so much as other human beings.

His sense of smell was acute. In many of his verses and much of his prose his strongest disgust arises from his reactions to unpleasant odours. The city street is intolerable because of the fetid kennels,[4] a lady's dressing-room is equally so because she neglects her person.[5] The rank sweat on Brobdingnagian maids almost overpowers him, and thus we are forced to the conclusion that the human race, and especially the female sex, was, for Swift, "fundamentally an evil-smelling"[6] one.

This physical revulsion is a strong and persistent characteristic and implies that Swift, at some very early period, received a shock to his extreme sensibilities, causing him to be obsessed with the animal properties of human bodies. This obsession, like the silvery tracks of a snail in her night journeys, leaves its traces on much of his work. Perhaps his strong, possessive country nurse transgressed in propriety before the infant child, too young in her estimation to take

---

[1]*Cadenus and Vanessa*, Poems II, p. 412.
[2]*Letter to a Very Young Lady on Her Marriage.*
[3]*Observations Upon Lord Orrery's Remarks*, Delany, p. 173.
[4]*Description of a City Shower.*
[5]*The Lady's Dressing Room.*
[6]Rossi & Hone, p. 402.

any notice. Her dying relation, to whom she was recalled from Ireland when she stole Jonathan away with her, may have lain in the room with him: his uncle Godwin in senile decay may have so distressed the young schoolboy that he could never again regard humanity with equanimity. The cause must remain conjectural but the results are sown over all his writings, in some of which he essayed to rid himself of this unpleasant preoccupation. The result was often unfortunate. One lady, upon reading a poem of his, promptly fainted. He was exceptional even amongst the outspoken writers of his day: in fact "almost singular in this respect and (his frankness) forms the strong outline which distinguished him from every other writer."[1]   Barrett quotes from a pamphlet which appeared in Swift's lifetime disparaging *A Tale of a Tub*, whose author accuses Swift of "taking the air upon dunghills, in ditches and in common sewers, and at My Lord Mayor's dog-kennel." Swift's writings, even to men of his own time, were what we call strong meat. His friend Delany charitably alleges that his offensive pieces were:

> "the prescriptions of an able physician, who had the health of his patients at heart, and laboured to attain that end . . . by all the most nauseous, and offensive drugs, and potions, that could be administered,"[2]

without understanding the basic nature of Swift's preoccupation.

But if Swift's friends, servants, and readers, suffered from his overscrupulosity, or from his grossness, he himself was the most unfortunate victim of this mental malady. The most exquisite nymph in the world was unapproachable, beyond certain flirtatious overtures, because simultaneously with her image there sprang up in his mind the associated one of filth and loathsome odours. This lamentable condition is clearly expressed in *The Lady's Dressing Room*.[3] In poems such as these, and in certain prose passages, Swift writes like

[1]*Essay on the Early Part of the Life of Dean Swift*—Reverend John Barrett, D.D., 1808, pp. 28-9.
[2]*Observations upon Lord Orrery's Remarks*, 1754, p. 198.
[3]Poems II, p. 529.

one who feels himself tainted from birth, smeared with obscure, faecal matter. This obsession explains his fundamental
horror at being part of the human race, so closely allied to the
Yahoos, and, for me, makes any belief in his alleged marriage
impossible.

Sir Shane Leslie has suggested the antithesis between
Donne's and Swift's attitude to physical love, which may be
perceived on comparing the former's passionate *Elegy* with
the latter's poem *On a Beautiful Young Nymph Going to Bed*.[1]
The comparison leaves one stunned. Donne's ardour, sen-
suality, and frank abandonment to carnal delights carry one
away with their poetic fire and his own infectious joy. Swift
repels.

That Swift knew his Donne is obvious, for he made use of
his predecessor's title, which he modified, and four out of
five of his adverbs. But how cramped, mean and obsessional
are Swift's feeling, attitude, lines and words compared to the
earlier poet's. Desire becomes suppressed out of all recognition into avowed disgust, and where Donne writes:

> "*Licence my roving hands and let them go
> Before, behind, between, above, below.
> O my America! my new-found-land. . . .*"

Swift contrasts:

> "*No noisom Whiffs, or sweaty Streams
> Before, behind, above, below
> Could from her taintless Body flow.*"[2]

We turn away in revulsion from Swift, who defeats his own
ends in attempting to expose a contemporary evil. We
cannot stomach what was unendurable to him, and like a
caricature which over-emphasizes that which it seeks to mis-
represent, art is lost in grotesqueness, and instead of being
stimulated the senses are nauseated.

---

[1] *The Skull of Swift*, pp. 12-13.
[2] *Strephon & Chloe. Poems*, Vol. II, p. 584.

VIII

Upon his third and final return to Moor Park (in 1696) where he remained for three years, Swift found himself received more as an equal than a dependant. Even the cook respected him, waiting in seemly fashion upon him for his orders for dinner, and he had rooms of his own which enabled him to live alone "in great state."[1] He had ample time for exercise, study, writing, and meditation, and he spent eight, sometimes ten, hours a day at his books and papers. *The Battle of the Books* and *A Tale of a Tub* were perfected and work continued on Sir William's *Memoirs*, *Letters* and *Essays*. A list of books which Swift read at this time shows us his taste in literature. History ranks first, the classics and works of travel second and third. Surprisingly we find that the metaphysical poet Sir John Davies attracted him, but there is a marked absence of theological and philosophical reading, with the exception of ecclesiastical history.

His eye observed everything and that inner eye of the mind noted, compared and criticized. The rooks tossing above him, with their accurate morning and evening assembly for discussion, flight to the feeding grounds, and outlying nurseries, their method of choosing a leader and advocate, and other domestic habits, much amused him.

He found time for a kind of primitive analysis, the fruits of which were summed up in those curious *Resolutions When I Come to be Old*.[2] These are seventeen in number and indicate what he considered were the weaknesses of his character against which he must guard. They open with the decision, always foremost in his thoughts as the chief pitfall:

"*Not to marry a young Woman.*"

There follows the revealing resolve:

"*Not to be peevish or morose, or suspicious.*"

The fifth is the frightening one:

[1]Letter to Stella, or Her Mother, 1698. Ball, Vol. I, pp. 21-2.
[2]Hayward, pp. 467-8.

"Not to be fond of children, or let them come near me hardly,"

and another is related to this:

"Not to hearken to flatterers, nor conceive I can be beloved by a young woman—et eos qui hereditatem captant odisse ac vitare."

What is the meaning of this strange, forbidding interdict with regard to children? It strikes an alarming note in one on the threshold of full manhood. Fear of poverty, of ridicule, of failure, made him write that first resolution, but a greater fear augmented the lesser. "One's immortality lies in one's children," wrote Brahms a century and a half later, cursing the poverty and inhibitions which had prevented him too from mating, and as a melancholy rejoinder, tragic in its intensity— "Is life worth while when one is so much alone?" These fearful barriers which Swift erected to safeguard himself were the coign stones of the prison which was to shut him in with ever-darkening walls, and in the determination to save, he paradoxically lost himself. Distrusting the strength of his own emotions, he denied them existence at their source, castigating them as a weakness rather than an enrichment of life. His own emotional safety and happiness must come first: he dared not give himself lest he suffer in the giving, or in the renunciation, or loss of that gift, no matter how precious. Thus the first resolution is linked with the fifth.

During Swift's absence at Kilroot, Lady Temple had died, and with her death ended one of the most perfect of recorded histories of love. Sir William outlived his wife by four years and his loneliness was probably one of the factors which had induced him to urge Swift to return to Moor Park. But if the household had lost one beautiful woman it had gained another, for little Hetty Johnson was grown into a lovely girl of fifteen, soon to become a roguish, full-bosomed maiden with something of the charm of Nell Gwynne. The eyes, large and lustrous, have steadiness as well as warmth, the long but amusingly broad-tipped nose, the full underlip, and the pleasing roundness of the face, the dark hair and dark eyes, suggest one of the "brown" maidens of Donne's or Herrick's

amorous verses. The set of the head on the shoulders implies
a queenliness of bearing for which the sitter was noted in
later years, and betokens grace in movement. "She had," says
Swift in that most moving of all elegies written on the night
of her death,

> "a gracefulness somewhat more than human in every
> motion, word, and action. Never was so happy a con-
> junction of civility, freedom, easiness and sincerity."[1]

Since Restoration beauties and those of succeeding reigns
flowered early, Stella may have been anything from sixteen to
twenty-six when the portrait was painted, but Swift's memories
of her when he returned to Moor Park for the last time and
when her promising beauty struck him square, tell us as much
as the painting.

> "She was sickly from her childhood until about the age
> of fifteen; but then grew into perfect health, and was looked
> upon as one of the most beautiful, graceful and agreeable
> young women in London, only a little too fat," he adds
> with characteristic, unflattering honesty. "Her hair was
> blacker than a raven, and every feature of her face in
> perfection."[2]

The image of Varina fell away. Try as he might, Swift
could not depress Stella to her rightful age of child. He
felt her charms of mind and body; of the mind which he had
helped to form, of the body which had unaccountably ripened
like one of Sir William's favourite peaches, and was now tan-
talizingly near to him.

These months of early summer, when he was in accord with
Temple and discovering the womanly charm of the girl whom
he had always regarded as child, may have been amongst the
happiest or the most tormented of Swift's life. He gives no
clue to his state of mind. The gardens of Moor Park with
their shaven emerald lawns, covered green walks, flights of
easy stone steps, plantations of fruit and nut trees, their
mellow walls and orangeries, their fountains and "shady

[1] Hayward, pp. 725-34.
[2] Ibid.

Plate I

Portrait of Stella as a young girl, by an unknown artist

wildernesses" were a kind of Paradise fitter for Marvell to celebrate than any contemporary poet. But even such a setting as this failed to rouse the hesitant lover into immediate action.

When Swift was nearing thirty-two and Stella nineteen their patron died. He remembered both his protégés in his will, bequeathing to Stella the revenue of certain lands in Ireland, and to Swift the sum of one hundred pounds, a promise of preferment from the King, and the privilege of publishing his posthumous works, with the profits which might arise from these.

Unfortunately public taste is fickle and Temple, whose style in Swift's and others' estimation had "advanced our English tongue to as great a perfection as it can well bear,"[1] began to lose popularity in the rising flood of prose and verse. The work of the essayists (Addison and Steele), of the novelists (Defoe, Richardson, Fielding and Smollett), of the poets (Pope, Gay, Parnell and Prior), of the philosophers (Locke and Berkeley), of the politician authors (Bolingbroke and Walpole), and of the dramatists (Congreve, Otway and Vanbrugh), succeeded and drove it from prominence.

Swift carefully edited his former patron's works, which appeared in several volumes during the next ten years, and humbly dedicated Temple's *Letters* to the King. But some devil of contrariness and disappointment continued to dog him. The King ignored the dedication, and Swift antagonized Lady Giffard, who alleged that he had printed some of her brother's work "against his wishes and from an unfaithful copy." Swift successfully countered this charge, but such disagreements did not make for amicable relationships and the feud continued with acrimonious letters exchanged between Swift and Sir William's nephew, afterwards Lord Palmerston, of which the following sentence is an example—"My Lord, if my letter were polite, it was against my intentions, and I desire your pardon for it."[2]

---

[1]*Preface to The First Two Volumes of Sir William Temple's Letters*, 1700. Temple Scott, Vol. I, p. 216.

[2]Swift—Letter to Viscount Palmerston, January 29th, 1725. Ball, Vol. III, p. 302.

IX

If, as Swift says later, he "retired to" Temple's house for the sole motives of benefiting from his patron's "conversation and advice, and the opportunity of pursuing his studies,"[1] why did he remain dependent upon Sir William for so long? For ten years, intermittently, the older man overshadowed the younger while he attempted to establish himself. Some have suggested that Swift returned because of Stella, but this is unlikely as she was only a child at first, and Swift was never attracted by children. Apart from other barriers, any romance was impossible because of Stella's age; it was in the beginning "such a little thing."[2] It was only when Temple died and Swift returned once more from Ireland to find Stella a castaway like himself, uncertain of her role in life, that it became predominant. Others have alleged that Swift remained for the simple reason that he had no other way of earning his daily bread. But this was not true either, for his salary was purely nominal; he could have entered the Church at any time that he wished, or applied for a secretaryship elsewhere. Others suggest that he remained from fear of losing both place and preferment, that, since he did not run well in harness and was ambitious, he had hopes of leaping into a position of prominence through Sir William's agency rather than relying solely on his own merits.

The reasons lay in Swift's character. The weaknesses which undermined his strength and prevented him from being the contented, successful man he aspired to be, causing him "Still to be cheated, never to be pleased. . . ."[3] forced him into emotional and actual dependence upon Temple. First came his legacy from early transplantation, a divided nature which displayed itself in indecision: secondly, his inability to confront the will of another until he had hardened himself:

[1]Swift—op. cit.

[2]*Swift, Stella and Vanessa*—Margaret Woods. Vol. LXXIV, Nineteenth Century and After. Constable & Co., 1913, p. 1230.

[3]*Occasioned by Sir William Temple's Late Illness and Recovery*, 1693. *Poems*, Vol. I, p. 55.

and thirdly, his attachment to Sir William with alternate strands of love and hate.

Swift longed for something fixed and defined to which he might adhere, by which he might be supported. The calamities of life bent and overpowered him: like a young, unstaked sapling planted in the open he felt the cold, destructive winds tearing at his roots. He had not, as yet, developed his own will sufficiently to withstand other people's. He seems to have feared identifying himself with their wishes and interests, especially when these were antagonistic to his own undefined and fluctuating ones. "Nor with hired thoughts be thy devotion paid," was one of his earnest prayers. He was perpetually divided between his loyalties: Ireland and England, Dublin and Leicester, later Dublin and London, Kilroot and Moor Park, quarrelled within him. He brought the perverse pugnacity of the Celt to the Anglo-Saxons, and a hard north-country commonsense practicality to the indigent Irish. His trait of being his own worst enemy, which had very nearly ejected him from Trinity, and from the graces of his uncle Godwin, worked within him to destroy the good in his relationship with Temple, from whom he fled, either in a temper or with the excuse of illness. Then, bored with the banalities of life in Kilroot, he resigned his Irish prebend with hopes of English preferment and again clung to Temple.

His emotional dependence upon his patron is nowhere more clearly displayed than in that revealing sentence in the *Journal*, in which he reminds Stella of how he used to tremble and be on tenterhooks for days if he fancied Sir William angry with him.[1] This hypersensitivity caused him to anticipate reproof or rebuff, and such was his vulnerability that he translated Temple's coldness or inattention into active disapproval aimed at him. If Temple had a fit of the spleen, was troubled with his old enemy the gout, was saddened by memories of his lost children, or disappointed by the meagre appreciation of his own services to the State, and was glum or silent, Jonathan was instantly frosted by his elder's mood. He was your "man of glass"[2] who, if you but breathe on him, grows

[1]Williams, p. 231.
[2]*Solid Philosophy*, by Sergeant, 1697.

misty and moody, returning an impure image of his own true countenance.

For a short time after coming to Moor Park he had allowed himself almost to love Temple. In dire need of a father, a mentor, to whom he might commit himself, and whom he might reverence and serve with affection, he had seen Temple as the great man he once had been, the man who would stay the hunger in his heart. But he expected too much—appreciation, compliance, recommendation for the highest positions for which he was not yet fitted by experience. Temple, baffled by this sullen, resentful, suspicious creature with his moods of exaltation and aspiration, his queer habit of alternating mole-like study with violent exercise, found that for once his gifts of charm, tact and persuasion had been foiled and were worthless. His failure must have saddened him. Doubtless he looked for affection and gratitude, and Swift, who imagined emotional extortion, denied them, withholding himself rigidly. If this interpretation is correct, each blackmailed the other for appreciation and affection and neither understood what was at work. The more Temple implied his wishes the more Swift drew back, fearing the apparent imposition of another's will and a loss of liberty. Only when Swift, on his own initiative, entered the Church was the band which held them loosened, for then Swift felt himself externally free: he might go and come as he wished and if Temple was inattentive or cold he could throw over his obligations to him.

For with Temple, Swift had begun to hope and Temple, like everyone else, had disappointed him. Through the rime of his disillusion he began to see that no one was worth considering but *himself*. He must depend only on *himself* for preferment and prosperity. He was finished with exploitation and frustration: his interests must in future come before those of others, time must not be lost in hanging on false promises and faint rewards.

His hypersensitivity hardened into insensitivity where others were concerned, for if he dared think of their needs he was swayed too much, stifling his own. He had maintained his equilibrium with such difficulty that if the actions, the

character, the will of another interfered with his own he
regarded them as a threat to his safety. Therefore the feelings,
the needs of others unless he chose to champion them, were
incommoding, and dangerous.

Woe to anyone who ignored or rebuked him. Varina
temporized and what was the result? He placed the onus of her
doubts, her indecision and apparent dismissal of him at her
door: he made her acceptance of him impossible by his bru-
tality, but the world should see that she, not he, was to blame.
Cousin Dryden laughingly assured him that "he would never
be a poet" and the sensitive, aspiring youth who had dared to
put forth his inquiring antennae was snubbed into instant, dismayed reaction. The nascent poet wholly lost heart and,
although he wrote verse in plenty, he never again essayed
poetry of exalted style or enthusiastic tone. It took but a
single rebuff to discourage him, and that so profoundly that
he refused to make a fool of himself a second time. When
Sir William neglected him, underestimating his qualities
(and Lady Giffard rebuked him), he vowed perpetual banishment from his thoughts and life of the whole of Temple's
family.

> "I thought I saw Jack Temple and his wife pass by me
> to-day in their coach; but I took no notice of them. I am
> glad I have wholly shaken off that family." [1]

(Later, however, he softened and in 1736-7 corresponded
in amiable fashion with the formerly despised nephew of Sir
William.[2]) He could not hate them sufficiently, and the
energy which should have been used in a steady confrontation
of his alleged enemies, a quiet acceptance or rejection of their
implied criticisms and censure, was used first in flight, and
then in a prolonged spate of hatred which gnawed at his heart,
corroding it more than that of the hated.

He reverted more profoundly than ever to the cynicism
which had begun to form in him long before he wrote his letter
of passionate protestation to Varina—

> "Philosophy advises us to keep our desires and prospects

[1] Williams, p. 9.
[2] Ball, V., pp. 416-7.

of happiness as much as we can in our own breasts, and independent of anything without. He that sends them abroad is likely to have as little quiet as a merchant whose stock depends on winds, and waves, and pirates, or upon the words and faith of creditors, every whit as dangerous and inconstant as the other."[1]

One sees in these two sentences how apt Swift was to look to someone else for his happiness, and when, having placed an undue strain upon the relationship, with expectations impossible of fulfilment, the individual seemed to fail him, he swung away in bitterness, upbraiding and despising those who disappointed him, rather than altering his own anticipations. Ignorant of the fact that he was doing it he searched for another to live his life for him, and it is this need to annex, possess, and almost inhabit another being which brought unhappiness to the women whom he believed he loved, and cheated him of his own contentment.

X

Sir William and Swift were indeed a strange pair and the wonder is, not that they disagreed, parted, and came together again into a belated Indian summer of understanding, but that they worked in unison.

For Temple was a lover of truth, solitude and meditation; gardens, music—("seldom without it in his own family")[2]—women and children; who delighted in making others at ease, and whose charm was so irresistible that "he never had a mind to make anybody kind to him that he did not compass it."[3] Even an enemy remarked of him that he was glad Sir William was not a woman "because he was sure he might have persuaded him to anything."[4]

On the other hand, Swift, although ruggedly sincere, was inclined to be secretive, was unable to bear solitude without uneasiness, admired action rather than reflection, was wholly unmusical and never interested in gardens. He planted hollies

[1]Ball, I, p. 17.
[2] and [3]Lady Giffard's *Character of Sir William Temple.*
[4]Lady Giffard's *Life of Sir William Temple*, p. 19.

and willows at Laracor and elms in the Dublin Cathedral precincts, to the mortification of his parishioners at his disturbance of ancient tombstones, but of gardening in the gentler sense he derived little pleasure, as far as we know. He prayed that women and children might not impede him in his uncertain course in life; and although he often attempted to play the mediator, his whole method of doing so was antithetical to Temple's, for it was one of stirring people into consciousness by pricking and prodding them into vexatious activity.

Temple had been a passionate lover and claimed unashamedly the support of a wife and sister, delighting in their service and company, repaying them with devotion and constancy; Swift repressed his emotions to such an extent that he himself did not recognize their existence and called himself "cold" and fastidious.

Temple was fearless of opinion, "not minding whom he pleased or angered." Swift cared terribly whether he received approbation or disapprobation; if he appeared to be ruthless and unmindful of his own vehement intrusions it was because he would not admit this weakness, and felt it necessary to wipe his adversaries from the slate with a bitterly determined thoroughness which admitted of no further reckoning. Temple stood outside party and faction, keeping an even balance between dissentient bodies: Swift hurled himself in where others feared to tread, attacking a party, ridiculing an individual, marking them down as a beast does its prey.

Meditation drew Temple, and a philosophical consideration of principle and value—how truth, for instance, might be full of an intrinsic beauty and was not to be wooed merely for the rewards she might bring. He studied and inquired, exploring the realm of ideas, the inner recesses of heart and mind, finding a kind of poetry in the exploration: he was objective and reflective. Swift disliked philosophy and science, was impatient of theory, and, eager to be a realist, contemptuous of temporizing and procrastination. He found it easiest to express himself in action and, if this was denied him, in verbal medicine—written prescriptions made up of subtly poisoned phrases. It is almost as if he judged the whole of mankind to be suffering from a mental malady allied to his own physical one, a deafness of the mind so complete that nothing could penetrate it, and, since cursing and shouting were useless, the infiltration of medicinal oils, whose ingredients taken in sufficient quantities would either kill or cure, was advisable.

Temple was a born diplomatist, a fine example of the old school of cultured and aristocratic courtiers who accomplished their ends by means of personal charm and ability: Swift was the born politician in a newer, harder, more party-ridden age, on the eve of commercial, industrial and agricultural development.

Swift's tendency to go counter to those around him, more especially if he was made to feel indebted to them, reveals itself gradually in his religious and political views, upon which he takes a stand after Temple's death. Where Temple, influenced by the Dutch, advocated religious toleration as the most fruitful soil in which spiritual trees might grow, Swift firmly adhered to the tenets of the Established Church and regarded dissenters, Jews and atheists as unfit for office. While Temple stood for preferences beginning to be labelled "Whig"—an alliance with Holland, continental protestantism, admiration of the Prince of Orange—Swift abhorred the Dutch, whom English poets of the past fifty years had been at pains to picture as "mutinous" or "crouching and cruel," and actively disliked William the Third.[1]

A constant complaint made against Temple by the older biographers of Swift is that he was pompous, pedantic, self-centred and boring, insensitive to the latter's abilities, oblivious of his needs and welfare, and solely concerned with making use of him. They accuse the older man of having brought out the worst in the younger, and imply that Swift actually did Temple a favour in remaining with him. So that when, years later, Swift breaks out impatiently with "Faith, there's no such thing as a fine old gentleman," they assert that he indicates Temple; and when in the privacy of the *Journal* he snarls at Sir William, his sister and descendants, their pity is for Swift and not for Temple.

[1] See Rossi and Hone, p. 67 et seq. The finest analysis of Temple's influence on Swift is in Quintana, *Mind and Art of Swift*, Oxford University Press, 1936, pp. 10-28.

Yet how could the man who invented the hoax of "shara-waggi"[1] and fooled even Horace Walpole ever be boring? This was a name given by Temple to a theory which he alleged the orientals practised of harmonizing contrasts, of employing a studied irregularity, in landscapes or buildings; and the name, which he declared came from the Chinese, entered on immediate popularity. "But in the end it appeared that there never was such a word or one remotely like it."[2] It is interesting to see it cropping up in articles to-day and to find that Temple's theory is being studied and applied in England and America and on the Continent.

Swift's splenetic outbursts are those of a man suffering from repressions who regards his imagined "imprisonment" with resentment. It speaks something for his admiration for Temple that he never directly assaults him but only makes allusive explosions. His irritability was an indication of his bruised and roughened character. Deprived of a sound belief in himself, unable to accept or reject fearlessly, submitting to the will of others with outward pleasure but inward dissatisfaction, he was determined at long last to assert himself and clamoured arrogantly for the attention and respect which he half knew that it was fitting he should receive. Intent upon shielding himself, upon wounding rather than receiving further wounds, he turned to revile those who had once been kind to him.

During the years with Temple, Swift began imperceptibly to withdraw into misanthropy, almost as a conscious protest. If, before, he had suspected that he was a fool and others were knaves, now he knew that they were knaves and that he was not a fool. He raised and hardened his conception of himself in order to displace the opinions and judgments of others: now he, Swift, was just and sane, whilst others were corrupt and unsound. The *Digression on Madness* in *A Tale of a Tub*, which he wrote while at Moor Park and Kilroot, is the first symptom of a growing attitude of separation from humanity, an isolation to become more absolute than that of a lost polar

[1] *Essay on Gardening.*
[2] Margaret Barton and Osbert Sitwell on "Taste", *Johnson's England*, Vol. II, ed. by A. S. Turberville. Clarendon Press, 1933.

explorer. For the latter in his heart and mind remembers his fellow-beings with a feeling of consanguinity, of warmth and trust, and has a yearning to mingle and be one with them, which Swift, owing to his estrangement from himself, slowly lost.

CHAPTER THREE

. . . a dangerous tendency, it seems to me, that carries religion into politics and, almost inevitably, coarsens religion into a sort of celestial politics and diplomacy. One world is enough to my feeling, and I should wish religion to digest and transmute this life into ultimate spiritual terms rather than commit us to fresh risks, ambitions, and love affairs in a life to come. . . . Fixity of tradition, of custom, of language, is perhaps a prerequisite to complete harmony in life and mind. Variety in these matters is a lesson to the philosopher and drives him into the cold arms of reason: but it confuses the poet and saint, and embitters society.

SANTAYANA

I

TO look to another human being for happiness, or to a particular country, place, or household for a feeling of security, Swift now knew was fatal. People deserted one, or died; they cheated one with false implications and promises, or, valuing you for your talents rather than loving you for your real self, kept you in fruitless dependence.

Yet something misguided, something human in him forced him to continue to look to others for appreciation and contentment, as if he could not believe in himself unless others first did so. It was all an early misconception—of what life is, of what man is, of the nature of one's duty to oneself as well as to others. The world as Swift had known it had little of the fairytale quality, yet in a child-like way he still looked for a happiness he never found, and his bitterness and frustration suggest a search in the wrong direction.

"The various opinions of philosophers have scattered through the world as many plagues of the mind, as Pandora's box did those of the body; only with this difference, that *they have not left hope at the bottom.*"[1]

[1] *A Tritical Essay upon the Faculties of the Mind.* Temple Scott, Vol. I, pp. 291-6.

Not only the ancient philosophers but present-day statesmen, lawyers of one's own family, the very women who had
borne and suckled him, had confused and discouraged him so
profoundly that he went about seeking employment, preferment and honourable service, convinced that life was a battle
in which the adversaries were better armed than he and apt to
use deceitful methods—a scoundrelly lot who would score
against him. His new experiences only confirmed his fears.

One of the most hopeful prospects before Swift on the death
of Temple was a promise which the latter had extracted from
the King that Swift should receive a prebend of Canterbury,
or possibly Westminster. Such a position would not only have
satisfied his ambition but would have been especially fitting,
since the younger branch of the Yorkshire Swifts, from which
he was descended, numbered amongst them Thomas Swift,
collated to the territory of St. Andrew, Canterbury, in 1569.
To one of Swift's disposition, inclined to regard himself as
homeless and unattached, a prebendal stall in the cathedral
city in which his great-great-great-grandfather had lived and
worked would have been more than gratifying.

Alas for royal promises! Even one's Sovereign could not
be trusted, nor his courtiers; for when Swift appealed to the
King through the Earl of Romney, the latter either forgot or
refused to carry the message and once more Swift was left
empty-handed. What was his reaction? Years later he
retaliated by calling Romney "an old, vicious, illiterate rake,
without any sense of truth or honour."[1] But, at the time,
some other more constructive action must be taken. At the
age of thirty-two he still had his way to make and, as he himself
puts it, "was as far to seek as ever."[2]

After waiting and hoping in vain for advancement from
this quarter Swift determined to accept a position offered him
by the Earl of Berkeley, recently appointed one of the Lord
Justices of Ireland, that of chaplain and private secretary.
But although he acted as secretary on the journey (which took
a considerable time, since Berkeley, in regal style, delayed in

---

[1] Temple Scott, Vol. XI, p. 380.
[2] Letter to Lord Palmerston. January 29th, 1725. Ball, III,
p. 301.

order to attend to matters on his estates in Gloucester before sailing from Bristol), Swift found, upon arrival in Dublin, that the secretaryship had been filched from him. A Mr. Bushe had persuaded Lord Berkeley that a clergyman could not properly fill the position, nor would it be of any advantage to him, and had then usurped the secretaryship himself. In a few months' time Swift claimed the Deanery of Derry, which now fell vacant. Again that serpent, the new secretary, blocked his advancement, conferring the rich Deanery upon another candidate who had bribed him with a thousand pounds. Just as Temple in his lifetime had been told that he might have the embassy to Spain for the sum of six thousand pounds, Swift was informed that, could he supply another thousand, he might still be appointed Dean. This custom of mixing bribery with the attainment of even ecclesiastical positions, disgusted Swift. Besides, he had not the money. Zeal, ability, devotion to the work, counted for nothing. Is it to be wondered at that he was enraged and that he felt that once more he had been cheated? Turning on his heel with "God confound you both for a couple of scoundrels,"[1] he left his lodgings in the Castle and took revenge with his most dangerous weapon, his pen. The pair of poems said to have been written at this time[2] are gross in the extreme, and it is in writings of this kind that Swift acts like an animal who relieves itself upon the carcass of a despised adversary.

Lord Berkeley hastened to make amends. Swift was given the pickings of the Deanery and in six months' time accepted the livings of Laracor, Agher and Rathbeggan. It has been suggested that Berkeley pacified Swift in this manner since he was afraid of his pen, but there is no proof that he ever read the verses in which the mean, dark and venomous side of Swift's nature ignobly reveals itself. It is possible that he liked Swift or had the perspicacity to see his ability.

[1] *Life of Swift*, by Sheridan, p. 29, and Ball, Vol. I, pp. 31 and 33 n.

[2] *The Discovery* and *The Problem*. Mr. Williams thinks that the victim of *The Problem* is more likely to have been the Earl of Romney, who had failed to carry Swift's message to the King. See *Poems*, Vol. I, p. 65.

II

Before the resident chaplain was to become vicar, much friendship and merriment sprang out of his intercourse with Lord Berkeley's wife and family. For the Earl himself Swift had little use, and with his usual acerbity he summed up the character of the man whom he both envied and contemned, in a private note calling him "Intolerably lazy and indolent and somewhat covetous."[1] But for the Countess he had respect, and for the three daughters, Lady Mary, Lady Betty and Lady Penelope Berkeley, a playful affection. Lady Penelope died young and was buried in the Dublin church in which Vanessa was to be laid to rest: Lady Mary was soon married to Thomas Chambers, sometime Master of the Mint, but young Lady Betty and Swift instantly struck up a friendship which was to last until his death. She was a girl of spirit and beauty and when Swift, as she alleged, "deafened them with puns and rhyme" Lady Betty did not hesitate to retaliate with doggerel verses of her own.

Once more he was a member of a household, not incorporated into it, but by means of his wit and charm floating very pleasantly on the surface of intimacy. With his need to exercise power over other weaker natures, he set about making slaves and suppliants of Lady Betty, her mother and the female domestics. One of his most delightful poems, in a vein of humorous raillery which he used all too seldom (probably written at Dublin Castle in 1701) tells how Mistress Frances Harris, one of the Countess's gentlewomen, lost her purse. The house is turned upside down; the loser, gasping for breath with the eagerness of her distracted search and her spate of words, succumbs and is put to bed. The Steward pompously remarks that such domestic tragedies are common occurrences:

"... I remember when I was at m' Lady Shrewsbury's
Such a thing as this happen'd, just about the time of gooseberries."

Everyone is appealed to, no one can help, until in despera-

[1]Remarks on "The Characters of the Court of Queen Anne": Temple Scott, Vol. X, p. 279.

tion the suggestion is made that Mrs. Harris should consult an astrologer. The chaplain, who she vows is as good, is of course Swift himself.

> "*So the Chaplain came in; now the Servants say, he is my Sweet-*
> *heart,*
> *Because he's always in my chamber, and I always take his Part;*
> *So, as the Devil would have it, before I was aware, out I*
> *blunder'd,*
> Parson, *said I, can you cast a* Nativity, *when a Body's plunder'd?*
> (*Now you must know, he hates to be call'd* Parson, *like the*
> *Devil*)."[1]

It is a brilliant caricature of the muddle-headed gentle-woman and other members of Lord Berkeley's household. Swift had a peculiarly clear insight into the minds and characters of servants.[2] Perhaps he felt more at ease with their unpretentious ways than with those of his superiors since he hated cant, convention and empty formality. Mistress Harris, the steward, the valet, the housekeeper, the footman's wife, the housemaid, the chaplains (Swift and his rival), and Lady Betty Berkeley all appear, drawn by the garrulous tongue of the gentlewoman who gives away her own character in every line.

With such delightful nonsense, presage of Swift's more biting, maturer wit, he amused the ladies whose society and admiration he could not dispense with. It was well for him that he had this gift of effervescence, of throwing off such lively trifles, for this quality, in contrast to his gloomy and brooding cynicism, acted as a safety valve and relieved the excessive pressure caused by unnatural restraint.

Amongst Swift's duties as chaplain was the reading of holy works to Lady Berkeley. One day, weary of the "heavenly Meditations" of her ladyship's favourite author, Robert Boyle, he substituted the "most solemn waggery" of his own

---

[1] "*To Their Excellencies the Lords Justices of Ireland, The Humble Petition of Frances Harris* (who must Starve and Die a Maid if it Miscarries)." *Poems,* Vol. I, p. 72.

[2] See his *Directions to Servants.* Temple Scott, Vol. XI, pp. 307-64.

Meditation upon a Broomstick, which he read "with an in-flexible gravity of countenance" and "the same solemn tone which he had used in delivering" Boyle himself.[1] The Countess, no judge of style, swallowed it up neatly. Upon discovering some time afterwards that she had been taken in, she laughed good-naturedly at herself, declaring it to be a "vile trick that the rogue" had played on her, adding that Swift "never baulked his humour in any thing."

Yet the *Meditation* was bound with an odd twist of tragic irony. Swift describes the broomstick, once flourishing in a forest with verdant boughs and tenacious roots, now turned upside down,

"and by a capricious kind of fate, destined to make other things clean, and be nasty itself . . . SURELY MAN IS A BROOM-STICK . . . a topsy-turvey creature, his animal faculties perpetually cock-a-horse and rational; his head where his heels should be; grovelling on the earth, and yet, with all his faults, he sets up to be a universal reformer and cor-rector of abuses, a remover of grievances, rakes into every slut's corner of nature, bringing hidden corruptions to the light . . . his last days are spent in slavery to women, and generally the least deserving. . . ."[2]

Here Swift parodies himself. He was probably aware as he wrote that he did so, but not to what extent his pre-occupations, fears and final desperation were foreshadowed. The roots of the topsy-turvey broomstick, which have withered away and been inverted, symbolize the dried and sapless emotional life of the man who starved and killed his tap-root in order that reason and intellect alone might guide him. He fears unbridled emotion, distrusts his powers of control, and constantly sees himself being "run away with," so that he describes man as a creature whose "animal faculties" irrationally ride him: yet the reverse became true of Swift because of these very fears coupled with repressive powers. This preoccupation with inverted faculties appears again in

[1] *Life of Swift*, by Sheridan, p. 39.
[2] Hayward, p. 458 (capitals omitted).

The Digression on Madness,[1] and later in *Gulliver*. It was the foundation of the tragic conviction uttered to Arthur Young, that like a blasted tree which they regarded, he, Swift, "would die at the top."

Like the broomstick he was destined to spend his life in the service of others. Without any fixed aims of his own he adopted their needs and interests, fighting for them like some valiant mercenary. Unable to believe at first that he *could* succeed and then hardening into the opposite belief that *only* he could help others, he appropriated first Temple's literary and political disputes, then those of Bolingbroke and the Tory Party, the Established Church in Ireland, and finally those of Ireland herself. He becomes the champion of the oppressed, ill-educated and poor, the mad and crippled, of starving poets, discarded soldiers, unfortunate printers, improvident curates, unwise statesmen and disinherited sons. A tenth of his small income in the first year of his life at Laracor goes in gifts and charity: his benevolence is princely. He never deserts an office without seeing that it is filled by someone more deserving. He goes out of his way to pester those in power for preferment—not for himself—but for others, and denies himself the comforts of daily life to relieve the paupers to whom he feels allied in common need and the fate that overhangs them. Their "looped and windowed raggedness" tears at his heartstrings and he seeks to avert it for himself by acts of perpetual unselfishness. There is something both pitiable and terrible in the compulsive altruism by which Swift tried to counteract his ingrowing parsimony; the indulgence of assisting others freed him from censure in his own eyes. Could he but have seen it, more attention devoted to his own disordered inner life would have repaid him and those near to him a thousandfold.

Like the broomstick he swept out the kennels of others. A

---

[1]op. cit., pp. 329-31. "Having to no purpose used all peaceable Endeavours, the collected part of the *semen*, raised and enflamed, became adust, converted to Choler, turned head upon the spinal Duct and ascended to the Brain . . . my *Phenomenon* of *Vapours*, ascending from the lower Faculties to overshadow the Brain, and there distilling into Conceptions . . . *Madness*, or *Phrenzy*."

victim of disturbed sensitivities, he raked over and studied other men's vices, weaknesses and physical aberrations, in the effort to rid himself of the constant absorption, and to help them improve themselves. If, unlike the broomstick, he failed to wear out his last days in slavery to undeserving women it was only by heroic efforts. He prevented himself from falling a victim to humiliating servitude; he escaped. But at what cost? At the cost of all that is beautiful, natural and serene. Only by this means did he avert that fatal sentence which he was tempted to pass on himself, "wherein he was at once the judge and the criminal, accuser and executioner."[1]

Thus his days, and not only his last days, were spent in a slavery far more tragic than that of any inanimate article. The fop involved in the volatile passions to which he is in bondage wears himself out in a profligate misuse of his powers. The miser hoards his coin, as the Yahoos hoard their shining stones which serve no purpose, earn no increase, and remain hard, sterile and unrewarding. Swift's enslavement, for all his eager service, belongs to the latter class. The chains which fettered him, permitting him to leap upward and forward, backward, and in tantalizing circles of prescribed limitation, were his groundless but seemingly real fears, and his fundamental misconceptions with regard to the human race—especially the wielders of distaff and broomstick.

III

Swift set out from Dublin for Laracor, a distance of about twenty miles, on foot, halting for the night at Kells where he was struck by the nationality, name and place of birth of the innkeeper, an Englishman called Jonathan Belcher, who had come from Leicestershire. Swift was astonished at the triple coincidence, but especially impressed by the man's happy acceptance of his lot.

"Have you long been out of your native country?" asked Swift.
"Thirty years, Sir."

[1]*Critical Essay upon the Faculties of the Mind.*

"Do you ever expect to visit it again?"

"Never."

"And can you say that without a sigh?"

"I can, sir, for my family is my country."

"Why, sir, you are a better philosopher than those who have written volumes on the subject. Then you are reconciled to your fate?"

"I ought to be so: I am very happy. I like the people, and though I was not born in Ireland, I'll die in it, and that's the same thing."

"Ipsis Hibernis Hiberniores!"[1] exclaimed Swift, after a long pause.

He envied the innkeeper's disposition which allowed him to remain fixed in a single sphere and occupation, rooted in his family; he marvelled at the philosophic trend of mind which enabled him to equate birth in one land with death in another, to relinquish and accept simultaneously. How fortunate were those of simple heart!

Descending upon the curate at Laracor without warning or ceremony, Swift announced himself brusquely, bullying him and his wife into instant submission and indicating from the start that he expected to be treated with more than ordinary respect. He made them his vassals before they might attack or maltreat him. This was his usual method of imposing himself upon others and if they made no resistance, but took his behaviour in good part, he warmed to them, exerted his charm, and made them subsequent friends and admirers.

The church in which he was to serve equalled in simplicity that of Carlyle's first pastor and tutor, John Johnstone, the old "Shepherd of Annandale." Like the Scottish meeting-house, the Irish building was earthen-floored, thatched with reed instead of heather. Against the western wall stood a huge chimney to carry the smoke from a smouldering turf fire. With its square windows and plain square door, its horse-box pews for the sprinkling of gentry, and rough wooden benches for the poorer parishioners, its crude half-circular altar, its communion plate of tin and pewter, it was a building in which the saintliness of a George Herbert or a

[1] *Swiftiana.* Wilson, London, 1804. Vol. I, p. 58.

Thomas Traherne might have kindled flames of celestial fire, but hardly one to satisfy the worldly ambitions of Jonathan Swift.

In looking back upon the congregation of the small Scottish church—"rude, rustic, bare"—which he had known as a child, Carlyle wrote:—

> "Strangely vivid are those old faces whom I used to see every Sunday . . . heavy-laden, patient, attentive, fallen solitary most of them."[1]

These were the crofters and cottagers, the weavers from as far south as the city of Carlisle (a distance of sixteen miles over the border) who came to hear the minister preach, hanging their dripping plaids to dry in the porch.

Swift's congregation, composed of the English settlers, their servants and former dependants, was probably smaller. In moments of bitterness he reckoned that it consisted of fifteen persons, "most of them gentle and all simple." He does not appear to have become intimate with any members of his congregation, who at first were probably intimidated by his domineering airs. There is no evidence that he regarded them, even in retrospect, with the affection which Carlyle obviously felt for his fellow-worshippers.

He led a regular and orderly life, reading prayers twice a week and preaching on the Sabbath day. Few came to the prayer services, and an anecdote relating to one of them, when no one attended, lingers to preserve for us Swift's peculiarly sardonic humour. Turning to his clerk he opened the service with the words:

"Dearly beloved Roger, the scripture moveth you and me. . . ."[2]

To receive such scant appreciation of one's gifts and of one's ministrant intentions was galling, but Swift continued to perform his duties conscientiously, and, in time, his fidelity to duty, his reputation, and his forceful delivery won him as

[1] *Reminiscences*, ed. by Charles Eliot Norton, Vol. I, pp. 40-1 and II, pp. 13-16.
[2] *Remarks on the Life and Writings of Dr. Jonathan Swift*, by Lord Orrery, 1751, p. 20.

large an audience as it was possible for the sparsely populated countryside to muster.

But if he thought to content himself by humbly performing his duties, Swift was mistaken. His experience at Kilroot might have taught him to suspect his own restless inclinations and inward dissatisfaction. The gap between his imagined successes and the actual level attained was too discouraging for him to contemplate with serenity. The melancholy which attacked him whenever he returned to Ireland in time wore off: he even grew fond of Laracor, yet the ambitious part of him must have looked upon life in Meath as excommunication from the elect. After the beauties of Moor Park, the grandeur of Dublin Castle, the live ebb and flow of London, Laracor must have seemed dull indeed. In all of these places he had been in touch with the shifting problems of the day, which lured him like darting shadows. Now, as at Kilroot, he was cut off from participation, and the excitement of participation.

His energetic and practical nature drove him to attempt the creation of order and beauty around him, in so far as his modest stipend would permit. He made the neglected parsonage more comfortable, enclosed a small garden, built a wall with a southern aspect upon which he planted fruit trees, like his monastic predecessors made a fishpond and filled it with trout, and dug a canal beside which he made a walk whereon he planted willows. In these recreations he buried his chagrin at being merely a country clergyman who was expected to be content with fishing, gardening, engaging in mild gossip, and playing at evening cards.

Many times in after years he was to show how fond he was of Laracor. From London in 1711 he wrote to Stella:

"Oh, that we were at Laracor this fine day! The willows begin to peep, and the quicks to bud. My dream's out: I was adreamed last night that I eat ripe cherries. And now they begin to catch the pikes, and will shortly the trouts . . . and I would fain know whether the floods were ever so high as to get over the holly bank or the river walk; if so, then all my pikes are gone; but I hope not."[1]

[1]Williams, p. 220.

His little Irish holding brought out the poet and the gardener in him more than any other place. He was happy there in his hours of active construction and when, in 1713, he went back to Laracor for a short period he wrote to Vanessa in London:

"My river walk is extremely pretty, and my canal in great beauty, and I see trout playing in it."[1]

He preferred, he said, "a field bed and an earthen floor, before the great house" then awaiting him in Dublin, and in one of those bitter moods of self-depreciation and discouragement, which those who loved him had to bear with, he called himself:

"fitter to look after willows, and to cut hedges, than meddle with affairs of state. I must order one of the workmen to drive those cows out of my island, and make up the ditch again; a work much more proper for a country vicar than driving out factions and fencing against them."[2]

To each of the women in turn he revealed his emotions, of joy and longing, or disillusion and despair, which he durst not show to others.

His efforts to improve Laracor included increasing the glebe from one acre to twenty, and endowing the incumbent of the living with tithes bought by himself to which he attached a singular condition—that if any other form of religion should supersede that of the Established Church, the money should be given to the poor, excluding Jews, Atheists and Infidels.

The construction of the canals, river-walks and walled gardens was a tribute to the influence of the Temples, and in its turn to that of Lucy, Countess of Bedford. It is a felicitous reflection that the outward beauty which a mind creates lives after it and spreads its widening ripples to shores undreamed of by the maker. For it was by one of those strange accidents of history which appear to be primed with an almost personal intent that Moor Park in Hertfordshire, upon which Donne's

[1]*Letter to Vanessa*, Freeman, p. 91.
[2]Ibid.

gracious friend and patroness had lavished so much loving
care, eventually passed to Dorothy Osborne's relations. Here,
along the terraces lying flush with the long windows (terraces
powdered with snow, for it was Christmas and the fountains
which played from their leaden cisterns were glazed with ice)
Sir William and Dorothy had walked on their long-awaited
honeymoon. Observant and appreciative, Temple noted the
disposition of the gardens and determined one day to imitate
what had given him so much pleasure. His labours at Moor
Park in Surrey, which he named after Lady Bedford's home,
in turn influenced Swift, who carried his impressions to
Ireland and in his limited and masculine fashion applied them
to the landscape.

> "I should be plaguy busy at Laracor if I were there now,
> cutting down willows, planting others, scouring my canal,
> and every kind of thing."[1]

Fortunately for Swift's peace of mind, the custom of the
day permitted him to be absent for long periods of time from
his parish. He seems to have been aware of the excess to
which he carried his absences since "he subsequently detailed
his presences in the Visitations and Chapters of these years—
as if to excuse himself from charges which he considered . . .
serious in the case of others."[2]

Sometimes he sought diversion in the town of Trim, with
its ruined abbey and twin-towered castle, only to determine
that the people there were "as great rascals as the gentlemen." He renewed his acquaintance with the Berkeleys in
Dublin Castle, and after the Earl was recalled to London
favoured successive Viceroys there, since he was their Chaplain also. The family of the Duke of Ormonde received him
with as much gusto as the Berkeleys, and the new Lord
Lieutenant had a daughter, Lady Mary, who was attractive to
him if for no other reason than that she put him in mind of
Stella.[3] Lord Pembroke did him the honour of punning with

[1]Williams, p. 197.
[2]Rossi and Hone, p. 132.
[3]Williams, p. 298.

him. But for at least four years out of the ten, following his
succession to Laracor, London claimed him.

Eight months after his induction, the Prebend of Dunlevin
was added to Swift's livings. Entry into the Dublin Chapter
enabled him to claim a Doctorate of Divinity. In the spring
of 1701 he returned to London with Lord Berkeley whose
domestic, if not resident, chaplain he had continued to be for
nearly two years.

IV

These were pregnant days. That malevolent goddess, whom
Swift had so early chid, turned her eyes upon him for an
instant and directed his genius into a fruitful channel. It was
the time of the impeachment of the Whig Lords[1] and, upon
discussing the subject with Lord Berkeley, a notion came into
Swift's head to write an impartial warning to the Commons
in which he should urge them not to condemn Lord Somers
and his colleagues lest they upset the internal balance of power
of the State. He used the method which he had employed while
working for Temple, drawing analogies from history, point-
ing the moral by reference to past calamities. The current
difficulties, he suggested, might be compared to the civil
discords in ancient Athens and Rome in which liberty had also
been endangered by tyranny.

Swift was feeling his way and the *Discourse*[2] was a clever
method of drawing attention to his powers without committing himself to either party, or any definite policy. The piece
was conceived and, like a child abandoned on the steps of the
Foundling Hospital, left to make its way in life. If it succeeded
and was a credit to its father then the parent might acknowledge it: if it disgraced him he might still withhold his name
and disavow it when convenient. He had used the same procedure over his share of the disgraceful *Tripos* at the University; and continued to do so three years later when *A Tale of a
Tub* and *The Battle of the Books* were finally published, and in
launching all his subsequent writings with a single exception.

[1]Lords Oxford, Halifax, Somers and Portland.
[2]*A Discourse of the Contests and Dissensions between the Nobles and the
Commons in Athens and Rome.* 1701. Temple Scott, I, pp. 231-70.

Plate II

Portrait of Swift, by Charles Jervas

For a long time past anonymity of this sort had been common amongst writers of religious, seditious or scurrilous works, which might endanger the lives or members of their authors. But with Swift, one feels that the procedure was adopted, not only for reasons of safety, but also out of vanity and a deep need for secrecy which permeated his being. An anonymous work often gathers more notoriety than an acknowledged one, and at the height of its popularity it is easy to step in and openly avow it, especially if other presumptuous individuals have the temerity to claim it. But above all it enabled Swift to live dangerously, to test his powers, and to realize from these experiences the gratifying sense that he was exceptional, more gifted and more courageous than ordinary men. In his own eyes he raised himself not only above the great mass of the common people but above the few who flattered themselves that they were talented and influential. It was like fencing in the dark, a perilous task, but one which might be attempted by those with a dash of madcap folly: one pricked one's adversaries and fled before they had time to unmask one, or even to discover that they were wounded, sometimes mortally.

He was in London when the *Discourse* was published and was thus able to relish its public reception. Having crossed over with Berkeley in April (1701) he returned again to Ireland in September, only to remain there for another six months before recrossing to England. Frequent crossings of this sort were common with those who had magisterial, clerical or other business to attend to, since England was the mother country imposing her will and methods of administration on her subordinate. Yet in Swift's case they appear to have been exceptionally frequent and one cannot help wondering whether they were not connected in some way with his poise and equilibrium.

"To men, driving through life at such a pace, the road in front splits like a cleft stick and the landscape on each side spins and scatters as they pass. For them, rest is impossible. Only a change of excitement rests them—only something which stimulates their imaginations in fresh directions."[1]

[1]Desmond MacCarthy on Dickens.

Swift's early disturbances had given him a tendency to oscillate, and by perpetual change, flight, and seeming escape, he maintained a precarious balance which eased and satisfied him since it gave him the feeling of being at liberty, unhampered by rigid ties to either country, profession, policy, or individual. Like a circus rider who takes the ring with a foot on two matched ponies, Swift must have drawn upon himself both the envy and ridicule of those who were less nimble and more conventional.

The *Discourse* was attributed first to the Lord Chancellor, then in forced retirement but much in the public eye, and secondly to Gilbert Burnet, Bishop of Salisbury. Swift says that it was the first time that he had troubled about either Whigs or Tories. While at Kilroot he had had some political arguments with his friend John Winder; with Temple and Berkeley he must have engaged in more serious discussions, but they were of a skirmishing nature and might have been indulged in by an intelligent fellow destined for any other vocation. Politics in the modern sense were still in the making: parties were variable and undefined, and a man might look for a long time at the principles of either party without seeing very clearly what they involved, or where one overlapped its rival.

Swift lay low and waited, doing nothing for a time to reveal his authorship. Not until the Bishop of Kildare had twice snubbed him for being nothing more than "a young man"[1] (with the implication that he did not know what he was talking about when he denied that Burnet had written the pamphlet) did he spring from his covert and reveal himself as the author. At a single stroke he mortified his ecclesiastical superior and inflated himself by appearing in his true colours.

When piqued and cornered he flung away disguise. In exactly the same way, three years later, when stupid "little parson-cousin Thomas" allowed it to be hinted that he was the father of *A Tale of a Tub*, a much more dangerous child to acknowledge, Swift, incensed, let it be known in a letter to his printer that the *Tale* sprang from no such feeble loins.

One further comment needs to be made on the *Discourse*.

[1]Scott, Vol. I, p. 72.

It was Swift's new method of wooing those in power. Heretofore he had approached them personally and been rewarded
with contemptuous neglect, or frigid oversight. Weary of
rebuff, he determined to show his ability without waiting for
others to appreciate it in service. Then the great, for a
change, might court him, grow envious, make advances, risk a
snub from Dr. Swift. This would be turning the tables with a
vengeance if it succeeded. And it did: Lords Somers, Halifax
and Sunderland, and other leaders of the Whig party flattered
and courted him and promised high places.

During these years (from 1688 to 1710 when he was rising
from obscurity to fame) Swift found time to visit his mother
at least once and possibly twice a year, as he walked southwards from Chester to London, or rode northwards before re-
embarking for Ireland. It is only when one studies the dates
of these constantly repeated journeys up and down England
and Ireland and across the bad-tempered channel, that one
realizes how tormented Swift must have been both in mind and
body. Fortunately, despite his distressing attacks of illness he
was constitutionally strong. Abstemious through a fear of
poverty, of illness, and possibly of virility, he is said to have
inclined to emaciation in later years, but his portraits in
middle life show him heavy-jowled, broad, and almost portly.
His mother welcomed and soothed him, and evidence of the
playful relationship existing between them comes from a single
anecdote relating to a visit of Mrs. Swift's to Laracor.
Arriving unexpectedly at her Irish lodgings she persuaded the
landlady to believe that Swift was her lover. One may
imagine what one likes—that Jonathan was enraged at her
behaviour, linking scandal with his cloth; or that the mother
bound the son to her with unwholesome emotional ties which
no woman succeeded in breaking. It is best to read into the
anecdote nothing more than the fact that Mrs. Swift had in
her a dash of that prankish humour which her son inherited
from her.

His affection and respect for his mother appear to have
been deep and sincere, and when she died some years later in
the spring of 1710, when he was on the eve of his greatest
triumphs, he wrote:

"*Mem*. On Wednesday, between seven and eight in the evening . . . I received a letter in my chamber at Laracor . . . giving an account that my dear mother . . . died that morning . . . I have now lost my barrier between me and death: God grant I may live to be as well prepared for it, as I confidently believe her to have been! If the way to Heaven be through piety, truth, justice, and charity, she is there."[1]

Perversity prevented Swift from expressing his deepest sentiments openly and, as if he might only pay sincere and poignant tribute to the unheeding dead, he placed this eulogy of his mother in a yearly account book intended for no eyes but his own. In the same way he had scrawled a tribute to Temple in the margin of a notebook on the night of his death —"With him" died "all that was good and amiable among men"[2]—and in like manner he commemorated Stella. It took the ultimate stab of death to wake and release his emotions.

V

While the statesmen and churchmen wondered and whispered over their "plaguy French claret" or mulled port as to who might be the author of the startling *Discourse*, Swift took a step which was to influence the rest of his life as well as those of three other people—Stella, Rebecca Dingley and ultimately, Vanessa. For, in the summer of 1701, he persuaded Stella and Dingley, to whom she had grown attached, and with whom she had lived in lodgings after Temple's death, to follow him to Ireland.

His arguments were eminently sensible and, so he maintained, directed solely towards the pecuniary welfare of the two ladies. Never for an instant does Swift let this practical basis for the "abduction," so hedged about with propriety that the scandalmongers were gagged into silence, melt from view. He admits that such a transplantation is for his own "satisfaction," but the main reason given is that Stella's income will thereby be increased and he probably seriously

[1]Temple Scott, XI, p. 387.
[2]Ibid, I, p. 212.

believed that he placed this consideration before the other more obvious and more natural one. Writing on the night of Stella's death, twenty-seven years later, when emotion at her immediate loss might have made him swerve from his original course, he still maintains (with an exactitude which is re- morseless when one considers the circumstances under which he writes) that his thought for her purse was the chief cause of her removal:

". . . I found she was a little uneasy upon the death of a person upon whom she had some dependence." (Sir William Temple). "Her fortune, at that time, was in all not above fifteen hundred pounds, the interest of which was but a scanty maintenance, in so dear a country, for one of her spirit. Upon this consideration, and indeed very much for my own satisfaction, who had few friends or acquaintance in Ireland, I prevailed with her and her dear friend and companion, the other lady, to draw what money they had into Ireland, a great part of their fortune being in annuities upon funds. Money was then at ten per cent in Ireland besides the advantage of turning it, and all neces- saries of life at half the price. They complied with my advice, and soon after came over."[1]

No one should ever accuse him of anything more than paternal, at worst, fraternal, intervention and protection.

Yet his cloth must come foremost and anything so equivocal as this arrangement must be guarded with all manner of regulations and stifling precautions. Thus it was that he and the ladies never met of a morning, that he and Stella never saw each other alone but only in the presence of patient Rebecca, that the ladies lived in Trim while Dr. Swift dwelt at Laracor, or lodged in Dublin while he inhabited the Deanery. True, Stella sometimes rode over and found the Doctor in his garden attired in his dressing-gown, but this could not shock a country accustomed to the indecorous behaviour of English peers or inured to the indecencies of Sovereigns who openly supported mistresses at the expense of the people.

In his midnight elegy Swift continues the story:

[1] *On the Death of Mrs. Johnson.* Hayward, pp. 725-6.

". . . but, I happening to continue sometime longer in England, they were much discouraged to live in Dublin, where they were wholly strangers. She was at that time about nineteen years old, and her person was soon distinguished. But the adventure looked so like a frolic, the censure held, for some time as if there were a secret history in such a removal; which, however, soon blew off by her excellent conduct."[1]

Comment would certainly be more frequent and more pungent since Stella was no cold bluestocking. Her appearance must have been provoking to say the least of it, if she still resembled her early portrait and Swift's description of her at fifteen or sixteen.

We read and re-read those vexing lines for a hint of a disclosure. We strain to catch some thought or emotion lying behind the action, if not Swift's, then Stella's, or even "dummy Dingley's," as one feminine writer has called her. But Swift's self-control froze his pen and his lips. The tongue of the idle gossip, the pen of the fanciful biographer, of the theorist and conjecturer, might wag or ply in earnest but the protagonists of that drama, enacted nearly two-and-a-half centuries ago, schooled themselves in reticence. Posterity is left to admire and to wonder. Yet we cannot help inquiring into Stella's and Dingley's thoughts, as well as into Swift's, for he benefited from the arrangement more obviously than they.

What tentative, what persuasive arguments must Swift have used to Mrs. Johnson? Stella was now independent. but was there not something particularly unusual in this decision whereby a young girl of promising talents and beauty, who might be insinuated into Court and London society, who might marry well, was whisked off to Ireland where she knew no one, and thrown back upon the companionship of either her companion Dingley or of her male 'abductor,' a being upon whom she must never fully and openly rely, or never make the slightest claim? If Stella's mother acceded, was it because of Swift's implied promises of marriage, or her daughter's belief in these? We know that Mrs. Johnson remained on friendly terms with Swift, sending him cakes,

[1] op. cit, pp. 725-6.

wax candles, and sweet water for his head when he was in London. But there is just the possibility that Mrs. Johnson did not agree and, if this is so, the character of Stella takes on a more spirited tone, for she must then have defied her mother's wishes and injunctions. Above all, is it not likely that the heart of a young girl, sensible and biddable though she might be to her imperious mentor, should love and admire the superior being who had not only taught her what books to read and how to shape her letters but who had also concerned himself with her "moral education"? Next to Sir William, she owed him everything, and it would be natural, even if unreasonable or against his strict injunctions and ominous forebodings, for her to love him. Being of a practical nature she may early have decided to throw in her lot with philosophic good humour, silently agreeing to love him without confessing, silently risking success or defeat. To be near him was sufficient and perhaps, in time, his heart would melt.

This seems the most likely reading. Swift, as a man of honour, which he prided himself on being, probably attempted to make it plain to her that he was unlikely ever to marry, that she must consider herself in no way bound to him and was, in fact, free to marry another whenever she inclined. Possibly he reserved a like liberty for himself. His treatment of a suitor for Stella's hand in a few years time suggests this. Nevertheless the cunning side of his nature, unable (because of its unfortunate attitude to a married relationship and its revulsion from physical intimacy) to take openly what it unconsciously coveted, stealthily achieved what the whole man had not the courage to bid for, a half-wife with means of her own, conveniently disposed to warm his house and look after his interests during his absence, and to withdraw tactfully to lodgings upon his return, in order to shield his, as well as her, reputation. The sensitive, fragile, unformed and timid creature, who wore the mask of bully and dictator to the world, thus begged for and received the imitation of a life which it dared not enter on fully, and the precarious balance between desertion and possession, loneliness and absorption was achieved.

But at what cost to Stella? The *Journal*, sole record of her reflected thoughts, meagrely interpreted by Swift, gives few signs of discontent. Her letters to him, by a strange irony, are all destroyed, probably by Swift himself after her death, or even before. It is only from stray straws of comment blown in at the doorway of time by observant commentators that we get any clue to her state of mind. And which of these is to be believed? We have to sift not only the evidence of the remarks themselves but also of the lives and reputations of the commentators. Laetitia Pilkington was often inaccurate and fanciful, Lord Orrery was malicious and biased, Sheridan was only a boy when he knew Swift, Delany was loquacious and eulogistic. Can we trust Samuel Rogers? In the *Recollections* of his *Table Talk* occurs this haunting statement:

> "Grattan's aunt was intimate with Swift's *Stella*, who would sometimes sleep with her in the same bed and pass the whole night in tears. *Stella* was not handsome."

That first sentence gives us a world of information. Its implications and pathos are more valuable than all the conflicting opinions on Stella's outward grace or beauty.

And what of Dingley? Was she, too, to wear away her remaining years (and she was middle-aged when she trapesed over to Ireland), in uncomplaining companionship with a young girl who took such unusual risks? Gossip would bandy her name about as well. She had little enough beauty, or fortune, and could ill afford to throw away her chances of matrimony as high-handedly as Stella. But we know so little of Dingley—"a lady of more advanced years" with whom Esther Johnson "had contracted an intimate friendship,"[1] are Swift's dry words as an ageing man. What powerful persuasions did he use over Dingley? Or was it once more "little Hetty" who ravished her away from more sensible paths? Dingley, as far as we know, was not in love with Jonathan Swift. The thought of a channel crossing was probably odious to her: she may have been fearful of the wild Irish 'savages': chopping and changing about from the Doctor's rectory to various lodgings may have destroyed her sense of having a home of her own and uninterrupted security: in fact

[1]Hayward, p. 725.

she may rightly have complained of inconsiderateness and jangled nerves. But we hear nothing of all this. Dingley remains endearing for her self-effacement, for her quality of uncomplaining adaptation to the vagaries of a pair of lovers crossed with more than moon-madness, even for her stupidity which Swift jibed at.

"It would take a stupid woman to play gooseberry for twenty-seven mortal years, to bear a continual pelting with praises and endearments ostensibly aimed at her, but really meant for somebody else: to sit daily in the same room with two people who would not have her join in their conversation and even hauled her over the coals if she listened to it: and then to be censured for turning to Tiger, the lapdog, for sympathy."[1]

She remains immortal because it was for her that Swift in London bought rasps of dark Brazilian tobacco, for her that rascally Patrick kept a linnet imprisoned in his Chelsea cupboard until he might carry it over the water.

"I went last night to put some coals on my fire after Patrick was gone to bed; and there I saw in a closet a poor linnet he has bought to bring over to Dingley: it cost him sixpence, and he is as tame as a dormouse. I believe he does not know he is a bird: where you put him, there he stands, and seems to have neither hope nor fear: I suppose in a week he will die of the spleen. Patrick advised with me before he bought him. I laid fairly before him the greatness of the sum and the rashness of the attempt; showed how impossible it was to carry him safe over the salt sea: but he would not take my counsel, and he'll repent it."[2]

Did Dingley ever receive the linnet? I fear not. By the end of the month Swift writes that the frost is so "smart" that "Patrick's bird water freezes in the gally-pot, and my hands in bed."[3] The following week he reports that the bird

". . . was very tame at first, and 'tis now the wildest I

[1] Margaret Woods.
[2] Williams, p. 156.
[3] Ibid, p. 178.

ever saw. He keeps it in a closet, where it makes a terrible litter—but I say nothing; I am as tame as a clout."[1]

The linnet grows wilder and wilder and by March:

"His wings have been quilled thrice, and are now up again; he will be able to fly after us to Ireland, if he be willing."[2]

I believe Swift hated to see the bird imprisoned and rejoiced in its increasing spirit. He had been too long oppressed himself not to shudder at even a linnet's caging. There is something infinitely appealing in his docility in keeping it and in his conspiracy with Patrick. Are they not like two great schoolboys plotting to bring their sisters gifts? There is humour, too, in his glance at himself and in his recognition of his own submissiveness. Under the spell of this tenderness, so surprising in a man of Swift's rough temper, Dingley was probably held prisoner as much as her mistress.

VI

The 'abduction' of Stella, a step taken openly before the eyes of England and Ireland, was Swift's real marriage. The alleged marriage to Stella which is said, on imperfect evidence, to have taken place in 1716 was no marriage in spirit. Nor was it, if it occurred, legally valid. It was a marriage null and void in any court of law since it was never consummated. The step which he took in 1701 was for him tantamount to marriage since it was all that Swift, crippled by his fears, revulsions and inhibitions, could achieve.

At least the 'abduction' had this merit, that it was a courageous and open act, and as honest a one as Swift's blindness might allow. If Stella was forced to face the volley of censorious comments which undoubtedly rang out upon her first appearance in Ireland, Swift had to face a similar one, more penetrating than that directed at an ordinary person since the reputation of his cloth was at stake. He did not believe in marriage, did not consider himself ready or fit for that state; very well then, he would not attempt it. Nor did he

[1] Williams, p. 181.
[2] Ibid, p. 209.

want an illicit relationship, which would cloud his ideals for his life as a clergyman and would of necessity grow insipid, even brackish. On the other hand, restless, lonely, morbid and unsteady, he longed for feminine companionship. The only compromise between these equipollent forces, drawing him like wind and tide in contradiction, was that curiously variable form of relationship, Friendship.

Swift cheated himself into believing that, provided the outward proprieties were rigorously observed, no damage might be done. A leading trait of Stella's, for which he never ceased to praise her, was one which he had early encouraged— that of sound commonsense. She would never embarrass him with tantrums and hysterical outbursts, fetter him with extravagances, hinder him with demands to which he could not attend. He held that the feminine nature might be taught to imitate the masculine, in which case men would have a far more tranquil existence with no tempestuous nonsense to disturb it. What is more, he would train and produce a woman to prove his theory, like a man who raises a new variety of stronger, more richly-coloured flowers, like one who breeds a new human species. The excitement and the rewards of the experiment would make it worth while. For the best part of thirty years he appeared to achieve this highly precarious success. Stella, apparently, did not complain as long as she was the sole recipient of his attentions. As far as we know, she did not cry out when he left her, attempt to recall him when he was gone, entice him with any of those more doubtful forms of feminine witchery, lean on him over-much for support. Possibly she was not aware of the effect which Swift's more dominant and aggressive character had exercised, and was continuing to exercise on her. Stunted into partial immaturity, forced to deceive herself as he did, she endured and acquiesced.

Yet for a girl of spirit this acquiescence must often have been torture, and that Stella was of a lively and courageous nature no one can deny. Swift himself pays tribute to her animation more than once:

"With all the softness of temper that became a lady, she had the personal courage of a hero. She and her friend

8

having removed their lodgings to a new house, which stood solitary, a parcel of rogues, armed, attempted the house, where there was only one boy. She was then about four and twenty: and, having been warned to apprehend some such attempt, she learned the management of a pistol; and the other women and servants being half dead with fear, she stole softly to her dining-room window, put on a black hood to prevent being seen, primed the pistol fresh, gently lifted up the sash; and, taking her aim with the utmost presence of mind, discharged the pistol loaden with the bullets, into the body of one villain, who stood the fairest mark. The fellow, mortally wounded, was carried off by the rest, and died the next morning, but his companions could not be found. The Duke of Ormonde hath often drank her health to me upon that account, and had always an high esteem of her.

"She was indeed under some apprehensions of going in a boat, after some danger she had narrowly escaped by water, but she was reasoned thoroughly out of it. She was never known to cry out, or discover any fear, in a coach or on horseback, or any uneasiness by those sudden accidents with which most of her sex, either by weakness or affectation, appear so much disordered."[1]

Stella is more fortunate than Vanessa because Swift's love for her, enshrined in the *Journal* and the elegy written after her death, reveal her character to us as seen through Swift's eyes. The *Journal* was begun some nine years after she crossed over to Ireland when he was in London. In it we see her, still a young woman, walking, riding, playing cards of an evening, sipping her wine and "toasted" oranges, already securely set in a little circle of Swift's intimate friends who seem to have accepted her unusual position, and admired her for her tactful and competent handling of it. In the elegy, Swift draws her portrait as a mature woman in the years immediately preceding her death, with delightful glimpses of her as she was when a child. He succeeds in performing that most difficult of all tasks, of presenting her to us in the round, with something of her blemishes as well as her virtues—always harder to do when affection obscures the true outline. Even his enemy

¹Hayward, p. 727-8.

Lady Giffard says:

> "I think nothing harder than to write anybody's character, and that of a friend is yet more difficult. If one tells truth, 'tis thought being partial, and if one does not, one is sure to be unjust."[1]

After emphasizing her spirit and admirable control, Swift speaks of her "gifts of mind."

> "I cannot call to mind that I ever once heard her make a wrong judgement of persons, books, or affairs. Her advice was always the best, and (given) with the greatest freedom, mixed with the greatest decency. . . .
> "There seemed to be a combination among all that knew her, to treat her with a dignity much beyond her rank: yet people of all sorts were never more easy than in her company."[2]

With characteristic honesty Swift sets down the fact that "her memory was not of the best." He goes on to relate her contempt for coxcombs, liars, and churchmen who profaned their calling by "breaches of honour." And here we see Swift's influence in moulding her character, for his hatred of insincerity and coxcombry was well known and, having entered the Church, he was always jealous of its advancement and reputation.

For all her softness there is something stern and unyielding about Stella as if she had, through long association with him, become imbued with some of Swift's own exacting fierceness. While noting that her servants loved and adored her, Swift adds that

> "her demeanour was so awful, that they durst not fail in the least point of respect. She chid them seldom but it was with severity, which had an effect upon them for a long time after."[3]

With a coxcomb

> "she had no mercy, but was sure to expose him to the

[1] *Character of Sir William Temple*, p. 26.
[2] Hayward, p. 726.
[3] Ibid, pp. 727-8-9.

contempt of the standers-by; yet in such a manner as he was ashamed to complain, and durst not resent."[1]

Before those of high station who had lapsed from her ideals

"she could not conceal her indignation, nor hear them named without showing her displeasure in her countenance."[2]

In her criticism of his, or other people's, writings she was, says Swift, "sometimes too severe, which is a safe and pardonable error." Swift had met a match in Stella; she countered his strength with an equal strength and although she may once have been his pupil, her own gifts, developed by him, in some ways rivalled his. We may, in fact, owe Stella more than we know in Swift's very writings, for he says:

"Neither was it easy to find a more proper or impartial judge, whose advice an author might better rely on, if he intended to send a thing into the world, provided it was a subject that came within the compass of her knowledge."[3]

Next he commends her composure in company:

"She never had the least absence of mind in conversation, nor" (was) "given to interruption, or appeared eager to put in her word by waiting impatiently till another had done. She spoke in a most agreeable voice, in the plainest words, never hesitating, except out of modesty before new faces, where she was somewhat reserved; nor, among her nearest friends, ever spoke much at a time. She was but little versed in the common topics of female chat; scandal, censure, and detraction, never came out of her mouth. . . . She had not much company of her own sex, except those whom she most loved for their easiness, or esteemed for their good sense: and those, not insisting on ceremony, came often to her. But she rather chose men for her companions, the usual topics of ladies' discourse being such as she had little knowledge of, and less relish. Yet no man was upon the rack to entertain her, for she easily descended to anything that was innocent and diverting. . . . Although her knowledge, from books and company, was much more

[1], [2] and [3] op. cit., pp. 727-8-9.

extensive than usually falls to the share of her sex; yet she
was so far from making a parade of it, that her female
visitants, on their first acquaintance, who expected to discover it, by what they call hard words and deep discourse,
would be sometimes disappointed, and say, they found she
was like other women."[1]

In other words, for most women Stella was anomalous and
an object of curiosity. Small wonder when the fashionable
lady of Queen Anne's reign spent her mornings reclining in
bed, receiving her male as well as female guests; her after-
noons in dressing; her evenings in dining and card-playing
till midnight.

A contemporary pamphlet gives us a picture of the type of
woman Swift abhorred, and Stella avoided.

"Pray Madam, what books do you read?"
"Lewd plays and winning romances."
"Who is it you love?"
"Myself!"
"What, nobody else?"
"My page, my monkey and my lapdog."
"And why do you love them?"
"Why, because I am an English lady, and they are
foreign creatures: my page from Genoa, my monkey from
the East, and my lapdog from Vigo."[2]

Walking in the Mall, paying calls, shopping in the New
Exchange where the lisping little vendors pursued one with
their cries of "Ribbanths, Glovths, Tippeths," ogling the
beaux in Covent Garden Market, dancing, flirting, gossiping
their aimless way through life—these were the occupations
and pursuits of Stella's English contemporaries, whose Irish
cousins aped them.

Swift, with his ambitions for a more sensible, companion-
able race of women, taught Stella to despise this shameful
waste of time and life, taught her to use her mind and to
enjoy it, to be able to converse on current as well as past

[1]op. cit., pp. 733-4.
[2]*Social Life in the Reign of Queen Anne.* John Ashton. Vol. I,
pp. 90 and 97.

affairs: to neglect finery and fripperies, to economize for the sake of the poor.

"She became, and continued all her life a most prudent economist: yet still with a strong bent to the liberal side, wherein she gratified herself by avoiding all expense in clothes (which she ever despised) beyond what was merely decent. . . . She bought clothes as seldom as possible, and those as plain and cheap as consisted with the situation she was in: and wore no lace for many years. Either her fortune or judgement was extraordinary, in the choice of those on whom she bestowed her charity: for it went further in doing good than double the sum from any other hand. And I have heard her say, she always met with gratitude from the poor: which must be owing to her skill in distinguishing proper objects, as well as her gracious manner in relieving them.

"But she had another quality that much delighted her . . . it was a pleasure she could not resist; I mean that of making agreeable presents, wherein I never knew her equal, although it be an affair of as delicate a nature as most in the course of life."[1]

Stella was the perfect pupil who mirrored her tutor's precepts. In only one thing did she disappoint him—her inconvenient sex. If only she had been a boy, the child of some dear friend, he might have enjoyed her company with less comment and restraint. It is this longing of Swift's to turn his women into men that makes him break out in the *Journal* with "Why are not you a young fellow and then I might prefer you?,"[2] to declare laughingly that she and Dingley "are not women,"[3] and to call her repeatedly "Sirrah," an appellation of a contemptuous and imperious nature, half-humorous, half-affectionate, customary for boys or young men. It is this need which causes him to urge Vanessa to "act like a man of this world" when she is despondent,[4] and, in the long poem which he wrote for her, to draw the Queen of learning,

[1]Hayward, pp. 730-1.
[2]Williams, p. 246.
[3]Ibid, p. 90.
[4]*Vanessa and her Correspondence with Jonathan Swift*, edited by A. Martin Freeman, Selwyn & Blount, 1921, p. 135.

Minerva, as a goddess bewildered by Vanessa's sex since she

"*Mistakes Vanessa for a Boy.*[1]"

Once again he declares:

> "*That innocent Delight he took*
> *To see the Virgin mind her Book,*
> *Was but the Master's secret Joy,*
> *In School to hear the finest Boy.*"[2]

These were the expressions of a mind and heart restrained by fear. "He who understood society as a thief understands his jemmy, with the same grim stealth, or as a hangman knows his knots, did not comprehend so much about the heart of a girl."[3]

VII

Stella had not been three years in Ireland before she received an offer of marriage from another clergyman, the Reverend William Tisdall. Surprisingly he was a friend of Swift's but not a very congenial one. His father was Sheriff of Carrickfergus; his cousin, "Black Phil," was an eminent lawyer, and Tisdall, wordy and argumentative, prided himself on his controversial powers, comparing the success of some of his tracts in Ireland with that of Swift's in England. This alone would be likely to rouse Swift's contempt, but that he should consider himself a rival for Stella's affections was such presumption that it could only be treated with indifference. Besides, Tisdall was indiscreet. He had unwisely shown a letter of Swift's concerning the reactions of London to the *Bill Against Occasional Conformity* to the Lord Primate, Archbishop Marsh; it therefore behoved Swift to handle him in this matter with circumspection. His tone in his opening letters to Tisdall[4] sent from London, is jocular enough; he

---

[1] and [2]*Cadenus and Vanessa*, Hayward, pp. 768 and 777.
[3]*Stella, Vanessa and Swift*, Lady Gregory. 19th Century and After. June, 1933.
[4]December and February, 1703-4. Ball, Vol. I, pp. 40-5.

laughs at Stella's bad puns which Tisdall has repeated to him, sends her and Dingley messages, and bids Tisdall to "put them upon reading."

"And be always teaching something to Mrs. Johnson, because she is good at comprehending, remembering, and retaining."

But the third letter[1] is at once more serious and involved than the others. Tisdall had sounded Swift as to his chances of success with Stella, and Stella had revealed her offer to him. It was a situation which urged Swift, against his will, into a declaration of his feelings and intentions regarding Stella, and with characteristic adroitness he avoided being cornered and unmasked, avoided the emotional impact.

". . . my conjecture is, that you think I obstructed your insinuations, to please my own, and that my intentions were the same with yours; in answer to all which, I will, upon my conscience and honour, tell you the naked truth.

"First, I think I have said to you before, that, if my fortunes and humour served me to think of that state, I should certainly, among all persons on earth, make your choice; because I never saw that person whose conversation I entirely valued but hers; this was the utmost I ever gave way to. And, secondly, I must assure you sincerely, that this regard of mine never once entered into my head to be an impediment to you; but I judged it would, perhaps, be a clog to your rising in the world; and I did not conceive you were then rich enough to make yourself and her happy and easy. But that objection is now quite removed by what you have at present, and by the assurances of Eaton's livings. I told you indeed, that your authority was not sufficient to make overtures to the mother, without the daughter's giving me leave, under her own or her friend's hand; which, I think, was a right and prudent step. However, I told the mother immediately, and spoke with all the advantages you deserve. But, the objection of your fortune being removed, I declare I have no other; nor shall any consideration of my own misfortune of losing so good a

[1] April, 1703-4. Ball, Vol. I, pp. 45-8.

friend and companion as her, prevail on me, against her interest and settlement in the world, since it is held so necessary and convenient a thing for ladies to marry; and that time takes off from the lustre of virgins in all other eyes but mine.

"I appeal to my letters to herself, whether I was your friend or no in the whole concern; though the part I designed to act in it was purely passive, which is the utmost I will ever do in things of this nature, to avoid all reproach of any ill consequence, that may ensue in the variety of worldly accidents. Nay, I went so far both to her mother, herself, and I think to you, as to think it could not be decently broken; since I supposed the town had got it in their tongues, and therefore I thought it could not miscarry without some disadvantage to the lady's credit. I have always described her to you in a manner different from those, who would be discouraging; and must add, that though it hath come in my way to converse with persons of the first rank, and of that sex, more than is usual to men of my level, and of our function; yet I have nowhere met with a humour, a wit, or conversation so agreeable, a better portion of good sense, or a truer judgement of men and things, I mean here in England; for as to the ladies of Ireland, I am a perfect stranger. As to her fortune, I think you know it already; and if you resume your designs, and would have farther intelligence, I shall send you a particular account.

"I give you joy of your good fortunes, and envy very much your prudence and temper, and love of peace and settle-ment; the reverse of which has been the great uneasiness ot my life, and is like to continue so. . . ."[1]

Tisdall must have been thoroughly baffled. He had begged Swift, his possible rival, to act as his intermediary with Stella's mother, and even with Stella herself. Swift, with apparent good humour and courtesy, had complied. He pre-tended to protect Tisdall, who was junior to him, from a rash imprudence, as if he were a son. While praising Stella openly to Tisdall, he made no claims upon her, declaring that his "fortunes and humour" prevented him from marrying her.

[1]Ball, Vol. I, pp. 46-7.

Swift very cleverly implied that he had been so solicitous for Stella's welfare that he had even, for once, attended to gossip. People had seen Tisdall going and coming at Stella's lodgings in William Street; it might therefore be just as well for her reputation that the matter should be concluded by Tisdall marrying her. This may serve as an example of Swift's almost naïve blindness with regard to the position in which he placed Stella, for had not his name been linked with hers for nearly three years in much more equivocal circumstances?

But beneath the bland surface were troublesome and deceptive currents. While appearing to relinquish Stella, Swift, in reality, claimed her with a finality which made any attacks upon his and Stella's relationship futile. He had already bound her to him with "hoops of steel"[1] and could therefore afford to disregard other suitors. He appears to leave the decision to Stella and her mother; but Stella had already deprived herself of any freedom of choice or action by committing herself so profoundly to Swift that she even brought him her proposals for consideration. She was, in other words, waiting for Swift to decide, hoping to stir him into normal reaction by means of jealousy. But Swift seldom responded to emotional stimuli. In fact he shrank from them like one overcharged with electrical current who dreads further shock.

Nothing occurred, the matter subsided. Tisdall dropped away into the position of a subsidiary actor in the drama. He was no longer a protagonist: indeed he had never stood a chance of being one while Swift was on the stage. He remained friendly with both Swift and Stella, with this disadvantage, that the pair upon whose strange relation he had intruded made little jokes about him behind his back. Furthermore, Swift revenged himself upon Tisdall for his impudence, as he had upon some peers of the realm, by making obscene verses and references to him.[2]

The whole episode has its reflection nearly twenty years later when Swift has made Vanessa dependent on him, and when she also has her suitors. Men seldom vary in their

[1]Sir Leslie Stephen, p. 31.
[2]Ball, Vol. IV, p. 479, and Williams, p. 671.

tactics in lovemaking and Swift's deep-seated egotism, in both cases, made him impervious to jealousy. While appearing to relinquish he yet refused to openly claim, and while covertly claiming he could not surrender. The two counter-tendencies interlocked, preserving an unprogressive *status quo* which wore down those whom he ostensibly protected with a persistence more deadly than the sudden shock of complete rejection.

But Swift was never one to let the intricacies and embarrassments of a love affair, or its counterfeits, absorb the main stream of his energy. His goal was power, and the display of power, and from the days at Moor Park when Temple had implied so much for his advancement and achieved so little, he had never ceased, no matter what discouragement or excitement had threatened to distract him, to seek an outlet for the immense reservoirs which filled within him.

During the years with Temple he had often concerned himself with the problem of what conscience demands of us. Allegiance to the new sovereigns was difficult for many, for if they accepted William they were compelled to abandon the belief in divine hereditary right. Those who could not adapt themselves to the changes in thought and constitutional procedure gave up both position and preferment, maintaining that consistency and internal harmony were jeopardized by the changes taking place in the Church, the Tory Party, and the minds of individuals. Among those caught in this dilemma was Archbishop Sancroft, whose struggles Swift had watched from afar and to whom he addressed an *Ode*. It took him the best part of three years to write and in the end he left it unfinished. The fact that he found the subject so laborious and completion impossible may have been due to inconclusiveness in his own mind about the themes he was treating, as well as to a disinclination for the exalted and enthusiastic style which the Ode demanded.

Another of the non-jurors was Dr. Sherlock, who being more adaptable, saw fit to comply with the revolutionary government at a later date. The following lines on Sherlock's quandary (formerly attributed to Swift) occur in a manuscript from which some of his lesser poems have been taken:

"He who to two things takes an oath,
Is by the last absolved from both;
For each oath being an affirmation,
Both, as 'twas owned, make a negation.
Thus scientifically you see
The more you're bound, the more you're free.
As jugglers when they knit one more
Undo the knot they tied before[1]*"*

Swift, in the ensuing years, was to be tried by rigorous tests in three major fields, the religious, political, and sexual. The vacillation and self-reconciliation of other men was therefore bound to interest him and it is to be remarked that in *A Tale of a Tub*, fermenting in his head three or four years after the *Ode*, he speaks of the man who is "so ready to *give* his word to every body that he never *keeps* it."[2]

I am not implying that Swift stooped to juggling with oaths, although his enemies and detractors often enough accused him of it in the political sphere. But one is not pre-occupied with something from which one is wholly free, and Swift seems to have suspected in himself a weakness which, if it was not checked, might prove his downfall—the tendency to comply with more than one policy or individual simul-taneously. This so-called inconsistency laid him open to attack from men more singleminded.

Young as he was, he had in his time seen plenty of double-dealing in Court circles and he despised those whom he found involved in it. His ideals were high and he was unhappy when he could not live up to the highest. But he suffered from a compulsive need for freedom, as he conceived it, and, driven by conflicting forces, was obliged to adopt ruses by which he might escape to apparent safety. He therefore avoided taking his religious vows, or his political oaths as long as possible, and in the sexual sphere allowed himself a questionable licence by never making promises except negative ones.

[1]Scott. Vol. I, p. 70. *Poems*, Vol. III, p. 1057. Harold Williams rejects the-poem as unworthy of Swift.
[2]*Digression on Madness*, Hayward, p. 339.

CHAPTER FOUR

*You are aware that the gods owe you something which they
have not paid you as yet, all you have hitherto received at their
hands being insufficient. It appears also that you can help
yourself to the lacking portion of happiness. Cut into the
world's loaf then with sharp knife, with steady hand. But at
what cost? Living flesh as sensitive to pain as yours, living
hearts as precious as yours, as capable of feeling wrong, must
be carved and cloven through. Their blood, if you dare spill
it for your sake, doubtless it shall make you fat.*

CHALFONTE

I

IN the years 1710-1713 Swift became one of the unacknowledged rulers of England. He achieved what he had long
coveted, infinite, gratifying power. A mere country clergyman
—an Irish hedge-parson; a man of letters, courting scorn and
ridicule from the aristocracy if he revealed his profession; a
commoner, without wealth, rank, or office; he found himself
at last in the position which he most desired—that of a man
courted and wooed by others possessing these envied gifts of
fortune. Patience, assiduity, skill; energy, versatility and the
smouldering fires of resentment, had driven him to eminence,
and, now that he had reached a tardy but magnificent manhood,
power repressed and genius hidden burst out like heads of
pent-up steam.

He was an unavowed king amongst men. His social
superiors—the heads of princely houses, the officers of state,
their wives and daughters, reigning beauties of the day—
were forced to make advances to this commoner whose
insolence, in retrospect, appears fantastic and a trifle pitiable
since it lacks proportion, restraint, and certainly humour.
Those whom he cajoled and bullied seem mere automata,
running like figures in a comedy to do the bidding of an unbalanced giant.

The men whispered and complained: the ladies wept and

retired, but in the end Swift had his way. The principal
Secretary of State was fetched from the House of Commons by
the Lord Treasurer at Swift's express command in order that
Swift might inform him "with his own lips"—not of any
significant ministerial change in this "shaking season for
places"—but only that if the Secretary of State dined late he
would not dine with him.[1] The Lord Treasurer at a court
levee, bearing his robes and staff of office, was forced to wander
inquiringly from room to room to look for the poet Parnell
whom Swift had refused to present to him on the grounds that
"a man of genius" was "superior to a Lord in high station"
and that it was therefore becoming that the Lord Treasurer
should seek out the Irishman and introduce himself.[2] He
snubbed the Duke of Buckingham, whose pride amounted
almost to megalomania, by refusing to make his acquaintance
because the Duke had "not made sufficient advances":[3]
and when Lady Burlington declined to sing for him he
remained inattentive to her until she had repaired her
omission.[4]

The *Journal to Stella* discloses unashamedly these extraordinary reversals of customary behaviour, the splenetic outbursts, and the motives lying behind them. An informal and
indiscreet chronicle of the times, and an intimate but inhibited
recital of Swift's love for Stella, the *Journal* is also an unconscious revelation of its author's character.   To Stella
Swift dared to reveal himself as the irascible, revengeful
being whom others feared and regarded with awe.   Close-
locked in intimacy, they exchanged comments, criticisms and
jests, not always innocent or harmless, about the great people
of court and society: Stella knew and understood what agonies
of suspense and repression (as a boy in Ireland and as a young
man at Moor Park) had caused these violent explosions of
feeling: she accepted them without trembling, cavilling, or
remonstrating, and Swift sailed into her harbour like a ship
serene though dangerously crowded with sail.

[1]Williams, p. 190.
[2]*Observations*, Delany, pp. 28-9.
[3]Williams, p. 273.
[4]Scott, Vol. I, p. 440, based on Laetitia Pilkington.

Plate III

Facsimile of the handwriting of Swift

In his very first letter to her from London he shows this mounting, unconfined humour.

"The Whigs were ravished to see me, and would lay hold on me as a twig while they are drowning, and the great men making me their clumsy apologies, &c. But my Lord Treasurer received me with a great deal of coldness, which has enraged me so, I am almost vowing revenge."[1]

And later:

"I use them like dogs, because I expect they will use me so."

It takes a Frenchman to interpret these explosions. As Taine, with understanding tenderness, remarks:

"People were astonished or amused at these outbursts. I see in them sobs and cries, the explosion of long, over-whelming and bitter thoughts: they are the starts of a mind unsubdued, shuddering, rebelling, breaking the barriers: wounding, crushing or bruising everyone on its road, or those who wish to stop it."[2]

Only to Pope, more feminine than masculine by tempera-ment, does Swift show a frankness in any way comparable. The friendship between them which began in 1712 and grew more contorted towards the close of Swift's life, after the death of Stella, elicited letters and stray sentences of a biographical nature which plump the image we form of him from reading the *Journal*.

"I will tell you . . . that all my endeavours, from a boy, to distinguish myself, were only for want of a great title and fortune, that I might be used like a Lord by those who have an opinion of my parts—whether right or wrong, it is no great matter."[3]

Swift sought to establish a dictatorship of genius and it is to his credit that he claimed for other men of literary and intellectual talents a recognition equal to that which he sought

[1] Williams, pp. 5-6.
[2] Taine on *Swift*, in The History of English Literature.
[3] Ball, Vol. IV, p. 78.

for himself. His imperiousness was overweighted, it was often exasperating, but it was never petty, for behind the blustering insistence upon respect and admiration lay the vast resources of his powers, the ability to see current evils more clearly than most, and a large-hearted sincerity ready to attempt a remedy. The weakness of Swift's character, the obverse of its greatness, lay in his desires for revenge and humiliation; personal animosity and unconscious hatred clouded and embittered his outlook. His disbelief in the nobility of man, his recognition of the sordid, selfish, corrupt sides of human nature poisoned his attitude to life. Unable to distinguish the sources of his resentment, or the proper objects for its dispersal, he carried forward a quarrel of twenty and thirty years earlier into mature life, and this quarrel, which had begun as a personal one—against his uncle for expecting gratitude, against Sir William for expecting deference and submission—became diffused, and spread into a general quarrel with many whom he encountered, whose motives and ambitions he mistrusted. Thus half the joy of having won admittance to the higher world, which he had secured by sheer force of character, lay in avenging long-stored, secret humiliations, in sensing the exquisite pleasure of defiling the inner sanctum and outraging those who dwelt in it.

Swift's eccentricities, his unhappy nature, and his strange appearance, marked him out for attention. People could not fail to notice an intent, dissatisfied figure walking up and down the coffee-houses, oblivious of company, as if the crowded floors were empty boards set for a lone actor. Sheridan relates this anecdote concerning Swift's habits in London prior to his rise to fame:

"For several successive days . . . a strange Clergyman came into the coffee-house, who seemed utterly unacquainted with any of those who frequented it; and whose custom it was to lay his hat down on a table, and walk backwards and forwards at a good pace for half an hour or an hour, without speaking to any mortal, or seeming in the least to attend to anything that was going forward there. He then used to take up his hat, pay his money at the bar, and walk away without opening his lips. After having observed this singular behaviour for some time, they concluded him to be out of his senses; and the name that he went by among them was that of the mad Parson. This made them more than usually attentive to his motions:

"One evening, as Mr. Addison and the rest were observing him, they saw him cast his eyes several times on a gentleman in boots, who seemed to be just come out of the country, and at last advanced towards him as intending to address him. They were all eager to hear what this dumb, mad parson had to say, and immediately quitted their seats to get near him. Swift went up to the country gentleman, and in a very abrupt manner, without any previous salute, asked him:

"'Pray, sir, do you remember any good weather in the world?' . . .

"'Yes, sir, I thank God, I remember a great deal of good weather in my time.'

"'That is more . . . than I can say: I never remember any weather that was not too hot, or too cold; too wet, or too dry; but however God Almighty contrives it, at the end of the year 'tis all very well.'

"Upon saying this he took up his hat, and without uttering a syllable more, or taking the least notice of anyone, walked out of the coffee-house. . . ."[1]

This was good 'publicity' as a modern critic would say, but Swift's apprehensive and easily-wounded nature, his hypersensitivity, had made him wary and self-encased. He no longer rushed headlong at individuals or situations whence he hoped for an amelioration of his difficulties, or the opportunity for an expansion of his powers. His misfortunes and maladjustments caused him to ignore men, names, and appearances, which would register on a mind less callous from constant wounding. He had had to insulate himself against people, their moods, vacillations and bunglings, so that, wrapt in his own world, he failed to notice the watchful eyes and supercilious glances directed towards him, and, as we shall see, the distinguishing features of the women he encountered, or even their reactions to him. Although gifted with feminine intuitiveness he was also cursed with a curious

[1]Sheridan, pp. 40-1.

obtuseness which occasionally isolated him from those around him.

One of the men whose company he particularly relished at this time was Addison, whose acquaintance Swift had made three years earlier. The friendship quickly ripened. Addison was blessed with a warmth and tranquillity of temper which soothed and steadied Swift, who told Delany that:

> "often as they spent their evenings together, they neither of them ever wished for a third person, to support or enliven their conversation."[1]

Addison responded in kind and inscribed the fly-leaf of a copy of his *Travels*:

> "To Doctor Jonathan Swift, the most agreeable companion, the truest friend, and the greatest genius of his age, this book is presented by his most humble servant, the author."[2]

The placidity of Addison's nature tamed Swift, he basked in his urbanity, granting him privileges which others might envy. Addison corrected his verses, making him "blot out fourscore, add fourscore, and alter fourscore"[3] in a poem of not two hundred lines. Addison must meet Mrs. Johnson, which he did through Swift's introduction when Secretary to Lord Wharton at Dublin Castle: Addison might praise her without fear of reproof: Stella might admire and even imitate Addison. Exiled in Ireland early in 1710 it was to Addison that Swift had turned, writing fondly:

> "If you will come over again, when you are at leisure, we will raise an army, and make you King of Ireland."[4]

But ruffled by political differences their respect and affection for each other cooled until they became mere "civil acquaintances," although their friendship never suffered the severe check which Swift's with Steele experienced, or the deteriora-

[1]*Observations*, Delany, p. 32.
[2]Scott, Vol. I, p. 83.
[3]*Baucis and Philemon*. See Delany, *Observations*, p. 19.
[4]Ball, Vol. I, p. 189.

tion of that with Pope. He delighted also in the wit of other companions—his old friend Congreve, Gay, Prior and the other "wits." Swift's friendships were never lethargic, absorptive affairs: he was energetic in serving those whom he admired or loved, obtaining remunerative posts for Congreve, Gay, Steele, and Ambrose Philips, assisting Pope, who acknowledged his indebtedness, benefiting Parnell and Berkeley, defending his printer Barber, promoting men of his cloth like Trapp and Winder, and half a hundred others unrelated to him by blood ties, bound only to him by affection. His altruism became annoying, so much so that Bolingbroke jestingly declared later that Swift never came to the Tory ministers "without some Whig in his sleeve for advancement." He loved merit and pitied failure, and since he had known what it was to be poor, unrecognized, and discouraged, he went out of his way to be kind to young and starving poets, amongst whom the names of Harrison and Diaper stand out with particular pathos since Swift arrived too late to be of lasting service to them.

Yet, even in this tireless effort for others, possessiveness creeps in: he writes to Stella of Harrison,

"I [am] very much afflicted for him, for he is my own Creature."[1]

But if we carp at Swift for this need to annex while fostering others—(half genuine, half compulsive disinterestedness—as if he were always attempting to staunch his own wounds)—we are grateful to him for the happy influence which he exerted over his companions. A single instance of the result of this influence may speak for many—the writing of *The Beggar's Opera*. This "Newgate pastoral amongst the whores and thieves"[2] was a subject after Swift's own heart, but Gay treated it with a lightness which excelled the sterner touch of the satirist. What Swift had essayed fifteen months before in *Gulliver*, Gay achieved in a different medium in the *Opera*, and Swift showed his bigness of heart by writing to congratulate Gay in the following strain:

[1]Williams, p. 619.
[2]Ball, II, p. 330, and IV, p. 21.

"*The Beggar's Opera* has knocked down *Gulliver*. To expose vice and to make people laugh with innocence does more public service than all the Ministers of State from Adam to Walpole."[1]

How great was Swift's influence on Gay it is hard to say. The Barnstaple lad and the boy from Dublin had this for common experience—that they were both brought up by an uncle, and there is something akin in their temperaments as well. Gay's flippant epitaph on his tomb in Westminster Abbey:

> "*Life's a jest and all things show it*
> *I thought so once, and now I know it. . . .*"

is a lighter version of Swift's pronouncement that life is "a ridiculous tragedy—the worst kind of composition."[2] They were both products of contemporary cynicism.

All these rich energetic friendships indicate that Swift, despite his handicaps, had much to give. His ability to understand and conquer women was balanced by a capacity for the subjection of men as well. So much has been written about the unfortunate sides of his nature that it is good to lay emphasis on the virile, healthy aspects, if only for a moment. If he was sometimes overbearing, blustering and rude, he was also polished, consummately tactful and intuitively gifted to an extraordinary degree: if he was occasionally cruel, blind and even obtuse he was at least sincere, and people like Arbuthnot, physician and author, paid unstinting tribute to his "plain and open ingenuity in all (his) commerce." In studying his weaknesses, we have always to bear in mind a comment of that wise lover of mankind, Samuel Johnson, who remarked that "it is hard not to call a sick man a scoundrel."

II

In order to understand Swift's extraordinary, almost meteoric, rise to fame it is necessary to go back and recapitulate

[1]Ball, II, p. 330, and IV, p. 21.
[2]Ibid, IV, p. 217.

some of his disappointments. Among the years immediately
preceding his entry into the larger political world that of
1708 was, as he himself admitted, fraught with suspense and
big with import. He noticed with envy that men who were his
juniors received sinecures of three and four hundred pounds
a year whilst he reaped only fulsome but empty promises. He
was, as he later wrote, "caressed by ministers of state,"[1] yet
neglected. He contemplated going to Vienna as secretary to
a projected embassy headed by Berkeley: he thought, like
Donne, of escaping to Virginia.[2] A colonial bishopric would
bring more satisfaction than the position of hedge parson in
Ireland, above which he had not risen since entering the
Church fourteen years earlier. His mind was constantly
strung taut, like a bow bent for use, by promises dangled
before him. The see of Waterford fell vacant and it was
mooted that Swift was the man to fill it with honour: and when
Waterford was snatched away, Cork was suggested and also
disposed of to another. Wearied by false alarums he grew
soured in temper.

Yet Swift at all times must have been a difficult man to
place. No one travels at ease with a satirist riding pillion
behind him. He was too gifted for menial offices, too honest
for those requiring tact rather than bluntness, too narrow in his
religious views to be fit for conciliation, too obsessed with
past humiliations to suffer being passed over mildly. Men
feared his tongue and pen and sought to placate, without
trusting him. His insight into the characters of others, combined with his terrible, denunciatory power, made them as
uneasy as if a Hosea or Nehemiah moved amongst them. They
knew that at any moment, should they displease him or should
he discover their weaknesses, a spate of words deadly in their
venom would pour out against them.

Possibly a second reason for their distrust was Swift's
indetermination. They sensed that, as yet, he meant nothing
whole-heartedly: that he had not thrown in his weight
politically on either side without equivocation. Since his real
goal was unlimited power he lacked a clear external aim. His

[1] *Cadenus and Vanessa.*
[2] Ball, Vol. I, p. 145.

avidity was like a consuming fire: it ate him up: he did not know how to diminish or direct the flames, nor did any one around him. Ill-weaned and overgrown, his ambitions were boundless and if they could not be satisfied he roared and ranted, or, turning the force inward on himself, retired in dudgeon to brood upon the ingratitude of man, or the malignity of fate.

Men approach such a creature warily, for the slightest tremor may produce an explosion so devastating in effect that the landscape becomes unrecognizable. Yet his superiors, admitting his talents, were anxious to make use of this driving power for the good of the Church, and chose him as their mediator. In June of this same significant year (1708) Swift, on behalf of the Irish bishops, approached the Lord Treasurer Godolphin about the tithes called the *First Fruits and Tenths*, a business which occupied him for the best part of seven years. These ancient taxes, which had formerly been levied on the Church in England by the Pope to finance the Crusades and had at the Reformation been appropriated by the Crown, had been restored to the English clergy by Anne, in 1704. Swift, ever anxious to advance the cause of the Church, and ever solicitous for the needy, at once urged Archbishop King to act in order to obtain a similar remission for the Church in Ireland. The Archbishop temporized, the Irish clergy clamoured, and ultimately Swift was charged with using his influence in England upon their behalf. And now Godolphin, interviewed, answered in vague language, implying that the Irish clergy must earn their reward. What assiduity, perseverance, patience and courage were necessary if one was to take part in matters of state and win over ministers. Swift went away dispirited, more and more convinced that Whig promises were only "mouthfuls of moonshine."[1] It was not until late in 1710 that the matter was concluded and Swift tardily commended for his share in the undertaking.

Meanwhile, he revealed his true literary strength in two ways which had only been hinted at before—the humorous, and the religio-political. His inclination for practical joking displayed itself in *Predictions for the Year*, an assault of a

[1]Archbishop King to Swift. Ball, Vol. I, p. 222.

farcical but cruel nature on a one-time cobbler called Partridge, a popular and prosperous astrologer. Swift, deploring the gullibility of the people and the power which quacks exercised over them, declared, under the rival name of Bickerstaff,[1] that he was not content with nebulous prophecies but would make accurate predictions. He began by predicting the day of Partridge's death: on the day assigned, the astrologer's death was duly announced. Partridge retaliated by asserting in his new almanac that he was very much alive: Bickerstaff assured the public that Partridge's printed statements were insufficient proof. London was convulsed. Swift's friend Congreve and the other wits were drawn into the controversy and published a conviction of the "Astrological Impostor," Bickerstaff. And so the matter continued until Partridge, who was no match for Swift, mournfully subsided. Swift's ability to take people in, and his reputation for dangerous doctrines spread to the continent. The Stationers' Office solemnly struck Partridge's name from its rolls, and the Portuguese Inquisition, with a gullibility which must have been deliciously gratifying to Swift, consigned Bickerstaff to the flames. Here was another display of that amazing ability to imagine consequences following on an initial assumption, and to elaborate details of those consequences, which he was to use so consummately in *Gulliver's Travels*. Although Swift had always despised logic he could confound the most ardent logician with his accuracy when he worked out the minutiæ of some fantastic hypothesis of his own until, under his persuasive force, the imagined and deceptive event, or world, appeared more real than reality. In this affair he was copying the method of a less known and somewhat disreputable predecessor, Thomas Brown, but the earnestness of the satire was his own.[2]

The attack on Partridge was not merely an experiment in wit. It was one of the many attacks which Swift was to make on those who ridiculed or attacked the established Church.

[1]See *Predictions for the Year 1708*; *An Accomplishment of the First of Mr. Bickerstaff's Predictions*; *A Famous Prediction of Merlin, The British Wizard*; and the *Bickerstaff Papers* in *The Tatler*.

[2]See W. A. Eddy, *Modern Philology*, 28 (1931), 163-8 and *Studies in Philology*, 29 (1932), 29-40.

Swift strongly disliked the type of cheap, ranting, popular propaganda of which Partridge's *Merlinus Liberatus* (1706) was an example, and in taking up the cudgels against him he fortified himself with a belief in the justness of a cause dear to his own heart.

The other pieces of writing were statements of his religious and political creed at this time, when he was about to be placed in a crucible which should test and reveal his essential beliefs.[1] As he sifted and weighed his real convictions his power grew, and in one of the pamphlets, the *Letter Concerning the Sacramental Test*, we see for the first time what tremendous vitality and originality Swift could bring to political writing. In it he speaks of the Catholic natives of Ireland, restrained by the Test Act, who resembled a "lion . . . fast bound with three or four chains, his teeth drawn out, and his claws pared to the quick," as being a less dangerous enemy than "an angry cat" (by which he meant the Dissenters daily growing in number and power)—"in full liberty at one's throat." Telling as this analogy was for Swift's audience, it is more so for us if we apply it to the man himself; one senses his feeling of having been fettered and maimed in life and his new determination no longer to curb his strength.

But if the year 1708 was significant for Swift, because of the revelation of his true literary powers employed in the cause of politics and religion, his appointment as mediator with the Lord Treasurer and other ministers, his growing familiarity with Court and literary circles, and the discovery of his true, but hitherto dormant, convictions, it had in store for him the seeds of great unhappiness.

London was crowded. Stella and Dingley, roused from their long hibernation on the other side of the channel, were in town, visiting the city for the last time: and in December, a widow whose name was probably already known to Swift, for

---

[1] *An Argument to prove the Inconvenience of Abolishing Christianity*: *A Project for the Advancement of Religion and the Reformation of Manners*: *Sentiments of a Church of England Man, with Respect to Religion and Government*: and *A Letter from a Member of the House of Commons in Ireland to a Member of the House of Commons in England concerning The Sacramental Test.*

her husband had formerly been Lord Mayor of Dublin, also crossed over from Ireland. This lady was Mrs. Van Homrigh,[1] who brought with her her four children, two sons and two daughters. The journey had not been without adventures: she had transported her family on board "with great danger" and had been forced to spend an irritating number of days— nearly a fortnight—in Chester, waiting for a coach. But at length they reached London and the mother wrote cheerfully from her lodgings at "The Two Green Flower Pots in Charles Street near St. James Square."[2]

Introduced by Sir Andrew Fountaine whom he had known at the Vice-Regal Court in Dublin, Swift soon became intimate with Mrs. Van Homrigh and her children. In the following year he was not only writing to "Mrs. Van," as he called her, but also to her elder daughter, fatefully named Hester, or Esther,[3] whom Swift called "Mishessy," and later *Vanessa*. She was then twenty-one years old but appeared much younger.

His failure to obtain the *First Fruits and Tenths* for the Irish clergy, and the disrespect and ingratitude with which the Whig peers treated him, caused Swift to retire to Ireland in sullen discontent for more than a year.[4] But life at Laracor, though Stella might be his companion, the may-trees bud, and the trout leap from unrippled waters, was insufficient to quench his thirst for activity.

In desperation he appealed to Addison to secure for him the position of Historiographer Royal. Any post was better than none. He solaced himself by playing piquet with his curate and the Vicar of Trim of an evening, tended his glebe fields, and performed his clerical duties with impatient exactitude. But before Addison had time to reply Swift was up and gone. With his sensitivity to change he felt the "shaking season for

[1] The name was originally spelt van Homrigh, grew into Vanhomrigh, and seems to have been pronounced by the English *vanummry*.

[2] Ball, Vol. I, p. 390.

[3] Both letters are now lost. Swift's and Vanessa's extant letters, now in the British Museum, begin three years later, in 1712. For mention of the former, see Ball, Vol. I, pp. 384-5.

[4] June, 1709—September, 1710.

places" about to announce itself, and was restless to be in the thick of the struggle. Ostensibly his business in London was that of the tithes: together with the Bishops of Ossory and Killaloe he had been chosen to intercede a second time with the Queen and leading ministers. Dissatisfied with his reception by the Whig peers, Somers and Godolphin, Swift determined to approach Harley, rumoured to be willing to head the new Tory cabinet. Within a fortnight he was able to break out jubilantly to Stella with:

> "I suppose I have said enough in this and a former letter how I stand with new people; ten times better than ever I did with the old; forty times more caressed. I am to dine to-morrow at Mr. Harley's; and if he continues as he has begun, no man has been ever better treated by another."[1]

III

In his second letter to Stella in the *Journal*, Swift had written "The Whigs were ravished to see me." How is it then that we find him, at the height of the power which he was shortly to exercise, an ardent Tory? To explain this apparent defection one must consider the political background of the period from which Swift cannot be extricated and recall those factors which had previously influenced him. The ultimate decision as to which political party he belonged to involved a preceding struggle, since Swift was attempting to find himself, to become fused into an integral whole which should not be split by violent animosity issuing from party or individuals, whether politician, churchman, or valued friend.

When Swift first fled to England at the time of "the Troubles," he had already absorbed the principles and prejudices of his class. He belonged to that Protestant group, now generally termed Anglo-Irish, whose survival almost literally depended upon the ejection of the Catholic James and the establishment of Protestant William. But the Revolution was, for Swift, one carried out in defence of the Church; the defence of the throne was secondary.

[1]Williams, pp. 58-9.

His subsequent training with Temple, whose long residence in and affection for Holland inclined him to "Whig" policies, his meetings with William and William's Whig ministers, all implied that if he should take an active part in political life Swift would declare himself Whig rather than Tory. His defence of the impeached Whig lords in the *Discourse* of 1707, and his expectations of preferment from these peers, follow consistently. When he hoped that his petition concerning the *First Fruits* might be heard, it was to the influential Whig ministers that he applied, and as late as September 1710 he was delighted by their recognition. Yet, six weeks later, he was in the arms of the Tory party. How does one explain this *volte face*, even if one does not call it the act of a renegade?

The causes lay, partly in the political confusion which existed throughout the entire reign of Anne, and partly in Swift's own irresolution heretofore. When he plunged finally he was on the eve of his forty-third birthday. This tardy revelation of his true convictions is indicative of Swift's early unsettlement, discouragement, and struggle to establish himself, to free and direct the repressed strengths within him. A man of talent often develops more hesitantly than the ordinary man since his very gifts confuse him, or because his peculiar, natural ability remains strongly at variance with education and environment. Thus one watches Swift develop, not with patronage, but with something of pity, as well as of fear: the odds against him are so heavy, and unconsciously he works against himself with such tenacious obstinacy. His need for secrecy, for a hidden integrity, is so marked, conflicting with the counterpart need to stand revealed and unassailable. He resembles an actor who wears the mask of a certain character only to throw it down on the rising of the curtain to act that of another—his *real* self—which up till that moment he has not known or dared to reveal.

Amid a drama seamed with intimate and disgraceful intrigues dependent on private emotion—(the Queen moved by the vagaries of the powerful Duchess of Marlborough, her cousin Mrs. Masham, bedchamber-woman to the Queen, artfully supplanting her ducal benefactress in royal favour;

Bolingbroke plotting with Mrs. Masham for the Pretender's return, and a simple chambermaid causing the fall of Oxford)—Swift moves, alternately high-hearted and witty or stern and perpending, revolving his own destiny, determining how to subdue self to principle, how best to rise without losing all integrity.

Until the change of ministry in 1710 when the Tories suddenly came into power, Swift maintained an original line in politics, declaring himself to be a "High-Church Whig." In his poem to the Countess of Winchelsea, then Mrs. Finch, whom he calls "Ardelia," he describes himself as:—

> ". . . the Thing you hate,
> A Whig and one that wears a Gown."[1]

But such a creature was, as Sir Leslie Stephen points out, an "anomalous hybrid." Swift, "counter, original, spare, strange," was attempting to keep his foot in two camps simultaneously. Up to now he had been able to achieve this by swearing allegiance to no party; but when faced with accepting the position of friend, confidant and adviser to Harley, head of the new Government, he could no longer temporize. The screws of outward events forced an inner decision. He had, if he was ever to emerge a fully-fledged and winged creature, to risk rising or falling by some single principle or ideal, to which all else must be subservient. The process was one of self-reconciliation which no one could perform for him.

The line which Swift was likely to take, when circumstances would no longer permit him to dally, is clear in retrospect, for the one consistent trait which he showed once he had taken Orders was his fidelity to the Reformed Protestant Church. It is a loyalty at times narrow, intolerant, even ferocious: it brings out all his pugnacity, and in this respect he is the child of his ancestors, three generations of whom had faithfully fulfilled their ecclesiastical duties no matter what losses or hazards threatened them. If his paternal grandfather was the

---

[1] *Apollo Outwitted. Poems*, Vol. I, p. 119. Scott substituted the word 'Whig', which Swift omitted in the *Miscellanies of 1711*.

loved character on whom he (consciously or unconsciously) modelled himself, their methods of defence of the Church were similar—entire, self-abnegating, courageous service. Swift's written words to Archbishop King stand as his unvarying creed:

> "No prospect of making my fortune, shall ever prevail on me to go against what becometh a man of conscience and truth, and an entire friend to the Established Church."[1]

Yet the very need to state this creed implies a fear that some word or action may be equivocal and open to misconstruction.

The catch was here—the Whigs to whom he had once professed political inclination, if not allegiance, were becoming increasingly hostile to the Church, unless it were a State Church. As representatives of business and monied interests they favoured a repeal of the laws which circumscribed the Dissenters, the great body of middle-class men from whom the banker and tradesman rose.

The war with France, which sapped the vitality of the country, was a Whig war whose fiscal burden fell on the land. Lastly, the Whig policy arising out of the initial acceptance of William was based on obedience to a legislative power rather than to a Sovereign: it favoured the Union with Scotland and alliance with Holland, above all, a Church accessible to civil decrees.

Swift slowly began to see that all these political doctrines were alien to his true inclinations. As a realist he hated and deplored a long and useless war pursued for the glorification of Whig peers: he hated the Scotch and mistrusted and disliked the Dutch. If he accepted the bias of Whig principles he had to discard his fundamental belief in passive obedience to King and State, and a landed aristocracy supporting them.

> "I ever abominated that scheme of politics . . . of setting up a monied interest in opposition to the landed."[2]

For him, Church and State were indissolubly linked, but

[1] Ball, Vol. I, p. 117. Letter of November 9th, 1708.
[2] Ibid, Vol. III, p. 121.

they stood in that order. The plots of the Whig lords to secure the Crown for the Pretender, the insults which they openly offered to the Queen, their scandalous reflections on the universities, but above all their undisguised contempt for the clergy and their dangerous support of free-thinkers, threatened that which next to himself he was most eager to protect, the Church of England, which Swift held must, in all that concerned religion proper, be above civil wrangling and civil decree. In *The Sentiments of a Church of England Man* (1708) he states his convictions on religion and government with an adroitness, moderation, candour and reasonableness which are telling both in sincerity and clarity.

Thus, although Swift appeared to be grossly inconsistent, and has been called a traitor to that party to which he first inclined by training and education, he was in reality wholly consistent to those innermost convictions which he had always held. He sacrificed party to principle, not principle to party, as one biographer puts it. If he appeared to desert the Whigs in a crisis, they were after all still nominally in power; and he went over to Harley and the Tories when there were probably "not ten men in London who believed that the new ministry would stand."[1]

Swift had long been alienated from Whig doctrines in spirit, but he had not clearly seen this, or had lacked the courage to declare himself. When, therefore, Harley, the new Prince of Tories (whose views coincided with Swift's), embraced him and backed his embrace with proofs, not promises, of immediate co-operation, Swift's hesitations were over. He felt an instant affection for Harley from which he never wavered. Nor did his policy ever change.

Yet in this struggle to determine and reveal his true convictions Swift showed one disturbing weakness, a tendency to want to have it both ways. In his anonymous *Letter Concerning the Sacramental Test* he double-crossed those who might be on his scent by inserting a passage suggesting that Dr. Swift was likely to write advocating abolition of the Test, whereas he was in reality strongly in favour of keeping it.

[1]Collins, pp. 65-8.

He confused the trail further by complaining to Archbishop King:

"The author has gone out of his way to reflect on me as a person likely to write for repealing the Test, which I am sure is very unfair treatment. This is all I am likely to get by the company I keep. I am used like a sober man with a drunken face, (and) have the scandal of the vice without the satisfaction."[1]

This attempt to slip his own person relieved him of the burden of being himself, and may have afforded him amusement at his own ingenuity, but it inevitably lost him a reputation for reliability. He had pricked his opponents with a poisoned weapon in the dark. Then he was surprised, grieved, and even resentful that they did not trust and reward him.

IV

Upon his arrival in London in 1710 Swift first lodged in Pall Mall but shortly after removed to Bury Street, near St. James' Square. Ignorant either of the length of his stay in town, or of his own disposition, he quietly remarks to Stella (in the *Journal*) that he supposes he will continue there while he remains in London. Restlessness, dissatisfaction with landladies, with ground-floor rooms, poor drains and smoky chimneys, with burglars and night disturbances, kept him removing. In the following spring he went to Chelsea to benefit from the fresh air and the exercise involved in walking to or from St. James's, but three months later he was back in Suffolk Street: in the autumn he was in Leicester Fields, in the summer of his second year in Kensington, so that he could be near the court "where dinners are found": in July at Windsor: then in "hedge-lodgings" in town again, from which he writes angrily to Stella who had misunderstood something he has written: and finally in Little Rider Street, near Bury Street, where he had thought to find permanent quarters.

Lodgings were fashionable and easy to obtain. Mrs. Van Homrigh, likewise unable to rest content at the *Two Green*

[1]Ball, Vol. I, p. 130. Letter of 6th January, 1708-9.

Flower Pots, removed three or four times to Swift's dozen. Upon one occasion Swift found her "all in a combustion, squabbling with her rogue of a landlord"; another time she became involved with a landlady whom Swift shrewdly surmised to be a "bawd" because of her eyebrows.[1]

While in Chelsea, Swift and Mrs. Van Homrigh lodged only five doors away from each other. His letters to Stella become punctuated with a simple statement which might be monotonous were it not so significant. "I dined with Mrs. Van Homrigh." The announcement is varied from time to time by slight modifications such as, "and came gravely home," or "It was bloody hot walking to-day, and I was lazy. . . ." "An insipid day," or "No adventure at all to-day." These barren statements were not entirely hypocritical, but partly indicative of Swift's dissatisfaction with a temporary political vacuum. His mind and emotions had not as yet been focused on Hester, or Vanessa. Yet, eventually, the excuses begin to appear a little too palpable: "It was such dismal weather I could not stir farther," and "a terrible rainy day, which prevented my walk into the city, and I was only able to run and dine with my neighbour,"—until finally Stella is pricked into comment.

On the first occasion Swift replies hotly:

> "What do you mean '*That boards near me, that I dine with now and then?*' I know no such person: I don't dine with boarders. What a pox! You know whom I have dined with every day since I left you, better than I do. What do you mean, sirrah?"[2]

This was just under two months after Swift had come to town, and about four months later Stella apparently speaks slightingly of the Van Homrighs. She had a sharp little tongue and, in her turn, made Swift retaliate:

> "You say they are of no consequence: why, they keep as good female company as I do male: I see all the drabs of quality at this end of the town with them; I saw two Lady

[1]Williams, pp. 333, 360.
[2]op. cit., p. 86.

Bettys there this afternoon. The beauty of one, the good breeding and nature of t'other, and the wit of neither, would have made a fine woman."[1]

Stella, opening the fortnightly packets written in that neat, intellectual hand and sealed with the minute head of a Roman goddess, would know that one of these Lady Bettys was Swift's old friend of the Dublin Castle days, Lady Betty Germain, and the other, Lady Betty Butler, the Duke of Ormonde's daughter; but, woman as she was, she would not be put off the scent by this show of fine names and company. The very fact that Swift was nettled told her that her barb had gone home, and she had the uncomfortable knowledge that his "florence" (wine) lay in Mrs. Van Homrigh's cellar, where it "turned sour with a vengeance," that he kept his best gown and periwig at Mrs. Van's "to be put on when I come to town, to be a spark," and that in her house, above all others, he "could be easy." All this intimacy, this (for Stella) dangerous sense of his feeling at home with strangers, had sprung up in six months after his crossing to Chester. If the knowledge of Swift's pleasure at being with the Van Homrighs galled her, Stella bore it with tact and forbearance, for there are no more retorts to her inquiries or complaints about them. Possibly she suspected nothing: she knew what a variety of friends, interests, "bussinesses" (as she spelt it, for which Swift reprimanded her), he had. Secure in the certainty that no other woman could play the unusual role which she did in his life, at ease amid the little circle of friends in Dublin to whom he had introduced her with pride, she went her charitable way, intent on minding Swift's affairs for him in his prolonged absence, biding his return with feigned patience. Possibly, too, Swift's adroitness baffled her, for in the *Journal* Mrs. Van Homrigh's name is mentioned more than a hundred times but Vanessa's only three. The first occasion is when some friends of Swift's play a joke on him:

". . . and when I got home, Mrs. Van Homrigh sent me word her eldest daughter was taken suddenly very ill, and desired I would come and see her; I went, and found it was

[1]Williams, p. 202.

a silly trick of Mrs. Armstrong, Lady Lucy's sister, who, with Moll Stanhope, was visiting there; however, I rattled off the daughter."[1]

There seems to have been some conspiracy on the part of the fashionable ladies of London, who delighted in punning and practical joking as much as the men about town, to throw Swift and Vanessa together. (This was in February, 1710, and by November of the next year Vanessa's cousin, Anne Long, the celebrated "toast" of the town then living in retirement at King's Lynn to escape her creditors, writes to Swift implying that Swift and Vanessa are intimate friends.)[2]

The second mention of Vanessa in the *Journal* comes twelve days later and runs as follows:

"This was Mrs. Van Homrigh's daughter's Birthday and Mr. Ford and I were invited to dinner to keep it, and we spent the evening there drinking punch. That was our way of beginning Lent. . . ."[3]

adds Swift, with a wry grimace at his own levity.
The third and last runs:

"Her eldest daughter is come of age, and going to Ireland to look after her fortune, and get it in her own hands."[4]

This statement is important for another reason—that Swift was consistently misled by Mrs. Van Homrigh as to her daughter's age. The widow was still young and pretty, ambitious to cut a figure in London society and bent on amusing herself. It was inconvenient to let people know Vanessa's real age, which was twenty-three not twenty-one, and it was easier to deceive them since she had come from Ireland only three years before. In this deception Vanessa, because she did not care, because she was too much under the

[1]Williams, p. 179.
[2]Freeman, pp. 62-5.
[3]Williams, p. 191.
[4]op. cit., p. 333.

influence of her mother, or because she was young for her age, apparently concurred.

Hester Van Homrigh was a girl of unusual character, certain to attract attention from the fashionable world because of her idiosyncrasies, and from Swift because he detected within her a mind of exceptional calibre rusting in disuse. The ladies of fashion and their beaux laughed at the girl for her lack of sophistication; she did not walk in St. James's Park as they did, or visit the play-house, and preferred to converse with men on philosophical, historical, or political subjects rather than share in the tittle-tattle of the day. The fops could not make her out: she was not interested in their discussion of the weather, the theatre, the latest arrivals from abroad, the gossip about particular people: nor did she relish their insincere, conventional compliments.

> *"Their Judgement was upon the Whole,*
> *'That Lady is the dullest Soul'—*
> *Then tipt their Forehead in a Jeer,*
> *As who should say—'she wants it here;*
> *She may be handsome, young and rich,*
> *But none will burn her for a Witch.' "*[1]

The women were equally at a loss to admire or understand her. They found her reading Montaigne whilst her lady's-maid combed her hair, unwilling to be distracted by a consideration of the quality, colour, or price of their recent purchases—ribbons, fans, gloves and lace—to listen to scandal, or advice on how to dress or paint.

> *"Away the fair detractors went,*
> *And gave, by turns, their censures vent.*
> *'She's not so handsome, in my eyes:*
> *For wit, I wonder where it lies.*
> *She's fair and clean, and that's the most;*
> *But why proclaim her for a Toast?*
> *A baby face, no life, no airs,*

[1] *Cadenus and Vanessa, Poems*, Vol. II, p. 698. ll. 358-63.

But what she learnt at country fairs;
Scarce knows what diff'rence is between
Rich Flanders lace, and Colberteen.
I'll undertake my little Nancy
In flounces has a better fancy.
With all her wit, I would not ask
Her judgement, how to buy a mask.
We begg'd her but to patch her face,
She never hit one proper place;
Which every girl at five years old
Can do as soon as she is told.
I own that out-of-fashion stuff
Becomes the creature well enough.
The girl might pass, if we could get her
To know the world a little better.'
(To know the world! A modern phrase,
For visits, ombre, balls and plays)."[1]

This is Vanessa as seen through Swift's eyes (in a poem which he wrote) *a year later*; but moving as he now did in that small circle of titled, wealthy and conspicuous people—he must have heard the comments of fashionable men and women on Miss Van Homrigh earlier. With his gifts of minute observation and mimicry and his feminine intuitiveness, he recorded or imitated the type of comment which the foolish passed on her. His description of the ladies ridiculing her for not wearing one of the new-fangled whale-bone petticoats—a crinoline, which he begged Stella not to indulge in—of their comment that if she wore handsome garters at her knees surely she need not fear if men observed her, probably delighted Vanessa; by such an invasion into the minds of others and by such mockery, he drew the women he loved aside from the world in which they moved into an imaginary world of his own which he created for them, a world of magical intimacy from whose windows they might look out and laugh at living men and women. The portrait in *Cadenus and Vanessa* is also that of Vanessa as he wished her to be, as he had formed her

[1]op. cit., II, pp. 408-31 (capitals omitted).

in their friendship (extending intermittently over four years), whereby he might flatter himself that he had made her "his own creature" just as he had made Stella.

Vanessa's gifts of mind were equal, and in some respects superior, to Stella's. She excelled in imagination and creative power. Her father was dead, like Stella's, and like hers had been a merchant, but one of unusual ability. Upon his coming out of Holland into Ireland he was made Commissary General of Stores for King William during the Irish civil wars, then Muster-Master-General, a Commissioner of Revenue, and finally, Lord Mayor of Dublin. A collar and medal of office, still worn by the Lord Mayors of this city, are fine specimens of the goldsmiths' art, and were obtained through Van Homrigh's influence without any expense to the city.[1] He was a Member of the Dublin Philosophical Society, and a practical philanthropist who displayed an interest in training boys for a life at sea. He was generous, intelligent and capable, and the services which he rendered William III did not pass unheeded: he received especial attention at the English court. Amongst his friends he had numbered Swift's superior, Archbishop King, the Earl of Athlone, who stood godfather to his second son, the Duke of Schomberg, Lord Berkeley, and the Duke of Ormonde. The daughters of these noblemen maintained a friendship with Mrs. Van Homrigh and her children while in London. But Vanessa's father had died in 1703 when Hester was only sixteen.

At the beginning of their friendship, in 1711, Swift found it necessary to reprove her for certain failings for which he had not the heart to take her to task to her face. He hit upon the plan of doing so in a letter to her cousin, Anne Long, which he left unsealed and begged Vanessa to forward. After praising her for her "principles" and congratulating himself on having corrected all her faults, he criticizes her for her frivolity, idleness, and inattention to the reading which he has selected for her. She sleeps too much, and is indiscriminate in her affections, showing an equal regard for Lady Ashburnham,

[1]For a full account of Van Homrigh, and details of the mayoral collar and medal executed by one of the Roettiers and bearing Van Homrigh's name as the donor, see Ball, Vol. III, pp. 453-9.

her dog, and Doctor Swift. She does not treat him with proper respect, hinting to her sister that she wishes to be alone with him: in fact, she is impulsive, demonstrative, indiscreet and childish.[1]

These small but significant remarks point the way to Vanessa's nascent love for Swift, and his attitude towards her, and give us an inkling of her character before he had finished moulding it. He chaffs her for being difficult to please—"you that can neither work, nor read, nor play, nor care for company."[2]

Vanessa begins to treasure anything that Swift has written. Miss Long complains that "Misshessy" has forgotten to forward to her a copy of Steele's *Miscellany*[3] which Swift had promised to obtain for her and Swift, quick to understand feminine weaknesses, reproves Vanessa by telling Miss Long that "Mishessy has cheated you in not sending you one of them, which I got on purpose and delivered to her with my own hand."[4] In the following year Vanessa begins to keep Swift's letters to her, to endorse them with numbers in order of date, and to keep drafts of some of her own letters written to him. Thus it comes about that two women with identical names (the one in Ireland, the other in England), were simultaneously treasuring, endorsing, and putting away with tender affection, letters from the same man. Thus, although they have come down to us through different agencies, and not by the inclination of Swift, we are able to see side by side in the British Museum, what neither Stella nor Vanessa was able to, a letter from him to the former addressed:

"To Mrs. Johnson, at her Lodgings—over against St. Mary's Church, near Capel Street, Dublin, Ireland."

dated August 7th, 1712, and endorsed by Stella on the date

---

[1] Freeman, p. 68.
[2] op. cit., p. 72. Letter from Swift to Vanessa from Windsor Castle, August 15th, 1712.
[3] Not Steele's, but his own, and therefore precious to Vanessa. *Miscellanies in Prose and Verse.* Published February 27th, 1710-11.
[4] Freeman, p. 67.

received, August 14th: while almost at the same time we
stare at one to the latter, addressed:

    ⌐ "To Mrs. Esther Van Homrigh, Junior,
              at her Lodgings over against Park Place,
                 in St. James Street, London,"

dated the day after Stella's endorsement, August 15th, and
carefully ear-marked by Vanessa as the second of her hoarded
letters.[1]

V

What was Vanessa's appearance? Lord Orrery, after the
death of Swift, declared that Vanessa was not handsome, but
then Grattan said the same of Stella. Taste in beauty changes
from one generation to another and individuals seldom agree.
In an early portrait of her we see a delicate and mobile face,
expressive of extreme sensibility rather than strength, the
eyes tender and quiet, the mouth set in contemplative acceptance. It lacks the roguishness of the younger Stella, and gains
something over the later in thoughtfulness and sweetness. In
all, it augurs a character certain to attract a man of Swift's
susceptibility but not one to match his toughened fibre.

As for Swift's appearance at this time, it was said of him
that he never laughed, that he sat unmoved while his jest
convulsed the company round him, but that his piercingly
azure-blue eyes had about them a "very uncommon archness."[2]
Yet even his masculine friends had to admit that severity was
his prevailing expression. "But when that sternness of visage
was encreased by rage, it is scarce possible to imagine looks,
or features, that carried in them more terror and austerity."[3]
We gather the impression of a personality which alternated
between extraordinary, compelling charm and a terrifying
blackness, which in one of his attacks of fury might make one
tremble, or fly in fear.

[1]Letter 51 of the *Journal* is actually addressed to, and endorsed
by, Rebecca Dingley, but as Swift's use of Dingley as a cover for
Stella is obvious the meaning is the same.
[2]Pope's description in Spence's *Anecdotes*, p. 119.
[3]*Remarks*, by Lord Orrery, p. 74.

His influence upon a young, undeveloped and pliant character like Vanessa's can now scarcely be estimated. He had, as Scott so eloquently puts it,

"a name blown wide abroad in the world. In private society, the varied richness of his conversation, the extent of his knowledge, his unequalled powers of wit and humour, even the somewhat cynical eccentricities of his temper, joined to form a character equally interesting from its merit and originality. His manners, in these his better days, were but slightly tinged with the peculiarities which afterwards marked them more unpleasantly, and his ease and address were such as became the companion of statesmen and courtiers."[1]

Judge then the effect which his appearance, his increasing number of visits, and his especial interest in her intellectual growth, must have had on this talented, moody girl, impressionable and hungry, not only for knowledge, but for impetus and direction in life, which she found both bewildering and insipid.

Above all, she was not combative. She did not contend with her mother for her proper place in the home, that of an elder daughter of a marriageable age. She allowed her mother to push her aside, almost into the nursery, since there at least she might be left in solitude, or with only her younger sister 'Mollkin' for companion, to dream out her thoughts and read what she pleased. She was both intelligent and receptive; if she was idle, sometimes melancholy and sometimes petulant, it was not because of innate spitefulness but for want of encouragement and the proper exercise of her native powers. No one after the death of her father took an interest in her mind, and Vanessa drifted like a sloop who has lost her moorings. If not at once, then soon after Swift's introduction to the family, she must have perceived his genius, been drawn to him, and determined that here was the man to help her in the course which she found so difficult to chart. Diffident and insecure, she committed herself and her future happiness to someone whom she believed she could lean on, but above all

[1]Vol. I, pp. 206-207.

Plate IV

Portrait of Vanessa, by an unknown artist

else respect and honour. The need to reverence the man she might love is marked in Vanessa's letters.

Swift appeared to respond, if not by word, action or intention, then by manner and implication. Vanessa's inexperience and her powerful imagination, which created an unreal being and an unreal state of affairs blotting out the real, prevented her from reading Swift's character aright. The danger which lay ahead for her was that which Stella had also experienced in her association with him, that whilst appearing to give himself fully to the companion of the moment—more fully than most—he inwardly withheld himself. Both women, ultimately, were fated to come away empty-handed, having begun their journey with expectations of the most intense yet, because they were thwarted, the most painful kind.

In both cases the girl, or woman, was fatherless and Swift, whose protective tender side was drawn to shield and guide her, involved her in a relationship which must be largely sterile. It excited and deluded each in turn since this mixture of part-father, part-lover-and-husband, aroused in each the false hope that she alone received his intimate confessions, or soothed and encouraged him.

On Stella the effect of his behaviour was bound to be less disastrous. He had met her when she was young and unformed. The impact upon her childish character of his more turbulent and powerful one had been so strong that he had overborne and made her his, once and for all. Absorbed almost into his very being she remained a separate individual, yet one moving always under the guidance, wishes, aims, of another. She was identified with him and could no more escape than the falcon from the wrist of its trainer. Soar and eddy as she might she must always return to his lure, limited in her realm of flight, experience, and development. Denied the liberty of mating with him, the one man whom she loved, she was yet, because of her allegiance, denied it with another. Even her home was not her own; she inhabited Swift's hungrily when he was absent, and dutifully transplanted herself to maiden quarters upon his return. Her reading, occupation, thoughts, and actions were all modelled as he would wish them, and although her own gifts and strength of character prevented her from becoming the mere shadow or automaton of her mentor she remained irretrievably and essentially his.

With Vanessa the result was bound to be different. She lacked Stella's stability, practicality, or docility. From the beginning of her acquaintance with Swift we find him complaining that he could not make her read with ease what he wished her to read, could not dispel her tendency to melancholy, or rouse her into competent activity. She was all fire, or all tears, which he could not control and which alarmed him. She was in fact, too like him—without his strength and driving power, without his ability to shut out the unpleasant, the disturbing, the realistic when it came too close to him.

Their temperaments, moods, and inclinations fitted like hand and glove, with this difference. Vanessa was willing to abandon herself, Swift was fearful to do so. Vanessa rose exultant, or sank to depths of misery pitiful to behold: Swift responded with pleasure, or upbraided her for being "splenetic", without being able to help her. He mistrusted emotion and knew too well the dangers of melancholic brooding. His panacea was exercise, always exercise, and accordingly he urges Vanessa, as he urged Stella, not to sit moping by the fire but to walk, ride and walk again, to drive away passion by exhausting the body.

From the beginning, she was destined to beat her wings against the bars of the cage which his apparent love for her and her obsession with him made. Her character had set too far for him to remould it into the convenient and unnatural shape which he desired it to take. Stella had met him when she was eight: he had returned to her at fifteen: at nineteen he had taken her away. But Vanessa was twenty-one when he met her, twenty-four when they became more closely involved. Immature and delayed in growth as she appears to have been, she was yet too old for Swift to annex and fundamentally alter. And when the ice-cold floes of his inhibited nature began to close around her Vanessa was destined, not to succumb with happy acceptance or silent resignation, but to fight for her life—with results that could only be tragic.

VI

"Ladies," Swift once declared scornfully, "make nets not cages," and now, although he escaped caging, he found himself snared in a net of his own making.   Increasingly he was forced, despite his better inclinations, to play a double part.

The reiterations of loyalty and affection for Stella, interspersed like white buds among the dark core of the political passages in the *Journal*, grew fewer and fewer. Swift may have felt himself to be slipping away from his anchor, from the ideals to which he had always adhered, from the figure of himself which he had built up so conscientiously year upon year.

"When my Letter is gone, and I have none of yours to answer, My Conscience is so clear, and my shoulders so light, and I go on with such courage to prate upon nothing to deerichar Md."[1]

But whether it was weariness with diplomatic evasions, ill-health, continued absence, or the presence of Vanessa near him, the expressions of affection lack the intensity of those in the earlier letters. There is nothing to compare with:

"I say Amen with my heart and vitals, that we may never be asunder again ten days together while poor Presto lives. . . . Dear life and heart, do you tease me?"[2]

or:

"I will say no more, but beg you to be easy, 'till Fortune take her course, and to believe that MD's felicity is the great end I aim at in all my pursuits."[3]

Across the pages of the *Journal* there would pass a shadow causing him sometimes to halt his pen, to play tricks with his own mind, subtly to delude himself as he had deceived and convinced his audience in his political tracts; his spectators in

[1]Williams, p. 484.
[2]Ibid, p. 147 and 149.
[3]Ibid, p. 276.

the Bickerstaff-Partridge duel; and eventually the readers of *Gulliver*. His quandary, rooted in the emotions and not the intellect, refused to yield to reason. Imagination was stronger than will, the unconscious than the conscious. If he regarded himself squarely he found himself in the humiliating position of being governed by the despised passions. Sir William Temple had once written:

> "And though passions are the stings without which they say no honey is made, yet I think all sorts of men have ever agreed they ought to be our servants and not our masters. . . . I could never ride a horse that galls my flesh or shakes my bones, or that runs away with me as he pleases, so as I can never stop at a river, or a precipice."[1]

and Swift, interpreting the words to fit his own needs, had silently concurred, echoing his mentor with the concept that love was only "a ridiculous passion which has no being but in play-books, or romances."[2]

Like the Russians who affirm that all who suffer from this malady should be locked away, just as those with infectious diseases are isolated until the period of contagion is passed; like the French who hold that love overweights a relationship and makes it more likely to founder than float; like Brahms, who wrung out of the agony of his loneliness the false philosophy that "All passions must pass away, but if not then they must be driven away," Swift tried to ignore and repress his unsatisfied longings. To explain his predicament with the intellect, to attempt to control it with the will, was not sufficient: nor did it relieve him to bury his head like an ostrich in the sands of oblivion: it only postponed a solution.

Two images of two women, confusingly named Hester, often distracted him. He must at least differentiate, and so with his habitual need to classicize and poeticize, and to make each one a being of his own, he called them "Stella" and "Vanessa," intimate names for their ears alone. The first was merely the Latin form of Esther but it would do, for she had

---

[1] *Letter to The Countess of Essex.*
[2] *Letter to a Very Young Lady on Her Marriage.*

always been his guiding star: the second was part surname, part Christian. Artificial designations were a commonplace of the day, but in Swift's case they were an absolute necessity: a man caught in thought between two women, like a ram between two butting ewes, must seek to clarify his mind at all costs.

And now since his first pupil was in Ireland and, being so apt, no longer in need of tutelage, and since Vanessa was both so near and so much in need of guidance, he undertook to train her as he had trained Stella. In addition to Montaigne's *Essays* he gave her Plutarch's *Morals*, the *Maxims* of la Rochefoucauld and Davila's *History of the Civil Wars*, which she confessed wearied her. "The mark will be in the same place where you left it," she writes merrily to him.[1]

But alas, Swift could no more refrain from indulging in subtle allusions, invasions of her privacy, than he could from mingling affection with instruction. In his first recorded letter to Vanessa he writes:

"I suppose this packet will lie two hours till you awake. . . . Now are you and Puppy lying at your ease, without dreaming anything of all this."[2]

A girl, ripe for love, would pause on these trifling assertions, delighting in the thought that so great a man might concern himself with such intimacies as a knowledge of her waking and slumbering hours. Wickedly heaping fuel on the fire he closes:

"Adieu till we meet over a pot of coffee or an orange and sugar in the Sluttery, which I have so often found to be the most agreeable chamber in the world."[3]

What was the Sluttery which appears so frequently in Swift's and Vanessa's letters? Mrs. Van Homrigh's drawing-room, declares one editor. But I picture a room of pleasant untidiness, some small, back-parlour, looking on to the garden

---

[1]Freeman, p. 80.
[2]Ibid, p. 64.
[3]Ibid, p. 65.

at the rear of the Caroline house, informal and intimate, where one might brew one's drink on the hob, loll at ease and laugh in relaxed contentment. One's whole impression of "Mrs. Van," derived from the *Journal*, is of a hospitable, happy-go-lucky woman, attempting to live more affluently than her pocket permits, careless of financial arrangements, a bad judge of human nature (who picks a bawd for a landlady), and finally burdens her children at her death with debts and collectors. The Sluttery smells of a certain easy-going informality in which the not too scrupulous mother might leave her daughters to play with the Dean while she prepared the drawing-room for evening entertainment.

From the beginning it is obvious that Swift perversely admired Vanessa for a certain masculinity of mental fibre, whether inherent or attributed. Miss Long had written amusingly:

> "But how can I pretend to judge of anything, when my poor cousin is taken for an hermaphrodite—a thing I as little suspected her for as railing at anybody."[1]—

so that Swift must previously have commented on Vanessa's laudably male qualities to Anne Long. He did not admire very feminine women. He had succeeded in robbing Stella of a large part of her feminine role in life. He had schooled her like a son of his own. Now it must be the same with Miss Hessy: no doubt the experiment would prove as successful. Alas, he reckoned without knowledge of feminine hearts or of Vanessa's character. In this case, he might in vain adjure her, when misfortunes eventually crowded down upon her, to "talk and act like a man of this world." His attempt to inject her with a masculine nature and philosophy which should prove a safeguard against passion and ultimate disaster was doomed in this case to failure.

Swift wrote the first of his recorded letters to Vanessa on December the 18th, 1711, when he had been in London for fifteen months. He wrote the same night to the beautiful Anne Long, who died four days afterwards, and also to Stella, his "little MD." At the close of his fortnightly letter he bids

[1]Freeman, pp. 63-4.

her "love Presto" and asks God to bless her. Despite the fact that he was not well, suffering from a succession of colds and chills, he was indefatigable. He supped or dined in the fortnight three times at the Van Homrighs (including Christmas Day), twice with the Queen's rising favourite Abigail Masham, twice with his "Society" (the famous Brothers' Club, a select affair formed "to advance conversation and friendship" to which none but "men of wit and men of interest" were to be admitted), once in the city, thrice with Erasmus Lewis (Lord Dartmouth's Secretary, who had introduced Swift to Harley), twice with "Mr. Secretary" (St. John), twice with "my Lord Treasurer" (Harley), and once with the Duchess of Ormonde.

It was a period of the most anxious uncertainty for Swift, the Tories, and the country in general. Influenced first by one favourite and then by another—(the current rivals were the red-haired Duchess of Somerset and the phlegmatic but shrewd Abigail Masham, whose nose rivalled the Duchess' locks in colour)—the Queen hedged and vacillated, hoping to gather courage to make a change of ministry. The Tories, like Swift, prayed that the rumour that the Duchess was off to Petworth for Christmas might be realized, and groaned when it was not. Prince François Eugène, partner of Marlborough in the Battle of Blenheim, was hourly expected in London: my Lord Privy Seal set out for Holland: and Lord Nottingham was "owl" enough to make a pother in the House about some "Grub-street speech" on him and to have the printer taken up.[1] Swift was the author of the "speech," in reality a ballad.

In between his visits to Court, where he was amused to watch the members of "both parties coming to observe each other's faces,"[2] to the pregnant coffee-houses, and to the tables and closets of the great, in addition to his private correspondence, Swift found time to polish off, amongst other pieces of writing, a tactless poem[3] (which got him into the Queen's bad graces a second time, since he openly called the

[1]Williams, p. 441.
[2]Ibid, p. 440.
[3]*The Windsor Prophecy. Poems,* I, pp. 145-148.

Duchess of Somerset, "Carrots from Northumberland"[1] and warned the public of her nefarious influence), and to attend to the fifth edition of his masterly *Conduct of the Allies*. This pamphlet had an astounding success. Within forty-eight hours the first edition of one thousand copies had run out: in five hours a second was exhausted, and within a few weeks six were in circulation.[2] It cannot be denied that the *Conduct* was one of the chief instruments in bringing about the end of the war between France and England and indeed this was frankly acknowledged abroad. Just over a year later Swift was able to write to Stella, as proof of this:

> "This day se'ennight after I had been talking at court with Sir William Wyndham the Spanish Ambassador came to him, and said he heard that was Dr. Swift—and desired him to tell me, that His Master and the K(ing) of Fr(ance), and the Qu(een) were more obliged to me than any man in Europe, so we bowed and shook hands &c. I took it very well of him. . . ."[3]

He closes his journal of December, 1711, in which he had related the astounding success of the *Conduct of the Allies*, with jubilation. The Queen, thank God, "was awakened at last." Swift breaks open the seal, tearing the paper in his excitement. "We are all safe," he writes by the lamps of the coffee-house, as he adds his postscript:

> "The Queen . . . has turned out the Duke of Somerset. . . . I want nothing now but to see the Duchess out. But we shall do without her. We are all extremely happy. Give me joy, sirrahs!"[4]

He might rightly beg Stella to "Give him joy," for the change of Ministry, so important for the country's welfare, was in no small part due to "Presto's" efforts. The great Duke

[1]Elizabeth, Duchess of Somerset, was in her own right Baroness Percy, sole heiress of the eleventh and last Earl of Northumberland. She was a friend of Swift's enemy, Lady Giffard.

[2]A seventh edition was called for early in the New Year. Besides this at least five Dublin editions are recorded. See Hayward, Nonesuch *Swift*: p. 348 and J. C. Collins, *Swift*: p. 88.

[3]Williams, p. 585.

[4]Ibid, p. 450.

of Marlborough had fallen. The same Gazette which announced the names of the twelve new peers also declared—"Her Majesty has removed the Duke from all his employments."

Throughout the faithful *Journal* Swift's tone to Stella is one of confident maturity which he shares with her, almost as an equal. He treated both Stella and Vanessa when it pleased him as if they were children, but there is less of the spoilt child peeping out in response to the pages of the *Journal* than to the early letters to Vanessa. Stella was only seven years Vanessa's senior, but Swift's relationship with her was older and more secure. If he regards Stella with ambivalent eyes, seeing her as half-child, half-woman—provoking, amusingly responsive, yet reliable and eminently practical—he pays her the compliment of trusting her with his private business affairs and details of the most stirring events of the times.

Vanessa might prove equally docile and rewarding. He might yet teach her to direct and control emotion in the same profitable way, without in the least being aware that there was about it anything of contortion. By August of 1712, the date of his next letter to her, she too had proved herself an apt pupil, dangerously diverting.

Her early letters to Swift are spirited and witty, with a kind of metaphysical wit unusual in the period, and something of Dorothy Osborne's raillery.

London Sept. ye 1st, 1712

"Had I a correspondent in China," she flaunts at him in the first letter surviving for us—"I might have had an answer by this time. I never could think till now that London was so far off in your thoughts, and that twenty miles were by your computation equal to some thousands. . . . I believe you have formed a new system and think there is no more of this world, passing your sensible horizon. If this be your notion I must excuse you; . . . if it be so, I must reckon myself of another world; but I shall have much ado to be persuaded till you send me some convincing arguments of it. Don't dally in a thing of this consequence, but demonstrate that 'tis possible to keep up a correspondence between friends, though in different worlds. . . ."[1]

[1]Freeman, pp. 73-4.

Such a letter must have surprised, piqued and delighted Swift, to whom the dalliances of a mental courtship were supremely attractive, like the ceremonious dancing and prancing of some mythical, oriental bird who has no need for mating. He was then at Windsor—

"a most delightful place, and at this time abounds in dinners. My lodgings . . . look upon Eaton and the Thames, I wish I were owner of them, they belong to a Prebend."[1]

Not content with her first sally Vanessa followed her letter with another on the following day, in which she reveals herself as something of a vixen. She vows to plague Swift for his determination to leave Windsor just as she, her mother, and sister approach it upon his suggestion. She upbraids him flirtatiously for his friendship with the wife of General Hill. It is a bantering letter with no real malice at heart, yet one senses beneath the playfulness her annoyance at his apparent rebuff, the stubborn interest in Swift which was to become her downfall, and a forewarning of that intensity of pursuit which eventually irked him.

The Doctor replies immediately on paper which he prophesies may smell of venison since he has paid the coachman to carry a haunch to Mrs. Van Homrigh. He acknowledges Vanessa's letter and mentions some business matters current between them. Swift, as we know from his relations with Stella, admired a woman who could handle her own financial and legal affairs, and Vanessa, quick to look for approval, used this as a bond between them. "You know I love law business," she writes in another letter. Poor girl, she had need to do so, for Mr. Partington, whom her father had chosen as executor, succeeded in spinning out a settlement of the former Lord Mayor's estate for more than thirty years after his death. Vanessa was finally forced into instituting a law suit against him in which she was never successful, and he resisted her executors for many years after her death. In 1712 special powers of sale had to be obtained by means of an Act of Parliament.[2]

[1]Williams, p. 553.
[2]Ball, III, p. 35. Note 4.

VII

The calm which Swift and every loyal Tory had hoped might follow on this party's accession to power did not follow. The leaders were dissentient and failed to reflect the general opinion of the nation. The political situation was as full of prickles as the back of a porcupine.

Swift grew despondent and alarmed, not only for himself but for the country as a whole. The Queen's health was increasingly poor: Harley wittily asserted that when she was ill the ministers were distracted, and when she recovered they behaved as if she were immortal. Nothing was settled with regard to the succession. The Jacobite serpent reared its head; Harley,[1] the prince of procrastination, dallied with it, and Bolingbroke enticed it. Even sensible Abigail Masham, influenced by Bolingbroke, was at last drawn into treasonable plots, and Swift, although he was kept in ignorance of half the back-stairs intrigues, was in despair as to how to reconcile leaders, favourites, ministers and subjects.

He was bitterly discouraged as to his own prospects. Harley made fluent promises of advancement and, like Swift's former patrons the Whigs, failed to fulfil them. Swift hated to think ill of a man for whom he had so much affection, but the fact remained that he was still unrewarded. He had not received a single penny from the Ministry, "nor did he expect it." Once when Harley had sent him a banknote for £50 Swift had haughtily rejected it, "disliking both the thing and the manner."[2] Financial reward was not what he wanted, although at the end he half-expected a thousand pounds from the Queen. Ironically others, Irish as well as English, came creeping to him with hopes of patronage. Unable to say no to anyone who appealed to him, Swift assisted the latest applicant[3] and then remarked wryly, "This is the seventh I have now provided for since I came, and *can do nothing for myself.*" His letters to Stella mirror his growing discontent.

[1]Robert Harley was created Earl of Oxford, Earl Mortimer and Lord Harley of Wigmore Castle, in May, 1711.
[2]Williams, pp. 182 and 208.
[3]Sacheverell, the Tory Martyr.

To add to his discouragement, attacks upon his orthodoxy began to increase. Steele, from whom he had now become estranged, cut him to the quick by calling him an infidel. Nottingham described him in the House of Lords as a divine "who is hardly suspected of being a Christian." The Queen, slipping into gouty decay, remembered *A Tale of a Tub* and could but agree with the Duchess of Somerset, when she resurrected it as evidence against Swift, that he was "a man of no principle either of honour or religion."[1]

When things went against him Swift was inclined to take to flight, to retire where his enemies could not find him. More than once he had warned Stella that he had a secret hiding place which he should use when necessity pressed. Now when he observed that the Tories were playing their dilatory game with him as well as with each other he delivered his ultimatum. If they would not prefer him he would desert them. A man grows tired of fighting unrewarded for himself, and disinclined to continue a struggle for others whose aims and policy are at variance. But at length they threw a sop to this Cerberus whose fierceness had so often protected them—the Deanery of St. Patrick's. Swift knew that this was no great prize. For one thing it involved him in considerable expense, and secondly, it implied banishment to the country from which he had always sought to escape. But his pride was at stake: it was better than returning empty-handed.

"To return without some mark of destinction, would look extremely little: and I would likewise gladly be somewhat richer than I am."[2]

He set out for Holyhead on May the 31st, 1713, on "Stay-behind's mare." His parting thoughts were for Vanessa and the little room where he had been so often at his ease.

"I promised to write to you," he opens with urgency, ". . . it is impossible for anybody to have more acknowledgements at heart, for all your kindness and generosity to me. . . . I have hardly time to put my pen to paper, but

[1]Duchess of Somerset to Lady Giffard, June 1709. *Martha, Lady Giffard, Life and Letters*, Julia Longe, George Allen, 1911, p. 248.
[2]Williams, p. 276.

I would make good my promise. Pray God preserve you and make you happy and easy—and so adieu, brat."[1]

Vanessa is concerned for his health. He had experienced another of his periodic attacks and had written to her that he hoped the journey northwards would restore him, promising to ride but little every day. She writes with fervour:

"Had I the power I want, every day that did not add as much to your health, till it was quite established, as Monday last, should be struck out of the calendar as useless ones. . . . You have not kept your promise of riding but a little every day. Thirty miles I take to be a very great journey."[2]

Swift was forced to think so, too, by the time he arrived at Chester, for he complains to Stella in the last letter of the *Journal* that not having been used to riding for the past three years it had made him "terrible weary. . . . I will be three days going to Holyhead; I cannot ride faster, say (what you) will."[3] If his term of endearment for Vanessa had been "brat," his for Stella was even more racy, for the very last words of the *Journal*, scratched on the inside of the cover, are "Agreeable Bitch."

He had the whole inn at Chester to himself, for "all the ships and people went off yesterday with a rare wind," and there was no prospect of another. He must therefore ride on to Holyhead on the morrow and, since he had no one with whom to converse, and the summer evening was long, he wrote to Stella and then to Mrs. Van Homrigh. He had already written to Vanessa from St. Albans, and to Moll from Dunstable, and now he amusingly addresses Mrs. Van,

"at the Sign of the Three Widows, in Pom-Roy Alley," for "I reckon Hess and Moll are widows as well as you, or at least half-widows. . . . Who will Hessy get now to chide, or Moll to tell her stories and bring her sugar plums? We never know anything enough till we want it."[4]

---

[1] and [2]Freeman, pp. 78-9, 80.
[3]Williams, pp. 670-1.
[4]Freeman, p. 81.

Then he vanished, as if the sea had swallowed him, for three long weeks. From Swift's point of view this was entirely comprehensible. His journey took nearly seven days more and he was a fortnight in Dublin. On June the 13th he was installed Dean of St. Patrick's: his time and thoughts were occupied with solemn matters. But to Vanessa, whose love was at the springtide of fulness, the days were interminable, and his silence unendurable. She tried to divert herself by receiving morning admirers at her bedside like the fashionable ladies; by "paddling" in the mud-splashed streets with Charles Ford, her Dublin friend, whom she had introduced to Swift and whom Delany describes as "the best lay scholar of his time and nation"[1], with reading books which Erasmus Lewis brought her, and by writing to Swift. She wrote to him four times in June.

It is obvious that Swift's revelation of his affection for her, disclosed in his long poem *Cadenus and Vanessa* written for her in the previous summer, and her interpretation of where this affection would lead, were already blindingly clear in her heart and mind. She writes extremely well. Her first letter to Swift in Ireland is a mixture of espièglerie and current political matters—the former hides the depth of her true emotion, and the latter attempts to bind Swift with mutual interests.

"I wish you had been here last Thursday: I am sure you could have prevented the bills being lost" . . . (These were the rejected articles in the commercial Treaty with France, and Vanessa was probably right in her estimate of Swift's influence). "Lord! how much we differ from the ancients, who used to sacrifice everything for the good of their commonwealth: but now our greatest men will at any time give up their country out of a pique, and that for nothing."[2]

She goes on to speak of Whig rejoicings, the coming elections, Harley's latest stubbornness, and then she mocks him:

"I know you'll say: 'What does the slut mean, to talk all this stuff to me? If I were there I had as lieve hear it as

[1]*Observations*, p. 97.
[2]Freeman, pp. 84-6.

anything she could say, but to pursue me with her nonsense is intolerable: I'll read no more. . . .' "[1]

This is so exactly in Swift's manner that it could not fail
to amuse him. She closes by telling him that if he will not
talk with her on paper she will again take up *Les Dialogues des
Morts* which Lewis has given her. . . .

> "for I find no conversation on earth comparable but yours.
> So if you care I should stay, do but talk, and you'll keep me
> with pleasure."[2]

It would be hard for Swift to refuse to answer so provoking
a letter had he not been occupied with more solemn business.
As for Vanessa, she was already so seriously infected with his
wit and conversational charm—(then universally recognized,
but difficult to imagine or recapture now from fossil examples)
—that everyone and everything else seemed intolerably dull
by comparison.

In her second letter she gives herself away by showing her
deep concern for his health. Her distress is accentuated by the
conflict which some promise he has extorted from her produces.
She is torn between her fear of offending him and her need to
break the promise, and here, almost at the outset of their
intimacy we catch a glimpse of that terrifying and silent
battle which continued between Swift and Vanessa until her
death ten years later—the battle of the passionate and impulsive nature with the supremely inhibited; of the emotional,
sometimes hysterical, character with the coldly rational;
above all, of the more nearly normal with the abnormal.
Driven blindly by her love, a love which did not, and could not,
understand what sort of man he was, she beat her heart out
against the impregnable walls which he had erected to guard
his flayed sensibilities. She pitted the whole of her being
against his barriers. But Swift was the stronger of the two
and the very strength of his perversity, like the strength of
some unnatural monster which is double that of a human being,
was bound to crush a weaker nature. Her distress is pitiful:

> "I have done all that was possible to hinder myself from

[1] and [2]Freeman, pp. 84-6.

writing to you till I heard you were better, *for fear of breaking my promise*, but 'twas all in vain; for had (I) vowed neither to touch pen, ink or paper, I certainly should have had some other invention. Therefore I beg you won't be angry with me for doing what is not in my power to avoid."[1]

Her fear of Swift was not merely one of his wrath, of his Jovian claps and peals of thunder forked by shafts of satiric lightning before which even courageous men trembled, it was a deeper and more pitiable fear caused by her emotional dependence, the fear of losing him.

Being what she was, she was quite unable to restrain her loving concern for his welfare, and when she wrote—"what is not in my power to avoid"—she spoke truth, for her emotions were stronger than her control. In her next letter she puts on a brave face in order not to vex him with what she knows he most dreads, a sign of melancholy.

". . . But I have already suffered so much by knowing that you were ill, and fearing you were worse than, I hope, you have be(en), that I will strive to change that thought, if possible, that I may have a little ease; and more, that I may not write you a splenetic letter."[2]

Anything would be better than this cruel silence. Reproof would be better than neglect. She bids him tell her openly if he thinks she writes too often. Then follow some pregnant lines:

"If you are very happy it is ill-natured of you not to tell me so, except 'tis what is inconsistent with mi(ne) . . . . I have often heard you say that you would willingly suffer a little uneasiness, provided it gave another a vast deal of pleasure."[3]

Did some intuition warn her, or had she received a hint of Swift's association with Stella? It seems impossible that Vanessa and Swift could have common friends who had lived and were to live again in Dublin or near it, such as Charles

[1]Freeman, p. 87 (italics mine).
[2] and [3]Ibid., p. 88.

Ford, and that no mention of Swift's private affairs, common knowledge there, should ever reach Vanessa's ears. But whether her suspicion sprang from premonition or friendly warning, her nature was courageous and candid. She gave Swift an opening which he did not take.

VIII

If Vanessa was courageous in this situation Swift was not. He once remarked that cowardice was generally considered to be "a sign of cruelty,"[1] and how true this was in his treatment of both Stella and Vanessa becomes painfully obvious. Had he been able to make an open and final declaration of his feelings and decisions at this juncture, suffering might have been spared all three, and especially Vanessa. But Swift was caught between the diametrical drives of his character, which alternated between extreme sensibility and cruelty, altruism and egocentricity, enticement and rejection, expression and repression. Vanessa had rightly estimated the first of these characteristics, his uneasiness before another's pain and his wish to relieve it, but she had not, and could not, judge the severity of the second—his need to destroy the thing he loved in order (as he unconsciously felt) to protect himself. Should she recognize this it would ring the death knell to her natural and vital hopes.

If her emotions ruled her—and how much they ruled her she was painfully aware—it was exactly the opposite with Swift. Rational control was the precept by which he had lived for nearly half a century. The passions, if they obtruded, must be cut out like an offending eye, in order that the whole body might not become malignantly offensive. His letter from Laracor, whither he had retired after his installation, in answer to hers, is a masterpiece of self-concern and displays the alternating currents which confused and tormented her, now drawing her towards him tenderly, then brutally repelling her.

"I had your last spleenatic letter. I told you when I left

[1] *Letter to a Very Young Lady on Her Marriage.*

England I would endeavour to forget everything there, and would write as seldom as I could. . . . At my first coming I thought I should have died with discontent, and was horribly melancholy while they were installing me; but it begins to wear off, and change to dulness. . . ."[1]

It was, or it should have been, as plain as a pikestaff. Swift did not wish or intend to be a lover. Had Vanessa been older, or wiser, in other words a different person, she might have seen a man too sick to respond with ardour, undivided affection, or loyalty. The word "splenetic" which Swift was fond of hurling at her whenever she made a faint whisper of complaint against his wounding treatment, covered a multitude of his constant fears for himself. *He* might be "horribly melancholy," "die with discontent," or be afflicted with "dulness," these were privileges permitted by virtue of his seizures and the public treatment he had received; but Vanessa's health (which inclined to the tubercular), her discouragements and despondencies, often consequent on his behaviour, must all be ignored. "I am riding here for life," he writes, "and think I am something better." In other words, being the egoist he was, he was too ill to trouble himself with the sufferings of others close to him. He might grieve for young Harrison or Diaper, and go out of his way to assist them and their relations, but should a woman express her natural inclination to look to him for happiness or security, he instantly denied her the right. Relationships of intense and prolonged intimacy were insupportable to him: they strained his already weakened temper. He therefore threw up defences behind which he retired, and over which he hurled epithets and warning sentences by way of protection, but he did not do the one thing which would save both him and his partner-adversary further pain—withdraw completely.

To appeal to Vanessa's pity at the same time that he rejected her was both unkind and hopelessly confusing. To her alone, as far as we know, he revealed his gloom at being installed Dean of the Cathedral, his bitter determination to stay on at Laracor, "preferring a field bed and an earthen floor before

[1]Freeman, p. 90.

the great house which they say is mine"—(the Deanery in Dublin). The spectacle of this great man castigating himself as being "fitter to cut hedges . . . and to order workmen to drive out cows" from his Island, and make up ditches. . . . "work much more proper for a country vicar than driving out factions and fencing against them" was for her alone. "I must go and take my bitter draught to cure my head, which is spoilt by the bitter draught the public hath given me." How he revelled in self-torment and self-pity! How he worked on her sensitive heart, only to repulse her love and compassion when he had evoked it! If he was aware of it, Swift did not care. It is safer and kinder to assume that he did not see what he was doing.

The bitterness and despondency visible in Swift's letter to Vanessa arose from an accumulation of causes, the main ones being the galling circumstances under which he had received his promotion, and his inauspicious reception in Dublin. His preferment, which he rightly felt should have been granted joyfully and spontaneously in reward for all his services, had been dependent not only upon the wishes of the Queen, but upon the influence of Lord Oxford, the Duke of Ormonde, patron of the living, the Archbishop of Dublin, and even Lady Masham.   Upon realizing Swift's determination to leave London "unless he had something honourable immediately given" to him[1] Oxford secretly stopped the warrants for three vacant deaneries (Wells, Ely and Lichfield) whose disposition had already been settled, and begged Ormonde to exercise his influence with the Queen to obtain the Irish one for Swift. Lady Masham, not given to displays of emotion, upon hearing that Swift was to be sent out of the country, burst into tears and pleaded with the Queen to prefer him in England. (Oxford, temporizing, suggested the vacant canonry at Windsor.) But the Queen remained adamant. Her horror of Swift, which she could ill conceal, prevented her from promoting him near her. It must be the Deanery of St. Patrick's, or nothing.

Then Ormonde began to vacillate. Stearne, who must be promoted if Swift was to succeed him as Dean, had been dis-

[1]Williams, Vol. II, p. 660.

respectful to him, his patron; he did not deserve advancement. For an instant Swift must have hoped that the solution would be to make *him* Bishop of Dromore, leaving Stearne in Dublin. Ormonde twice begged him to name some other deanery. Weary of the whole matter, Swift bowed in resignation.

"I desired, he would put me out of the case, and do as he pleased; then with great kindness he said he would consent, but would do it for no man alive but me, etc., and he will speak to the Qu(een) to-day, or to-morrow. So perhaps something will come of it. I can't tell."[1]

In order to obtain the Deanery Swift was actually forced to recommend to Harley, Bolingbroke, and the Duke of Ormonde, the very man he was ousting, and the tiresome business was complicated by arguments and disagreements with Stearne occasioned by Swift's liability to him as incoming tenant. "I shall buy Bishop Stearne's *hair* as soon as his household goods," he shouts in vexation to Stella: adding, "I shall be ruined, or at least sadly crampt, unless the Queen will give me a thousand pounds: I am sure she owes me a great deal more."[2]

This was an additional anxiety, for Lord Oxford had promised him this sum as a premium upon his entering the Deanery, but when upon the Queen's death the ministry fell the promise remained unredeemed. Thus Swift, who hated above all things to be indebted to any man for praise, promotion, financial assistance, proofs of love and friendship, unless won by his own merit, who knew that he had enough ability to equal ten Stearnes, found himself forced, not only to accept, but to secure for himself, a prize which was almost an indignity. His suspense and rage at the vacillations, humiliations, and vexatious business affairs connected with taking up the Deanery, brought on an attack of illness which reduced him to sullen misery.

To add to his chagrin, his reception in Dublin was far from auspicious. He was aware of the silent hostility of invisible people—the Whigs who regarded him with suspicion, and the Dissenters with a dread which was not unreasonable since he

[1]Williams, p. 663.
[2]Ibid, p. 669.

had never spared them; jealous rival prelates who resented his imperious manner, envied his preferment, and were ungrateful for his unwearying efforts over the *First Fruits and Tenths* from which they had benefited. "I remit them their First Fruits of Ingratitude, as freely as I got the other remitted to them,"[1] he wrote in an excess of bitterness which one can easily appreciate.

Upon the day of his installation some verses which will serve as an epitome of all the rancour and malice which surrounded him, and which must have "grated him to the heart" (an expression Swift often used) were nailed to the Cathedral door. They were by another churchman:[2]

> "Today, this temple gets a Dean,
> Of parts and fame uncommon;
> Used both to pray, and to profane,
> To serve both God and Mammon. . . .
>
> This place he got by wit, and rhyme,
> And many ways most odd;
> And might a bishop be in time,
> Did he believe in God. . . .
>
> Look down St. Patrick, look, we pray,
> On thine own church and steeple;
> Convert thy Dean on this great day,
> Or else, God help the people!"[3]

To aggravate matters, there was his disillusionment over Steele's ingratitude, Steele, who owed to him the retention of his lucrative office under the government, assistance in his literary ventures, and protection from verbal and written insult. "Do him a good turn and he is your enemy forever"— was Swift's biting riposte and the beginning of many fierce personal attacks which he proceeded to make upon his one-time protégé. And to crown all, the shame which he could not express, and could not even face, at the necessity to wound

[1]Williams, pp. 387-8.
[2]Jonathan Smedley, Dean of Killala.
[3]Scott, I, pp. 161-2.

first Vanessa and then Stella, if an intimacy with both was to continue, perplexed and distressed him.

His homecoming to Dublin must have been a sad and difficult one for Stella, who had never once upbraided him for being absent so long, who had in fact assisted him to be at ease when she knew that he was likely to feel guilty and uncomfortable at his own procrastinations and broken promises:[1] who had faithfully attended to his business affairs in his absence, even those clerical ones in which it might be considered unfitting for her to meddle:[2] who lived only for him and that his life might prosper, who rejoiced in his promotion and longed for the day of his coming.

If she consoled herself with thoughts that now, Dean of St. Patrick's, he would settle permanently in Ireland, be easy in mind over his increased resources and even—(if she dared to let herself think it)—revoke his resolution not to marry, it was a false consolation, for Swift showed less inclination than ever to fulfil the promises implied in the *Journal* or elsewhere, and in less than three months he set off again for London.

IX

In June, 1714, nine months later, Swift is writing to Vanessa from the house of a Berkshire clergyman, an old friend and acquaintance, whom he declares "he loves very well," complaining only that he is "such a melancholy, thoughtful man" that he "fears he will catch the spleen from him."

"You see," he opens,

"I am better than my word, and write to you before I have been a week settled in the house where I am. . . . This is the first syllable I have writ to anybody since you saw me."[3]

The only excitement in this land-locked hamlet is the arrival, not of the Pretender or the Duke of Cambridge, whose landings in England were imminent, but of the parson's wife

[1] and [2]Williams, pp. 233 and 668-9.
[3]Freeman, pp. 92-3.

who has been staying twenty miles off with her father. "I
never saw her, and perhaps the house will be worse when she
comes," suggests the misogynist. He looks forward to hearing from Vanessa,

> "not as . . . a Londoner but a friend . . . I send my man
> two miles with this to the post-town, so if there be a letter
> by chance from you I shall not be able to tell you so now."[1]

What was Swift doing in Berkshire on the eve of the death
of the Queen, and the fall of the Tory party? The answer lies
in the deterioration of the political situation during Swift's
absence, accentuated by the Queen and Lady Masham's
dissatisfaction with Oxford, the widening breach between
Oxford and Bolingbroke, the eagerness of the Whigs to import
a Hanoverian successor, and the intrigues of some of the
Tories to treat with the Pretender. The position is tersely
explained in Erasmus Lewis' previous letters to Swift in
Dublin, to which he had gone in June, 1713, for his installation:

> "We are all running headlong into the greatest con-
> fusion imaginable . . . I heartily wish you were here; for
> you might certainly be of great use to us, by your endeavours
> to reconcile. . . ."

Lewis followed this note in three weeks' time with another
more urgent:

> "My Lord Treasurer desires you will make all possible
> haste over, for we want you extremely. . . ."[2]

Swift could not resist the appeal. It was enough for him
that he was loved and needed. He left Dublin hastily (so
hastily that he offended the Archbishop, who threatened to
take steps to tether Swift to his Deanery) and returned to
London, barely three months after his installation. He would
try once more to exert that influence which had fascinated so
many at the height of his power, and to see if a mixture of
bullying and wheedling, of commonsense and charm, might not

[1]Freeman, pp. 93-4.
[2]Ball, II, pp. 55 and 57.

effect a reconciliation between Oxford and Bolingbroke. Good will, industry, and doggedness, reinforced his wish to escape from Ireland and to use those abilities which he could not employ to such extent in Dublin. Just as he had returned again and again to Temple, hoping that agreement and a good, working relationship might be established at last between them, so now he essayed to bring warring factions and individuals together.

But he underestimated the difficulties present, and failed to see clearly how antagonistic were the two leaders with whom he had worked in such close collaboration, and, as he thought, such honest intimacy. Although he finally brought about a meeting between them at Lady Masham's, and "seriously expostulated with . them" both, the hoped-for solution did not come. Swift was both amazed and saddened at the amount of intrigue which he now discovered, the plots and counter-plots which had ripened during his absence, and at the obvious deterioration of Harley, both mentally and physically. Always a mediator rather than a fighter, Harley had now lost all will to fight. His health had suffered since the attempt on his life three years earlier which had so shaken Swift, and in November, 1713, he lost his eldest daughter. The sincerity of Swift's affection for Harley—decorous, amiable, dilatory, yet perspicacious and able, a man so unlike one whom we would imagine Swift to admire—speaks plainly in his letter of consolation to the bereaved father upon this latter occasion.

Swift began to feel that it was not only useless but positively dangerous to interfere further in the political situation or to try to patch up the impaired friendship of his old leaders. The seeds of events which were, upon the death of the Queen, to lead to the imprisonment of Oxford in the Tower and Bolingbroke's flight to the continent, were already sprouting when Swift retired to his grave parson-friend in Berkshire.

"But if this place were ten times more worse, nothing shall make me return to Town while things are in the situation I left them,"

he tells Vanessa, and he confesses that he has "a mind to steal to Ireland,"[1] . . . which, when England fails him, becomes his refuge.

But he lingered on in Berkshire for another six weeks while all but his most intimate friends speculated about his hiding place. He occupied himself with writing *Free Thoughts upon the Present State of Affairs*, an honest statement of his attitude, coinciding with what he had not hesitated to say either publicly or privately, which might have had great and remedial influence had it then been published. He was concerned for Vanessa, whose mother had died leaving a highly unsatisfactory number of debts. Swift offered to lend her money through his friend Ben Tooke, and advised her about the debts. He wrote four letters to her from Berkshire and it speaks much for his tenderness and loyalty that he concerned himself for her welfare in such detail when his career, and that of his friends, was falling headlong to destruction.

On July the 27th Oxford resigned, leaving Bolingbroke triumphant with the reins of government in his hands. The proof of Swift's power, if final proof is needed, comes at this moment of dissolution when both Bolingbroke and Oxford appeal to him, the former holding out to him "hopes at once the most splendid and the most plausible,"[2] for political reinstatement and ecclesiastical promotion; the latter, a pathetically appealing offer of hospitality in disgrace and retirement at his seat in Herefordshire.

"If I have not tired you tête-à-tête, fling away so much time upon one who loves you.⋅ And I believe, in the mass of souls, ours were placed near each other."[3]

Swift did not hesitate in his choice. He was bound to Oxford by ties of touching friendship.

"I am writ to earnestly by somebody to come to Town, and join with these people now in power, but I will not do it. . . . I told Lord Oxford I would go with him when he was out, and now he begs it of me, and I cannot refuse him. I meddle not with his faults as he was a minister of state;

---

[1] Freeman, p. 93.
[2] Collins, p. 122.
[3] Ball, II, pp. 198-9.

but you know his personal kindness to me was excessive; he distinguished and chose me above all other men while he was great, and his letter to me t'other day was the most moving imaginable."[1]

But on the evening of the same day on which Swift intended to join Oxford—August the 1st—the Queen died. "What a world is this and how does fortune banter us,"[2] wrote Bolingbroke in despair. The visit to Lord Oxford never occurred. Swift remained on quietly at Upper Letcombe, like a dormouse safe in its nest of grass while palaces are burning, until the 18th of August, when he set out again for Ireland.

His last letter to Vanessa before departing exhibits his weariness with current affairs and his irritation with her. He had written to Stella eighteen months before to say that he Cardinal Wolsey.

"A weak old man, battered with storms of state,
Is come to lay his weary bones among you" . . . .

that he intended to retire for six months and then "steal over to Laracor," and now he says to Vanessa: "These public misfortunes have altered all my measures and broke my spirits."[4] Her pity, or her love, got the better of her judgment, and giving way to one of her impetuosities she paid Swift a surreptitious visit in his retreat, which only annoyed him. "You should not have come by Wantage for a thousand pound. You used to brag you were very discreet. Where is it gone?"[5] And then there follow directions for secrecy if they are to correspond while he is in Ireland. The seriousness of the political debacle, and his secretive nature, necessitated these drastic regulations.

"If you are in Ireland while I am there I shall see you very seldom. It is not a place for any freedom, but where everything is known in a week and magnified a hundred

[1]Freeman, p. 97.
[2]Ball, II, p. 214.
[3]Williams, p. 459
[4] and [5]Freeman, p. 99.

degrees. These are rigorous laws that must be passed through. . . . I say all this out of the perfect esteem and friendship I have for you. . . . I would not answer your questions for a million, nor can I think of them with any ease of mind. Adieu."[1]

His sojourn in England was over although he was not aware of it, for he was still too near the blaze to distinguish the amount of damage done, and like one blinded with stinging smoke, half thought to rescue something still invisible. He speaks to Vanessa of a possibility of returning to London "by the beginning of the winter," and of meeting her then. But there was no return, not for eleven years, and by that time Vanessa was dead.

It was the end of a dynasty, a reign, a party and a period and, for Swift, of all his hopes. There is something both tragic and ludicrous about the way in which his achievements are once more snatched from him just as he is about to realize their benefits—ludicrous because it is repetitive, as if Swift's "baneful goddess" really existed to tempt and torment him.

"This wonderfully abundant life has indeed a strange monotony of destiny. Destiny does not trouble to find new ways to slay Swift, new devices for stripping him bare; it repeats itself tirelessly, stupidly, pitilessly. . . .

"Swift had not only one life to live. There were for him many and many deaths, many and many slow, hard struggles towards resurrection—and as soon as he rose again the new life painfully won would be taken from him at a stroke. . . . his life did not *flow*. It met everywhere obstacles which it could not surmount, and was forced back upon itself. . . .

"Bolingbroke can be pardoned for his treason, Harley can be released from the Tower; Swift remained in an exile which was for him worse than a prison."[2]

[1]Freeman, pp. 99-100.
[2]Rossi and Hone, p. 219.

CHAPTER FIVE

Of what is't fools make such a keeping?
Sin their conception, their birth, weeping;
Their life, a general mist of error,
Their death a hideous storm of terror.

JOHN WEBSTER

I

DUBLIN, at the time of the fall of the Tories, numbered three Whigs to every one in the population of London. If Swift, in his retreat at Upper Letcombe, had been half aware of the impertinent and savage manner in which the curious and malicious sought him out, hurling squibs[1] after him like a pack of riotous school boys who pelt their fallen master, now he was fully conscious of the dangerous animosity of the Dublin Whig citizens. For Swift was a Tory, and therefore, in their intemperate judgment, a Jacobite and a Papist. Although he denied being a Jacobite it was well known that he had been intimately associated with Bolingbroke and Ormonde, both of whom were soon to be in the service of the Pretender, the one as Secretary, the other as General-in-Chief. His friendship with Oxford was equally known, and Oxford was as suspect as the former. People hissed and booed at him in the streets, some of them even pelted him with filth from the gutters. A misguided peer so far forgot himself as to attack the Dean, so that the latter had to appeal for protection while riding for exercise on the strand.[2] Swift found it expedient to keep his servants armed by night and to ride attended with them by day.

It was not for nothing that he had bade Vanessa beware prying eyes and poisoned tongues if she wrote to him; he was spied on by his own Archbishop, and his letters were inter-

---

[1] *A Hue and Cry after Dr. Swift.* Temple Scott, V, p. 480.
[2] See *The Dean of St. Patrick's Petition to the House of Lords against Lord Blaney*: Sheridan, pp. 183-4.

cepted and opened. He was constantly watched and constantly in danger. But this situation, far from making him cower like a hare frozen with fear in its form, brought out the most valiant sides of Swift's nature. When, upon the Duke's attainder, the Ulster King at Arms gave orders to take down the escutcheon of the Ormondes from the wall of St. Patrick's Cathedral, Swift sent the workmen packing, declaring that no such indignity should be offered so noble a house whilst he was alive to defend it. He offered to wait upon Oxford in the Tower, where he lay for two years. He maintained his friendship with the exiled Bolingbroke and Ormonde, and attempted to solace their deserted wives, who wrote to him affectionately. The House of Stuart no longer reigned, but, both in spirit and action, Swift resembled his fighting parson-grandfather who had defenced it so staunchly. The same fierce loyalty to a cause, an ideal, and a friend, activated the grandson.

But if he met these dangers with courage, "keeping up his noble spirit . . . like a man knocked down . . . still with a stern countenance . . . aiming a blow at his adversaries,"[1] they saddened and soured him; his defiance was tinged with self-pity, and as usual, he relieved himself in writing:

> " 'Tis true—then why should I repine,
> To see my life so fast decline?
> But, why obscurely here alone?
> Where I am neither lov'd nor known.
> My state of health none care to learn;
> My life is here no soul's concern.
> And, those with whom I now converse,
> Without a tear will tend my herse. . . .
>
> .   .   .   .
>
> Ye formal weepers for the sick,
> In your last offices be quick;
> And spare my absent friends the grief
> To hear, yet give me no relief;
> Expir'd today, entomb'd to-morrow,
> When known, will save a double sorrow."[2]

[1] Letter from Arbuthnot.
[2] *Poems*, Vol. I, pp. 203-4: *In Sickness* (capitals omitted).

One can but pity Stella if she tried to minister to this tearful being, who excluded her so completely from the circle of those who loved him—and presumably she was near him at Laracor, whither he went to regard the thefts and dilapidations which had taken place in his absence. He speaks sarcastically of his

"country seat, where I have an acre of ground . . . gone to ruin. The wall of my own apartment is fallen down, and I want mud to rebuild it, and straw to thatch it. Besides, a spiteful neighbour has seized on six feet of ground, carried off my trees, and spoilt my grove."[1]

"He gardened and sauntered; he turned over the Greek and Roman classics; he bandied nonsense with Sheridan and Esther Johnson; he went through a course of ecclesiastical history; he dabbled in mathematics."[2]

In Dublin he struggled to subject his rebellious choir and Chapter, and to pour oil on the troubled waters which surged between him and his Archbishop. When Pope writes glibly to him at the Deanery and reproaches him for not corresponding, Swift retorts with feeling:

"You know how well I loved both Lord Oxford and Bolingbroke, and how dear the Duke of Ormond is to me. Do you imagine I can be easy while their enemies are endeavouring to take off their heads! . . . You are to understand that I live in the corner of a vast unfurnished house. My life consists of a steward, a groom, a helper in the stable, a footman, and an old maid, who are all at board wages, and when I do not dine abroad, or make an entertainment, which last is very rare, I eat a mutton-pie, and drink half a pint of wine."[3]

How are the mighty fallen! The contrast between his life in London and now in Dublin was too depressing to bear contemplation. He was in an ill mood to bear with feminine vagaries.

[1]Letter to Bolingbroke before his exile. Ball, Vol. II, p. 240.
[2]Collins, p. 132.
[3]Ball, Vol. II, pp. 286-8.

Yet now, surprisingly, we find a letter addressed to Vanessa "at her lodgings in Turnstile Alley, near College Green, *Dublin*." Swift's worst fears as to his private affairs must have been realized, for College Green and Capel Street, where Stella lodged, were only a short distance from one another. The estate of Vanessa's father included a small property called Marley Abbey, on the banks of the Liffey, at Celbridge, about eleven miles to the west of Dublin. It was to this house that she and her sister Mary, whose fortunes were also diminished, expected to retire, alternating their periods of seclusion with visits to Dublin.

Swift cannot have wished that Vanessa should come to Ireland, but he could not prevent what it was natural that she should do. He endured her coming, her proximity, the complications which her nearness caused, as one more prank of a capricious Fate, who "seldom cares to humour our inclinations."[2] The perplexing and difficult game of being intimate with, and advising and protecting, two women simultaneously, to both of whom he was attracted, both of whom had claims on him, and who lived distressingly near each other, began in earnest.

It is strange how a man will deplore in others, and etch with accuracy, the very faults which he himself possesses without in the least realizing that he does so. The two weaknesses of Harley's character which Swift had drawn in his *Free Thoughts*, and which he had never hesitated to point out to Harley's face on what Harley called Swift's "whipping days," were procrastination and refinement. By refinement he meant

> "that over-subtlety of calculation which Swift thought inferior to plain common sense, and which, to use his favourite illustration, is like the sharp knife that mangles the paper, when a plain, blunt paper-knife cuts it properly."[3]

[1]Vanessa's first letter headed Celbridge is dated 1720—six years later.

[2]Freeman, p. 99.

[3]Sir Leslie Stephen, p. 115. See Swift's Letter to Bolingbroke, Ball, III, p. 41.

This over-subtlety of calculation was one of the reasons
which prevented Swift from marrying, which forced him to
give as an excuse for celibacy, his or a woman's age, his lack
of means, the woman's possible avidity, and all manner of
imaginary causes: it kept him from concluding his relationship
with Vanessa. It was rooted in several soils, his diffidence,
his hypersensitiveness, and an inner dependence. Thus his
morbid imagination prevented him from being able to
visualize himself as a contented domestic partner: he shrank
from giving pain with the result that, in this situation, he
caused even greater pain: and dreaded a severance like one
who fears an operation, even when that operation might be
the means of saving and not destroying a life.

Something of this same inability to terminate a relationship
quietly and finally, without conflict, was evident in his
behaviour towards Temple. This inconclusiveness, this
dependence strange in a strong man perfectly able to handle
other situations with expediency and clarity, can only have
been due to his need for affection. Swift had been so starved for
love as a child and a growing boy that affection, even though
misery attended it, was infinitely precious. Having (as he felt
it) been rejected and abandoned so often and for so long in
early years. he remained as a mature man the victim of
delayed emotions which tethered him against his judgment.

Throughout the remainder of his relationship with Vanessa
he displays a policy of perpetual small kindnesses, placations,
and appeals to her memory of past happy incidents, alternating
with gross rebuffs when these appeals are too successful.

A self-torturer, he faithfully demonstrates in his outward
behaviour his own inner torments by playing with Vanessa as
a cat plays with a mouse, now drawing her with circular
movements towards him, now letting her run in apparent
freedom a little distance before his counter-needs recall her,
until she cries out at him that he keeps her in a kind of
"languishing death."[1] His treatment is what Sir Walter Scott
calls "cruelty under the mask of mercy."[2] The need and
counter-need, the unconscious one to destroy and the conscious

[1]Freeman, p. 128.
[2]Scott, Vol. I, p. 240.

one to protect, are evident, even in small measure, in this letter, his first to her in Ireland. He will not go to Celbridge to see her "for all the world," but he will call upon her in Turnstile Alley in a fortnight's time: he is going to visit a friend, whose name and address he will not give her in order to avoid her importunities, yet he sends this note to welcome her in her lodgings: he will not promise occasions for future meetings, yet he reminds her of former ones.

II

Vanessa began to be troubled by other difficulties as well as her mother's creditors. Her younger brother Ginkel had died young; her elder, Bartholomew, who was in the Army and whom Swift jocosely called the "Captain" or the "Colonel," showed the family tendency towards extravagance and financially embarrassed his sisters: Mary, or Molkin, was fragile and in need of constant care. Vanessa's first thought for a supporter is Swift and she turns on him all the appealing force of her calamities.

Dublin, 1714.

"You cannot but be sensible, at least in some degree, of the many uneasinesses I am slave to—a wretch of a brother, cunning executors and importunate creditors of my mother's—things I can no way avoid being subject to at present, and weighty enough to sink greater spirits than mine without some support. Once I had a friend that would see me sometimes, and either commend what I did or advise me what to do, which banished all my uneasiness. But now, when my misfortunes are increased by being in a disagreeable place, amongst strange, prying, deceitful people, whose company is so far from an amusement that it is a very great punishment, you fly me, and give me no reason but that we are amongst fools and must submit. I am very well satisfied that we are amongst such, but know no reason for having my happiness sacrificed to their caprice. You once had a maxim, which was to act what was right and not mind what the world said. I wish you would keep to it now. Pray what can be wrong in seeing and advising an unhappy young woman? I can't imagine. You can't but know that your frowns make my life insupportable. You have taught me to distinguish, and then you leave me miserable. Now all I beg is that you will for once counterfeit (since you can't otherwise), that indulge(nt) friend you once were till I get the better of these difficulties, for my sister's sake; for were not she involved (who I know is not able to manage them as I am), I have a nobler soul than (to) sit struggling with misfortunes, when at the end I can't promise myself any real happiness. Forgive me; and I beg you'd believe it is not in my power to avoid complaining as I do."[1]

Her entreaties, importunate yet dignified, begin to have in them a note of tragedy, for she senses, without understanding, Swift's inability to live continuously at that level of intimacy and sincerity which make for constancy and reliability. She felt the oak on which she had leaned give way, and like one crossing a foaming river she knew not which she dreaded most, the savage torrent beneath her or the treacherousness of the bridge which she feared might not support her.

"Counterfeit that indulgent friend. . . ." She cannot endure to let the image she had adored be burnt from her heart. A false copy will be better than nothing, and she is reduced to pleading for this. "You have taught me to distinguish, and then you leave me miserable." 'Distinguish what?', one biographer asks, without giving an answer. To distinguish, surely, the vapidity of the ordinary world around her which Swift had taught her to depreciate and ridicule, sweeping her away into that world of his own which no other person had the charm to evoke, in which she was miserable without him, since he was both creator and companion: to distinguish a whole field of ideas, a set of values, which it was useless to attempt to share with other uninitiates, since they would not understand Swift's language or meanings. He had cut her off from the old world without making her safe in the new. It is like a process of birth, dangerously half-finished, and if Vanessa cannot bring forth a new being without his assistance, she will succumb.

How could Swift resist such entreaty, unless he fled completely? And now it was out of his power to fly. She

[1]Freeman, pp. 103-4.

touched him to the quick and his compassionate nature responded.

"I will see you in a day or two, and believe me, it goes to my soul not to see you oftener. I will give you the best advice, countenance and assistance I can. I would have been with you sooner if a thousand impediments had not prevented me. I did not imagine you had been under difficulties. I am sure my whole fortune should go to remove them. I cannot see you, I fear, to-day, having affairs of my place to do; but pray think it not want of friendship, or tenderness, which I will always continue to the utmost."[1]

What more could she want? His tenderness drew and attached her: it promised so richly. Yet her passionate response embarrassed him. Her desperation, which sometimes rose to fever-heat and ought to have alarmed him, annoyed and distressed him and actually prevented him from seeing what course to take with her. Thus he alternately pacified and rebuffed her.

The natural sequence to Vanessa's suffering and Swift's inability to make her happy would be an end of the affair, whether in misery on her part, or in exasperation on his. But neither the man nor the woman was able to act as wisdom and reason directed. Both remained victims of each other. Swift struck out in self-protection and Vanessa, blind to his condition since she was so desperately concerned with her own plight, increased the very evil which she strove to escape by holding up her heart "to be struck, and struck, and struck again."[2] She began to see how difficult it was to love, to try to hold, even to communicate with, a man whose underlying determination, albeit unconscious, was at all costs to suppress, exclude, and *escape*. Again and again she tries to break through the wall of glass dividing them until there comes a

[1]This letter is placed by Martin Freeman before Vanessa's to Swift, quoted above. But as it is without date and yet bears her endorsement 4th to match the 4th on hers it seems to me to follow hers rather than precede it chronologically. I suggest the same applies to the next pair of letters. Freeman, p. 102.

[2]Lady Gregory.

bitter cry, forerunner of her last tragic letters and prophetic
of her ending.

> "If you continue to treat me as you do you will not be
> made uneasy by me long. 'Tis impossible to describe what
> I have suffered since I saw you last; I am sure I could have
> bore the rack much better than those killing, killing words
> of yours. Sometimes I have resolved to die without seeing
> you more, but those resolves, to your misfortune, did not
> last long. For there is something in human nature that
> prompts one so to find relief in this world, I must give way
> to it, and beg you'd see me and speak kindly to me; for I
> am sure you'd not condemn anyone to suffer what I have
> done, could you but know it. The reason I write to you is
> because I can not tell it you, should I see you; for when I
> begin to complain, then you are angry, and there is some-
> thing in your look so awful, that it strikes me dumb. . . ."[1]

Swift replies that her letter has thrown him into confusion,
not because of its tenor, but because it was indiscreetly
delivered to him "when some company was with (him) on a
Saturday night." He is horribly afraid that this circumstance
may increase the gossip about them which is flying over the
town, linking his name with hers.

> "This morning a woman who does business for me told
> me she heard I was in—with one—naming you, and twenty
> particulars . . . I ever feared the tattle of this nasty town,
> and told you so, and that was the reason why I said to you
> long ago that I would see you seldom when you were in
> Ireland. And I must beg you to be easy if for some time I
> visit you seldomer, and not in so particular a manner. I will
> see you at the latter end of the week if possible. These are
> accidents in life that are necessary and must be submitted to,
> and tattle, by the help of discretion, will wear off."[2]

Some dignitary of the Church who would look unfavourably
on Swift's apparent indiscretions may have been dining with
him when Vanessa's servant brought her letter. Possibly
Stella was present. Swift began to live a nightmare life,
dreading that rumour would bear one woman news of the

[1]Freeman, pp. 105-6.
[2]op. cit., pp. 104-5.

other, that some unforeseen accident would precipitate their meeting, and worse, his ejection from the hearts of both, as well as from his Deanery.

III

With the exception of a single letter from Swift to Vanessa, which may or may not be assigned with accuracy to this period, there now occurs a gap of five years in their correspondence. How is this gap to be accounted for? One may imagine some of the letters to have been lost, but the fact that Vanessa endorses her last letter, seven, and the next, eight, implies that, willingly or unwillingly, she acknowledged the hiatus. One may surmise that Swift and she met so frequently in Dublin that Vanessa was contented and letters were unnecessary; that she was occupied with attentions from suitors for her hand,[1] whose offers Swift countenanced in the same way that he had accepted Tisdall's courtship of Stella without open interference; or that Swift's exactions became more severe and Vanessa's submission more complete. But these are conjectures, and the break in their written intimacy becomes significant when one finds that it was during this period that Swift is said to have married Stella.

So much has been written about the alleged marriage, so much gossip handed down, that it is difficult to sift fact from fancy. The motives, circumstances, and setting are mysterious and dramatic in the extreme. The whispered "last words" issuing through half-open doors, the secret recitals uttered behind those discreetly closed, and passing from one individual to another in two or three generations, confuse and mislead us. The stock elements of melodrama surround the statements—deathbed scenes, dying words, hearts broken with disillusionment and long disappointment, embittered by jealousy, or blocked by hatred. Biographers appear to accept or reject the marriage capriciously, according to their temperaments and what they wish to believe; a few, like Sir Leslie Stephen, are impartial.

[1] Dean Winter and Dr. Price, subsequently Archbishop of Cashell. Scott I, p. 229.

"The fact is not proved, nor disproved. . . . The evidence seems to be very indecisive. Much of it may be dismissed as mere gossip, but a certain probability remains."[1]

Since the legend has never been entirely refuted, and rests on the word of two church dignitaries, it deserves consideration, if not belief. What then are the facts as related, the sources and motives?

Swift is said to have been married to Stella in the year 1716, by his old friend and tutor, St. George Ashe, Bishop of Clogher, and the ceremony is said to have taken place in the Deanery garden at Clogher, or Dublin, without any witnesses.

The causes for the marriage are said to have been Stella's ill-health, occasioned by Swift's apparent neglect of her and her jealousy of Vanessa, whose presence in Ireland she had discovered, and her desire to be Swift's in name, if nothing else. More astonishing still, she is said to have agreed to continue to live apart from him and to keep the marriage secret.

The sources for this rumour are the Bishop of Clogher and Bishop Berkeley, who was tutor to Bishop Ashe's son. The Bishop of Clogher, it is said, told his wife of the ceremony and she in turn, many years later, confided the information to her grandson, who repeated it to Bishop Berkeley. Thus, despite all investigations, "the fact of the marriage still rests on testimonial evidence three times removed."[2] After this the matter becomes almost family property, descendants of the original narrators, and of Swift's friends and relations, taking up the cudgels in turn.

The greatest argument, factually, against an acceptance of the marriage, lies in a single word in Stella's writing, for she signed her will, dated December 30, 1727, Esther Johnson, *Spinster*.[3] Is it likely that the woman whom Swift

---

[1] *Life of Swift*, pp. 134-5. The original statements are to be found in Orrery, p. 22 et seq.; Delany, p. 52; Deane Swift, p. 93; Sheridan, p. 282; Monck Berkeley, p. xxxvi.

[2] Marguerite Hearsey: *New Light on the Evidence on Swift's Marriage*: Publication of the Modern Language Association of America. Vol. XLII, pp. 157-61.

[3] This was destroyed in the Irish Civil War, 1922: a facsimile

and others praised for her honesty and piety would have perpetuated a lie of this magnitude for eleven years, even to shield the man whom she loved? In addition, against the marriage there is the verbal evidence of Dingley, Mrs. Brent (Swift's housekeeper), Dr. Lyon (one of his guardians) and Stella's executor.

We are therefore thrown back, in this highly controversial matter, on to secondary evidence—that existing in Swift's writings, and an interpretation of his character derived from these. And here let me say roundly that the great mass of evidence in Swift's work, even if one were to attempt to ignore the recorded facts of his life, furnishes (for me) ample proof that he was not married to Stella, Vanessa, or any other woman. There are those who suggest that it is indecent to pry into the love affairs of a man, even though he be long dead;[1] others maintain that since love reveals the supreme possibilities of a soul "it is more than an excuse for disclosure, it is justification, provided it be made with reverence."[2] But if a man reveals contradictions of behaviour in another side of his character he cannot help but do so in this central sphere: each is antechamber to the other. Furthermore, his work (most important source of self-revelation) will betray traces of the discord in both.

"The work of any particular creative writer may, or may not, contain incidents taken from his personal life, but that which gives tone, direction, individuality and depth to his creations is an intimate reflection of himself—of his mind and temperament. There are no exceptions. Therefore, whoever sets out to draw a portrait of such a writer looks for his likeness first in his works. His correspondence, behaviour and the impression he made on others may give the investigator hints, or furnish him with corroborations, but his main source will always be his books."[3]

exists in Sir William Wilde's *Closing Years of Dean Swift's Life*, 1849, p. 97. For her Will, see also Ball, IV, pp. 462-3.
[1] *Jonathan Swift*, C. Whibley, Leslie Stephen Lecture, 1917.
[2] *The Alleged Marriage of Swift and Stella*: Stanley Lane-Poole. Fortnightly Review, 1910.
[3] Desmond MacCarthy on Chekkov.

Swift is an excellent writer to study from this angle, for he reveals himself emotionally if not factually. When his need for secrecy prevented him from breaking into action and involved him in outward mystery, when the poison of his anger festered inwardly, then he unburdened himself with his pen, easing his perplexed mind and lacerated heart.

"He was constantly turning verses as a common part of his everyday life, so much so that no part of his writing is as complete an autobiography."[1]

Throughout both prose and verse, countless passages exist to show his deep aversion to physical intimacy, his dread of marriage vows which he envisaged as the shackling ties of a stale, distasteful, wrangling conjunction, and his determination never to let friendship spill over into love. A few examples, in addition to those already given earlier, will be sufficient. Strephon's *Chloe* is a "Goddess grown a filthy mate":

> *Her dearest Comrades never caught her*
> *Squat on her Hams to make Maid's Water.*
> *You'd swear that so divine a Creature*
> *Felt no necessities of Nature.*
> *In summer, had she walk't the Town*
> *Her Arm-pits would not stain her Gown:*
> *At Country Dances, not a Nose*
> *Could in the Dog-Days smell her Toes.*[2]

Corinna, "Pride of Drury Lane," is a mass of running sores and filthy artificiality—false hair, eyebrows, complexion, teeth, eyes, breasts and waist—even her cheeks are plumped by artificial contrivances. Sleeping between her dirty blankets she dreams of incarceration in a vagrant's or harlot's prison, of being beaten by the gaoler, or deceived by a bully, of being transported to Jamaica, or left unprotected:

> *. . . near Fleet Ditch's oozy sinks*
> *Surrounded with a Hundred Stinks.*[3]

[1]Harold Williams, *Poems*, I, p. xv.
[2]*Strephon and Chloe, Poems*, II, p. 584.
[3]*A Beautiful Young Nymph going to Bed. Poems* II, pp. 580-3.

The stray cats of the town, the hungry rats, even the city pigeons are introduced by Swift to steal from, or to befoul, the sleeping Nymph—and how ironic the name sounds when applied to such a creature!

> Corinna *in the Morning dizen'd,*
> *Who sees, will spew: who smells, be poison'd.*[1]

These may roughly be condensed into two remarks which Swift is said to have made, that he "never yet saw the woman he wished to marry,"[2] a polite echo of the other, "that he never yet saw the woman for whose sake he would part with the middle of his bed."[3] The unconscious revulsions had become crystallized into a conscious philosophy.

He who cares for further examples of Swift's obsession has only to read his description of the breasts of the nurse in the farmer's home in Brobdingnag—"than nothing could appear more nauseous."[4] Symptoms of a diseased mind, these passages record Swift's aching disenchantment with love and woman's body, which he thus dishonours.

It is obvious that he despised weakness, and the man who gave way to passion was for him the feeblest of all. To protect himself he constructed a hard, cold philosophy which, like the skilfully hinged and louvred armour of some mediaeval knight, appeared impervious to all attack. Swift's tragedy is that in the end he could not disarm himself and, like a slow-starving prisoner immured in priest's hole, chest, or anchorite cell, he watched life ebb away from him, though he fought stubbornly till the last.

Other causes as well as his aversions were at work to prevent him from marrying—the terrible fear of impending madness: the feelings of inadequacy which his bouts of sickness with their frightening symptoms gave him; and, when he came to Ireland after the Tory crash, his increasing conviction that he was prematurely aged and broken. His tendency to be a

[1]Ibid.
[2]To Dr. Lyon.
[3]Sheridan, p. 294.
[4]*Gulliver's Travels*, with an Introd. by Harold Williams, Everyman edition, 1941.

perfectionist and perpetually to delay a consummation of what most people regard as normal desires, his claustrophobic fears of being pinned, possessed and destroyed, likewise hindered him.

Added to all these reasons for celibacy was the diminution of his potency through long suppression. Whether the body through lack of virility failed to stimulate the imagination sufficiently to overcome his scruples, or whether the mind with its network of fears, evasions and weaknesses prevented the body from springing into action, does not matter. We are marvellously and delicately made, body and mind intertwining react subtly and invisibly, and in Swift's case, they worked disastrously against one another.

The explanations for his not marrying which people have been forced to invent in order to explain away the inward impediment by outward circumstances, are strained and fantastic. They include such suppositions as these: that Swift and Stella were natural children of Temple and therefore related:[1] that Swift was impotent, or syphilitic: that his choice between a scholarly and a domestic life was entirely conscious and arbitrary. If they accept the marriage they cannot explain the secrecy surrounding it, the purpose for concealment, the strange silence of everyone. They suggest in desperation that neither Swift nor Stella acknowledged the ceremony because, if either did so, it would be tantamount to admitting a previous liaison. These are the attempts of ordinary people, ignorant of abnormality, to account for Swift's actions by normal standards. It is easier for them to dress the story in the fustian and trappings of melodrama, or to substitute an outward rather than an inward impediment, than to comprehend the stern laws of being which mould a man's life, and if they are disobeyed slowly cripple it.

An examination of his *Letter to a Very Young Lady on Her Marriage* will help us to understand Swift better. It is a mature work published in 1727 and was probably addressed to Lady Elizabeth Moore, daughter of the Earl of Drogheda.

"The grand affair of all your life," Swift declares, "will

[1]Or that Swift was the son of Sir John Temple and therefore half-brother to Sir William. See Denis Johnston.

be to gain and preserve the friendship and esteem of your Husband"; and he assures this young girl that if she follows his advice she

> "will arrive in time to think rightly . . . and to become a reasonable and agreeable companion. This must produce in your husband a true rational love and esteem for you, which old age will not diminish."[1]

So he sets about "to divert" her "from falling into many Errors, Fopperies and Follies to which your Sex is subject." First and foremost she must cultivate the Mind; study what he recommends (history and travels); observe and learn from the taste and conversation of selected companions, male rather than female; read aloud, once more to men. She must listen to men of learning who have travelled on the Continent, are conversant with the classics and history, with French and English writers. She must know and respect her husband's income; she must esteem him for real, not imaginary, virtues.

The list of things which Elizabeth may not do is far longer. She must not at once throw off the "modest behaviour of a Virgin"; exhibit fondness for her husband in public, or uneasiness in his absence; be extravagant, or value foolish finery.

> "In your own heart I would wish you to be an utter contemner of all distinctions which a finer petticoat can give you; because it will either make you richer, handsomer, younger, better natured, more virtuous, or wise, than if it hung upon a peg."

She must not be dirty; nor waste her time in idle visiting: she must not confide in a favourite waiting-maid; in company she must not be a hypocrite and feign a false reserve; nor false cowardice like silly girls who are

> "afraid of their own shadows . . . scream in a barge when the weather is calmest, or in a coach at the ring . . . run from a cow at a hundred yards distance . . . fall into fits at the sight of a spider, an earwig, or a frog."

[1]Hayward, p. 444 et seq. (capitals omitted).

She must not be sentimental and expect "Charms and Raptures, which Marriage ever did, and ever will, put a sudden end to." Above all she must not imitate or consort with the "bold, swaggering, rattling ladies" of the town who think it amusing to taunt a man with his physical deformities, or family misfortunes. Swift veers away from such women in horror and, Hamlet-like, adjures her to get her to a nunnery[1] rather than associate with them.

"I would recommend you to the acquaintance of a common prostitute, rather than to that of such termagants as these. I have often thought that no man is obliged to suppose such creatures to be women: but to treat them like insolent rascals disguised in female habits, who ought to be stripped and kicked downstairs."

It is all an echo of his praises of Stella, of the woman he had formed and persuaded to stay by him in order to counteract his phantasies of a proud, possessive, tyrant sex. All the virtues he commends are hers, all the vices those which he feared and taught her to abhor. There is the same crying-down of love, the same vaunting of Friendship.

"A Wise Man . . . soon grows weary of acting the Lover and treating his Wife like a Mistress, but wants a reasonable Companion and a True Friend through every Stage of his Life."

But the colours in which the picture is painted are harsh and crude, as if the artist feared the least subtlety. "His hatred of sentimentalism and romance, his savage determination to tear aside all veils, to expose reality in all its hideousness, the self-laceration, weariness, discord, cynicism and disgust of our modern "literature of negation" are all evident.[2]

"As Divines say, that some people take more pains to be damned, than it would cost them to be saved; so your sex

---

[1] and [2] *The Essential Shakespeare*, Dover Wilson, p. 117. See the same author's *What Happens in Hamlet*, p. 134, for the Elizabethan connection between brothels and convents.

employs more thought, memory and application to be fools, than would serve to make them wise and useful. When I reflect on this, I cannot conceive you to be human creatures, but a sort of species hardly a degree above a monkey; who has more diverting tricks than any of you; is an animal less mischievous and expensive, might in time be a tolerable critic in velvet and brocade, and for aught I know would equally become them."

After this display of cynicism and misogyny we are asked to believe that their author, in a mood of penitence or submissiveness, gave himself in marriage in some idyllic garden setting.

We are told that Mistress Rochfort[1] did not care for the letter, or Swift's opinion of women. Do you wonder? For even if she took pains to follow all his precepts she could not, he told her, hope to arrive "in the point of learning to the perfection of a school-boy." Indeed there is nothing in the letter to show that he valued women for their inherent qualities, the happy complement of the male—their courage (other than mere physical courage), their gentleness, their intuitive gifts, their touching loyalty, protectiveness, and nobility. It is as if living flesh and blood impressed him less than his misconceptions, for there seems no memory of his mother's constant cheerfulness in the face of apparent disaster, the selflessness of Stella, the fidelity of Vanessa, even when "forced from him" by every imaginable "severity."

Compare his attitude with that of two other contemporaries, the first a man somewhat older than Swift, writing, like him, advice for a young girl, his daughter, who was to become the mother of Lord Chesterfield, the author of famous letters. Being of the older generation his language has about it something lively yet ceremonious, the flavour of Elizabethan English still clinging to the Restoration phrases. See the gentleness of his opening sentence:

> "An early sprouting wit requireth to be sheltered by some rules, like something to be strewed on tender flowers, to prevent them from being blasted."[2]

[1]She married George Rochfort.
[2]*Advice to a Daughter*, 1700.

And mixed with the gentleness there is quiet humour, for when his daughter grows up he urges her to accept her years graciously:

"Be not like girls of fifty who resolve to be always young . . . and resemble a certain creature called a grave hobby-horse, a kind of She Numps."

The other man is that rough old politician Defoe, who urges better treatment of women in lines more encouraging than Swift's:

"The soul is placed in the body like a rough diamond, and must be polished, or the lustre of it will never appear. And 'tis manifest that as the rational soul distinguishes us from brutes, so education carries on the distinction and makes some less brutish than others. . . . Why then should women be denied the benefit of instruction? . . . I cannot think that God Almighty made them so delicate, so glorious. . . . so agreeable and so delightful to mankind, with souls capable of the same accomplishments as men, and all to be only stewards of our houses, cooks, and slaves."[1]

Like his mediaeval predecessors in the church, Swift appears even to begrudge women souls. Any appreciation of their spiritual qualities, or the spiritual ideals and aims of marriage, is entirely lacking in the *Letter*, and the omission is surely remarkable when we remember Swift's calling. For what has all this business of petticoats, lappets, ruffles, mantuas, waiting-maids, gossip, extravagance and behaviour, to do with marriage excepting from the worldly point of view? Any talk of a marriage of true hearts and minds, the fusion of two separate natures into a whole, would have seemed to him arrant nonsense. In his scalded imagination love must either be a whirlpool of carnal delights to suck a man under, or a deep, abiding well of friendship such as one *man* might feel for another. There was nothing in between.

Thus one comes regretfully to the conclusion that if the ceremony of his and Stella's marriage was ever performed it "was nothing but a ceremony,"[2] the husk of an ear which

[1] *The Education of Women*, 1697.
[2] Sir Leslie Stephen, p. 135.

had never ripened, a mere event lacking psychological or spiritual significance. There was no change of heart or mind, no inner conversion, no flooding in of new light to enrich the cramped, impoverished character. For Swift with his warped mind knew nothing of growing souls like Donne's lovers, who "watch not one another out of fear" and delight in each other's expansion. He did not, and could not, by reason of the early accidents of life, give himself freely and wholly to any woman.

IV

In 1718-9 Stella was thirty-eight. (Swift who was in-accurate about dates and the passage of time said thirty-four.) Upon her birthday the Dean wrote some lines for her, a practice which he continued, with one exception, each year until she died.

> "*Stella this Day is thirty-four,*
> (*We won't dispute a Year or more*).
> *However Stella, be not troubled,*
> *Although thy Size and Years are doubled,*
> *Since first I saw Thee at sixteen*
> *The brightest Virgin of the Green,*
> *So little is thy Form declin'd*
> *Made up so largely in thy Mind.*
> *Oh, would it please the Gods to split*
> *Thy Beauty, Size, and Years, and Wit,*
> *No Age could furnish out a Pair*
> *Of Nymphs so graceful, Wise and fair*
> *With half the Lustre of Your Eyes,*
> *With half thy Wit, thy Years and Size:*
> *And then before it grew too late,*
> *How should I beg of gentle Fate,*
> (*That either Nymph might have her Swain*),
> *To split my Worship two in twain.*"[1]

One may say that this is no more than a charming playful way of teasing Stella for her maturity of years, mind, and size,

[1] *Poems*, II, pp. 720-1.

but if one looks below the surface the real theme is that of
divided worship which occupies Swift's tormented mind.

Stella's birthday was in March, and in May Swift answered
a letter of Vanessa's written in French, in the same language,
"couched in such terms that it is surprising that commentators
have not married him, secretly of course, to Vanessa instead
of (or as well as) to Stella. It is of no avail to call this a
literary exercise in a foreign tongue, or to say that the
exaggerated compliments were modelled on a similar set in
Vanessa's letter. Swift is here in earnest. The qualities
referred to in such glowing terms are precisely those for
which he had always admired her."[1]

> "Il faut vous connoitre long-temps de connoitre toutes
> vos perfections: toujours en vous voyant et entendant, il en
> paroissent des nouvelles qui estoient auparavant cachées . . .
> vous, qui estes incapable d'aucune sottise; si ce n'est
> l'estime qu'il vous plaist d'avoir pour moy. Car il n'y a
> point de mêrite, ni aucun preuve de mon bon goût, de
> trouver en vous tout ce que la Nature a donne á un mortel,
> je veux dire l'honneur, la vertue, le bon sens, l'esprit, la
> douceur, l'agrement et la fermité d'âme. . . .
>
> "Depuis que j'avois l'honneur de vous connoitre j'ay
> toujours remarqué qui, ni en conversation particuliere ni
> generale, aucun mot a echappé de votre bouche, qui
> pouvoit etre mieux exprimé; et je vous jure qu'en faisant
> souvent la plus severe critique, je ne pouvois jamais trouver
> aucun defaut ni en vos actions, ni en vos parolles. La
> coquetrie, l'affectation, la pruderïe sont des imperfections
> que vous n'avez jamais connu.
>
> "Et avec tout cela, croyez-vous qu'il est possible de ne
> vous estimer au dessus du reste du genre humain? Quelles
> bestes en juppes sont les plus excellentes de celles que je
> vois semèes dans le monde au prix de vous. En les voyant,
> en les entendant, je dis cent fois le jour: 'Ne parle ne
> regarde ne pense ne fait rien comme ces miserables.
> Sont ce du même sexe, du meme espece de creatures?' "[2]

Another year passes with a repetition of the tributes to
both women. Stella's birthday is celebrated with verses in

[1]Freeman, p. 31.
[2]op. cit., pp. 107-10. Swift's French was inaccurate.

which a variant of the theme of divided worship is again apparent. Swift likens Stella to a favourite inn which no one will desert for a poor, upstart rival.

> *"And though the Painting grows decay'd*
> *The House will never lose its Trade;*
> *Nay, though the treach'rous Rascal Thomas*
> *Hangs a new Angel two doors from us*
> *As fine as Dawbers' Hands can make it,*
> *In hopes that Strangers may mistake it,*
> *They think it both a Shame and Sin*
> *To quit the true old Angel Inn."*[1]

Fast on the heels of this statement of loyalty follows a letter to Vanessa with the following lines, which Swift, eager to disclaim, implies are another's.

> *"Nymph, would you learn the only art*
> *To keep a worthy lover's heart.*
> *First to adorn your person well,*
> *In utmost cleanliness excell;*
> *And tho' you must the fashions take,*
> *Observe them but for fashions sake.*
> *The strongest reason will submit*
> *To virtue, honour, sense and wit.*
> *To such a nymph the wise and good*
> *Cannot be faithless, if they would:*
> *For vices all have different ends,*
> *But virtue still to virtue tends:*
> *And when your lover is not true,*
> *'Tis virtue fails, in him or you;*
> *And either he deserves disdain,*
> *Or you without a cause complain.*
> *But here Vanessa cannot err,*
> *Nor are these rules applied to her:*
> *For who could such a nymph forsake*
> *Except a blockhead or a rake?*
> *Or how could she her heart bestow*
> *Except where wit and virtue grow?"*[2]

[1] *Poems*, II, p. 734.
[2] op. cit., pp. 732-3. The holograph reads "grew."

In his poetry to both women Swift pleads for mercy. Troubled in mind about the disloyalty which he cannot avow explicitly to either, he remains, if not inarticulate, still impeded by his sense of wrong-doing. He craves Stella's acceptance of the fact that he has been attracted to another, which by now she surmises to be true even if she cannot verify it, and tacitly asks her forgiveness. In the same indirect way he begs Vanessa to understand that if he is not faithful to her the fault lies neither in her nor himself. She is not to take his defections personally, nor to blame him, since he is the victim of forces he can neither understand nor control.

The attempt was not a conscious process of reasoning on Swift's part. He understood himself and the tricks of the mind too little for that. The Georgians were an outspoken, unsqueamish lot, who called their sweethearts names of endearment which freeze our blood with their lack of delicacy, or poetry. Swift's for Stella vary from "slut," "brat," "huzzy," "quean," "jade," to "agreeable bitch." Vanessa is a "desperate chip." They were a worldly set, with politics and a gratification of the senses as their chief concern, despising the complexities of emotion or anything which savoured of introspection. Too much analysis, or "anatomy", as their grandfathers would have called it, dismayed them and made them suspicious. But just as a child will symbolize in drawing or painting what interests or disturbs it, so Swift, distressed, unconsciously indicated his preoccupation with his divided affections.

His letter in French to Vanessa is succeeded by one from her full of espièglerie. The girl who had bewitched him seven years earlier with her mocking letter to Windsor—shines at him with the fascination of a creature half fey. Her mood was the counterpart of his own love of mischief and drew him like a will-o'-the-wisp.

"... I should think you knew but little of the world, to imagine that a woman would not keep her word whenever she promised anything that was malicious." (She has threatened to pester Swift with letters.). . .

"Once more I advise you, if you have any regard for your quiet, to alter your behaviour quickly, for I do assure you I have too much spirit to sit down contented with this treatment. Now, because I love frankness extremely, I here tell you that I have determined to try all manner of human arts to reclaim you, and if all those fail I am resolved to have recourse to the black one, which (it) is said, never does.

"Now see what inconveniences you will bring both me and yourself into. Pray think calmly of it. Is it not much better to come of yourself, than to be brought by force, and that, perhaps, at a time when you have the most agreeable engagement in the world? For when I undertake anything, I don't love to do it by halves. . . ."[1]

Something dangerous glints and gleams beneath the playful surface which Swift, underrating, mistook for raillery. The hatred which she felt for him when he failed to live up to the role of ardent lover which her imagination had designed for him (and which he, despite his assurances to the contrary, played by implication) is thinly disguised. The real woman stands out in those short, unembellished sentences in which she tries to make him see her character—her desperation, and total immersion in his shadow.

That her letters were not sent off without deliberation we know from the "foul," or rough, extant copies in which her spelling gives a quaint, live tone. Vanessa spells spirit *spirrite*; fury, incongruously, *furry*; human *humain*; and quiet *quiate*. "Revenge," she writes in this letter, "*hurryes* me least"; and a flavour of Irish pronunciation creeps into *inconveainances* and *agreaible ingagement*.

Swift replies that if she writes as well as this he will see her less:

". . . on purpose to be pleased with your letters, which I never look into without wondering how a Brat, who cannot read, can possibly write so well. . . . Send me a letter without your hand on the outside, and I hold you a crown I shall not read it. But, raillery apart, I think it inconvenient for a hundred reasons, that I should make your house a sort of constant dwelling-place. . . . For the rest, you need make use of no other black art besides your ink. 'Tis a pity your

[1]Freeman, pp. 110-1.

eyes are not black, or I would have said the same of them; but you are a white witch, and can do no mischief. . . ."[1]

His disinclination to open letters which he here refers to arose from a neurotic fear of their contents, as well as from weariness with business and clerical matters, and constant applications for his services or recommendations. Once, when Lord Orrery visited Swift's library, he found a letter of his own, written several years before, inscribed in Swift's hand with the words, "This will keep cold."[2] When Stella lay ill he could not bring himself to break the seals of his friends' letters for fear of their dreadful contents, and when Gay died he kept Pope's letter announcing the event by him for five days, "by an impulse foreboding some misfortune."[3]

V

The drama, like some age-old tragedy, quickens in tempo. The pace is too fast for Vanessa's strength. Even Stella's fortitude is tried. She attempts to ease herself, as Swift does, in writing.

On Jealousy

"*Oh! shield me from his Rage, coelestial Powers!*
This Tyrant that imbitters all my Hours.
Ah! Love, you've poorly play'd the Monarch's part,
You conquer'd, but you can't defend my Heart:
So bless'd was I throughout thy happy Reign,
I thought this Monster banish'd from thy Train;
But you wou'd raise him to support your Throne,
And now he claims your Empire as his own:
Or tell me, Tyrants, have you both agreed,
That where One reigns, the Other shall succeed."[4]

Swift scolds her for her hot temper, perverseness and

[1]Freeman, pp. 111-2.
[2]*Literary Relics*, G. M. Berkeley, p. xvi.
[3]Scott, I, p. 407.
[4]*Poems*, II, p. 738.   Published in 1724, the year following Vanessa's death.

Plate V

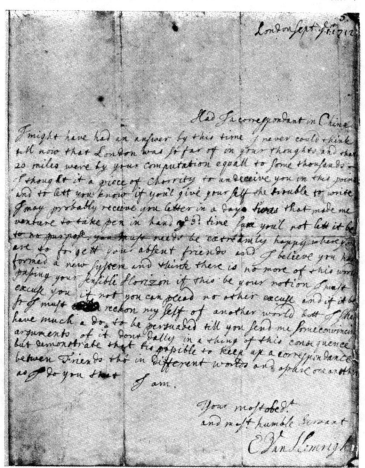

Facsimile of the handwriting of Vanessa (rough draft)

irritability, reproofs which must have been hard to bear in the circumstances.[1]

Vanessa writes her last letters, which mount in passion and desperation. Swift, in turn, eludes her more, invents devices for deeper disguises, withdraws and contradicts his withdrawal by tantalizing references to the past, placatory phrases and protestations of affectionate esteem mixed with sound advice. Her fluctuations between despair and ecstasy are pitiful to watch.

She attempts to force Swift with the violence of that very passion which causes her dependence on him, and he, sensing the unhealthy quality of her love, attempts to throw her off, to break the dependence and free himself as well as her. He has promised to write in a week, but lays little store by the promise, which he fails to keep. Vanessa, on the other hand, counts the hours of the week, which lengthens into a fortnight. Her distress saps her strength. She is so ill she feels near death.

Swift replies, accusing her of "quarrelling" with him, adding,

> "since you lay hold of my promises, and are so exact to the day, I shall promise you no more; and rather choose to be better than my word, than worse. I am confident you came chiding into the world, and will continue so while you are in it."[2]

He chaffs her because she has misdated her letter—"One would think you were in love."[3] (What a cruel thrust!) He fears that her passionate letters may fall into unscrupulous hands, and suggests an outlet for her stifled emotions. A series of dashes shall signify everything intimate which she wishes to call him; he shortens *Cadenus*[4] into *Cad* as a less obvious pseudonym for him and promptly adds four dashes which cloak a world of, for him harmless, for Vanessa, dangerous endearments. He even refers to himself as another

[1]*Poems*, II, p. 730.
[2] and [3]Freeman, pp. 116-7.
[4]The pseudonym he gave himself in his long poem, a play on *Decanus*, or Dean.

person. This is carrying secrecy to ridiculous lengths but the mask is an essential part of Swift's disguise, which enables him to make love irresponsibly. We are reminded of the "T'other I" and the Presto of the *Journal*.

Vanessa leaps like a trout to the bait. Her letter opens with five dashes which might look ridiculous were it not that one sees the terrifying amount of passion released by this artificial device. Swift is "good beyond expression." She will never "quarrel" again, but straightway sets about justifying misunderstandings between them, reasoning with him with irritating accuracy. She will try to please him by writing obscurely.

"I thought the last letter I wrote you was obscure and constrained enough. I took pains to write it after that manner. It would have been much easier for me to have wrote otherwise."[1]

Poor, poor Vanessa, who will quarrel no more, who will be reasonable and submissive, who will contort herself into any shape to please her tormentor, who will cease to be her very self if only she may extract a few words of alternating pity and cruelty from him. But her own emotions are stronger: she can no longer control them.

"I was born with violent passions, which terminate all in one—that unexpressible passion I have for you."[2] How well she understood herself. She declares that "solitude is insupportable" to her in her uneasy state. Swift seldom visits her, and sometimes five or even ten weeks elapse before she hears from him.

Now she is living at Celbridge. Her home, Marley Abbey, a gaunt, flat-faced building with niches for statues whose mock antiquity agrees with the false crenellations, is an imposing and dreary residence for a woman forced to live with an invalid sister, or in solitary, melancholy seclusion. This very seclusion renders her more susceptible to the excitement of Swift's visits, to anticipation of them, and brooding reflections on them. She wears herself out in intensity. The days when he

[1]Freeman, p. 118.
[2]Ibid, p. 129.

does not come are meaningless and empty: she lives through them as in a trance.

Many years later when Scott visited Celbridge he talked with an old man who had been gardener's boy. Everyone knew the Dean, although his cassock was rusty or his habit splashed with mud, and the bright-eyed, observant boy watched his sad mistress and the sombre clerical figure walking along the leafy paths, or sitting in shaded reflection high above the foaming Liffey. Vanessa, he told Scott, only seemed happy when Swift came, and she marked each of his visits by planting a laurel.

From the day that she had declared her love for him in the sluttery-schoolroom he had become the focal point round which her life centred. She neatly docketed and laid away his letters: she raised memorials to his comings, which were not only significant interludes in her life but the drug by which she lived. Like an addict of opium who curses his waking hours, who longs for the spaceless, timeless dreams in which visual and aural perceptions are heightened to acute intensity, Vanessa now lived only for these precious moments packed close with emotion. The bulk of life, outweighing those hours with a heavy preponderance, was meaningless and worthless.

Thus, against his will, she strove to make Swift responsible for her life and happiness. By letter and word she besieged him. She might as well have saved her breath, saved ink and paper, and all the reckless emotion which drove her. For she was fighting a losing battle with an adversary who did not wage war on the conscious level, but deep in the unreasoning unconscious; who had no sense of the passage of time, and who was determined never to submit, even though he destroyed those near him.

VI

Yet what a gift she had for writing, this moody, wayward, self-willed woman, prolonging her girlhood in pursuit of romantic love. If only Swift had urged her to write, to express herself in any other form than letters to him. But ladies did not write then, or if they did they laid themselves bare to ridicule. When the Duchess of Newcastle had published a book, Dorothy Osborne had held up her hands in horror:

> "If I could not sleep this fortnight I should not come to that. Sure the poor woman is a little distracted, she could never be so ridiculous . . . and in verse too."[1]

Mrs. Manley (mistress of Swift's printer, Barber, who succeeded Swift as editor of the *Examiner* and became Lord Mayor of London) was labelled "witty," "impudent" and "unvirtuous": and so was little Laetitia Pilkington, a protégée of Swift's, who dashed into print with her private memoirs to earn enough for her daily bread. "I am sorry to say that the generality of women who have excelled in wit have failed in chastity,"[2] was the frigid verdict of the Queen of the Bluestockings on authoresses in general.

Take this passage from one of Vanessa's letters. What is there in the letters of the period to compare with it?

> "I firmly believe, could I know your thoughts (which no human creature is capable of guessing at, because never anyone living thought like you), I should find that you have often in a rage wished me religious, hoping then I should have paid my devotions to Heaven. But that would not spare you, for was I an enthusiast, still you'd be the deity I should worship.
> "What marks are there of a deity but what you are to be known by? You are present everywhere; your dear image is always before (my) eyes; sometimes you strike me with that prodigious awe, I tremble with fear; at other times a charming compassion shines through your countenance, which revives my soul. Is it not more reasonable to adore a radiant form one has seen, than one only described?"[3]

Sir Leslie Stephen has remarked on the similarity of this passage with Pope's *Éloisa and Abelard*, which he suggests Vanessa may have read.[4] Undoubtedly she had read it. She

[1] *Letters* to William Temple.
[2] Mrs. Montagu to Mrs. Donnellan.
[3] Freeman, pp. 129-30.
[4] *Swift*, p. 133.

knew of Pope's friendship with Swift and would therefore be
interested in anything Pope wrote, but especially so in a
poem whose theme touched her heart with such peculiar
poignancy. (Swift may even have lent her the poem, which was
published three years before her letter was written.) But
Vanessa had no need to borrow or imitate phrases. Her plight
was that of Héloise with less fulfilment and delight; she had
only to imagine herself in the place of her mediaeval sister to
pour forth the adoration which Héloise was allowed to express
in unrestrained action. When Vanessa read Pope's lines they
spoke to every fibre of her being: her identification with
Éloisa was immediate and perfect and she translated it into
verse as well as prose.[1] This was both her explanation and
defence, as Swift's *Cadenus and Vanessa* had been his, for their
secret love-making. These are Pope's lines, in which Éloisa
speaks to her tutor-lover:

> "*Thou knowest how guiltless first I met thy flame*
> *When love approached me under friendship's name:*
> *My fancy formed thee of angelic kind,*
> *Some emanation of th'all-beauteous Mind,*
> *Guiltless I gazed, heaven listened while you sung:*
> *And truths divine came mended from that tongue*
> *From lips like those what precepts failed to move?*
> *Too soon they taught me 'twas no sin to love:*
> *Back throu' the paths of pleasing sense I ran,*
> *Nor wish'd an Angel whom I loved a Man:*
> *Dim and remote the joys of saints I see*
> *Nor envy them that heaven I lose for thee.*"[2]

But another comparison between Pope and Vanessa,
hitherto unheeded, is srtiking proof of her attitude to Swift,
and that she had read *Éloisa and Abelard*. Pope writes:

> "*But why should I on others' prayers depend*
> *Come thou, my father, husband, brother, friend.* . . ."[3]

[1] See her poem below and her letter supra, p. 281.
[2] and [3] *Éloisa and Abelard*, Pope, II, ll. 58-70 and 152-3. Published
1717.

and Vanessa, lamenting the Spring, echoes Éloisa's thoughts
even more exactly than in her letter to Swift:

> "*To me no more the breathing gale*
> *Comes fraught with sweets, no more the rose*
> *With such transcendent beauty blows,*
> *As then* Cadenus *blest the scene,*
> *And shar'd with me those joys serene;*
> *When, unperceiv'd, the lambent fire*
> *Of friendship kindled new desire;*
> *Still listening to his tuneful tongue,*
> *The truths which angels might have sung,*
> *Divine, impress'd their gentle sway,*
> *And sweetly stole my soul away.*
> *My guide, instructor, lover, friend,*
> *(Dear names!) in one idea blend;*
> *Oh! still conjoin'd, your incense rise,*
> *And waft sweet odours to the skies.*"[1]

Her idolatry of Swift is lamentable, if only for the reason
that it brought her so little happiness. Swift, flattered yet
embarrassed by its excessive nature, strove to escape rather
than attempt to alter it.

After her death, one of Swift's enemies[2] wrote that Vanessa
was "a pretended, vain, wit, who lived without God in the
world," and certainly her remark—"You must often have
wished me religious"—seems to agree with this superficial
summary of her unless one appreciates that by "religious"
she meant to be in a convent, that is, a nun. It is also said
that she refused to see a priest on her death-bed: if she could
not have Swift she would have no other. But if she erred on the
side of idolatry there was nothing petty or vicious about
Vanessa. For all her frailty she comes near the heroic. As far
as we know, she never allowed herself the luxury of biting
back, as Stella did. Her letters, when they are not tragic in

[1] Vanessa's *Ode to Spring. Poems*, II, p. 719 (Opening 6 ll.
omitted).

[2] Bishop Evans. (See article before referred to by J. H. Bernard.)
Lord Orrery, writing thirty years later, based his estimate of
Vanessa on Evans' malicious words.

the finest sense of the word, are graceful and humorous. Just as Dorothy Osborne's letters had revealed the intimate sides of life a generation earlier, in a manner which no one else had attempted, so Vanessa's give us passion and poetry which, despite their tragedy, we accept gratefully. The writers of the 18th century were lewd, bawdy and friendly, they were frankly sentimental or verged on pathos, but they were not lyrical or passionate.[1] Vanessa's letters have this additional value for us, they show us how Swift estimated her gifts and that she, like Stella, influenced him with her criticism. He shared *Gulliver* in manuscript with her, and once when he had chid her for "sitting moping with her elbows on her knees on a little stool by the fire" and urged her to show herself more in society, she plucked up courage and called on an acquaintance. Here is her account of her reactions:

"Since I saw you I have gone more into this world than I did for some time past, because you commanded me; and I do here protest that I am more and more sick of it every day than other. One day this week I was to visit a great lady that has been a-travelling for some time past, where I found a very great assembly of ladies and beaux, dressed (as I suppose) to a nicety. I hope you'll pardon me now, if I tell you that I heartily wished you a spectator; for I very much question if in your life you ever saw the like scene, or one more extraordinary. The lady's behaviour was blended with so many different characters, I cannot possibly describe it without tiring your patience. But the audience seemed to me a creation of her own, they were so very obsequious. Their forms and gestures were very like those of baboons and monkeys. They all grinned and chattered at the same time, and that of things I did not understand. The room being hung with arras, in which were trees, very well described, just as I was considering their beauty and wishing myself in the country with ———, one of these animals snatched my fan and was so pleased with me, that it seized me with such a panic, that I apprehended nothing less than being carried up to the top of the house, and served as a friend of yours was, but in this one of their own species came in, upon which they all began to make their

[1] See *Swift, Stella and Vanessa*, Margaret Woods.

grimaces; which opportunity I took, and made my escape."[1]

Swift, in reply, commended her description of the drawing-room scene, and identified himself with her in their tendency to fastidiousness.

> "The worst thing in you and me is that we are too hard to please, and whether we have not made ourselves so is the question. . . . We differ prodigiously in one point: I fly from the spleen to the world's end, you run out of your way to meet it."[2]

He might as well have written "whether *I* have not made *you* so," for his influence on her had been so strong that she could not look upon her companions without labelling them *bêtes en jupes*, as he did. He had urged her to mingle more with her fellows in order to dispel gloomy thoughts: but the antidote works like another poison against her recovery, because he has taught her to alienate herself from those very creatures, and drawn her so close. She no longer looks at the world through her own eyes: she ceases almost to be a real person: to have desires, direction, a character of her own. The tapestried trees, lovely in their blended stitching, are beautiful to her only because they remind her of the branches of those trees under which she and Swift have sheltered, in Chelsea, Kensington, Windsor, Dublin, Celbridge. Everything in life is valueless because it has become an inferior imitation of ecstatic but transitory moments spent with him.

In vain Swift tries to invigorate her with masculine standards, urges her to "be cheerful," "seize the moments as they pass," "be less romantic and act like a man of this world":[3] to "read, ride and laugh." If she rides she is tired, if she reads her frustration gets between her and the meaningless print. "I find the more I think the more unhappy I am. . . ."[4] "I do declare I have so little joy in life that I don't

---

[1] Freeman, pp. 136-7. Compare with *Gulliver's Travels*, Part II, Chap. 5.
[2] Ibid., pp. 138-9.
[3]   „   p. 135.
[4]   „   p. 137.

care how soon mine ends. For God's sake write to me soon, and kindly——"[1]

Vanessa was sobered, but it was a deceptive tranquillity arising, not from a happy acceptance of her narrowed, estranged life, or a temperate, stoical compromise with fortune, but from exhaustion. Unable to perceive any alternative to this dreadful state of fluctuating encouragement and discouragement, she longed to conclude it by death, which appeared her only means of escape.

Yet despite himself, "Little Heskinage," as he strangely called her, haunted the great man with her black magic as she had threatened to do, like the Héloise of Breton legend who is a sorceress. He confessed that when he was on horseback he saw her plainly, as she used to be seen "at ten in the morning" of the early days of their acquaintanceship—

". . . Now you are asking your questions round, and I am answering them with a great deal of affected delays; and the same scene has passed forty times, as well as the other from two till seven, longer than the first by two hours, yet each has *ses agrémens particuliers.*"[2]

At another time she came to his mind early in the morning. "Governor Huff," (his name for her when she chid him), "was with me at six o'clock this morning, but did not stay two minutes."[3] He suggests writing a chronicle of the last twelve years of their lives:

". . . from Dunstable to Dublin, with every single passage since. There would be the chapter of the blister; the chapter of Madam going to Kensington; the chapter of the Colonel's going to France; the chapter of the wedding, with the adventure of the lost key; of the strain" (which Vanessa apparently got with lifting too many books): "of the joyful return; two hundred chapters of madness; the chapter of long walks; the Berkshire surprise" (Vanessa's imprudent intrusion on his seclusion at Letcombe): "fifty

[1]Freeman, p. 141.
[2]Swift's last letter to Vanessa. Freeman, p. 143.
[3]Ibid, p. 126.

chapters of little times; the chapter of Chelsea; the chapter
of swallow and cluster; a hundred whole books of myself
and 'so low'; the chapter of hide and whisper; the chapter of
Who made it so?; My sister's money.' "[1]

With a blindness which is quite incredible he hopes to calm
her by paying her this compliment. He cannot see that to tell
over even these cold beads of comfort excites her to such an
extent that she rushes at him with revived affection.

"Tell me sincerely, did those circumstances crowd on
you, or did you recollect them to make me happy?'"[2]

As if he would tell her! Her urgency makes him shrink
back further. He shrivels under her touch. On his part the
intended chronicle was an attempt to fix the relationship in
time, place, and character, in order that it might not overflow
on to perilous shores. But he might as well have tried to curb
the ocean, for nothing is static, everything waxes and
diminishes, existing, not in spite of, but because of, change.

Their relationship was drawing to a close. Vanessa, in the
most tragic of all her letters, sinks to depths which are
pitiable to contemplate:

Celbridge, 1720.

"Believe me 'tis with the utmost regret that I now complain to you, because I know your good nature such that
you cannot see any human creature miserable without being
sensibly touched. Yet what can I do? I must either unload
my heart and tell you all its griefs, or sink under the unexpressible distress I now suffer by your prodigious neglect
of me. 'Tis now ten long, long weeks since I saw you, and
in all that time I have never received but one letter from
you, and a little note with an excuse. Oh —— how have
you forgot me!

"You endeavour by severities to force me from you;
nor can I blame you, for with the utmost distress and
confusion I behold myself the cause of uneasy reflections
to you. Yet I cannot comfort you, but here declare that 'tis
not in the power of time or accident to lessen the un-

[1]Freeman, p. 121.
[2]Ibid, p. 123.

expressible passion which I have for ——. Put my passion under the utmost restraint, send me as distant from you as the earth will allow, yet you cannot banish those charming ideas, which will ever stick by me whilst I have the use of memory.

"Nor is the love I bear you only seated in my soul, for there is not a single atom of my frame that is not blended with it. Therefore don't flatter yourself that separation will ever change my sentiments, for I find myself unquiet in the midst of silence, and my heart is at once pierced with sorrow and love.

"For Heaven's sake tell me what has caused this prodigious change in you, which I have found of late. If you have the least remains of pity for me left, tell me tenderly. No, don't tell it, so that it may cause my present death; and don't suffer me to live a life like a languishing death, which is the only life I can lead if you have lost any of your tenderness for me."[1]

One day a message is brought him at the Deanery which shocks and throws him off his balance. Molkin, Vanessa's sister, is dead. He had, on his last visit, "observed she looked a little ghastly,"[2] but conveniently ignored Vanessa's pleadings on her behalf.

"Poor Molkin has had two or three relapses, and is in so bad a way that I fear she will never recover. Judge now what a way I am in, absent from you and loaded with melancholy on her score. I have been very ill with a stitch in my side, which is not very well yet."[3]

Swift bids Vanessa:

"For God's sake get your friends about you, to advise and order everything in the forms. It is all you have to do. I want comfort myself in this case, and can give little. Time alone must give it to you."[4]

[1]Freeman, p. 130 (Paragraphing mine).
[2]Ibid, pp. 127-8 and 130 (Paragraphing mine).
[3]Ibid, p. 127.
[4]Ibid, p. 130.

But he does not go to comfort her. He eludes the spectacle of Vanessa's suffering: his first thought is for himself, not for her.

Yet from now on Swift shows increasing concern for Vanessa's health. He repeats his protestations of esteem, respect and devotion, and for once allows the word which she has longed for so passionately to creep in:

> "*Cad*—assures me he continues to esteem and love and value you above all things, and so will do to the end of his life, but at the same time entreats that you would not make yourself or him unhappy by imaginations."[1]

These were strong words, and for Swift, dangerous ones. They are the measure of his fears for her. At the close of the letter he repeats his declarations disguised in French:

> ". . . soyez assurée que jamais personne du monde a été aimée, honorée, estimée, adorée par votre ami que vous. I drank no coffee since I left you, nor intend till I see you again. There is none worth drinking but yours, if myself may be the judge."[2]

That strange elysian coffee which Swift refers to constantly. He drinks it again and again in imagination, sharing its remembered ecstasies with her who made it. It is the symbol of their stolen caresses, their shadowy embraces, which yet were no embraces since the spark which fired them had been ruthlessly snuffed out, which must never be acknowledged, even to her, except enigmatically and allusively. He assures her that "all her questions are answered in the affirmative"—that barrage of baffling questions which presses as insistently upon the mind of the reader as it did on Swift's. He reminds her that he thinks of absent friends, of whom she is one, with delight and has "hopes of seeing them happy, and of being happy with them."[3] Then the counter-stroke cuts in, the sweep of the scythe which mows down her crop as soon as the

[1]Freeman, p. 132.
[2]Ibid, p. 133.
[3]Ibid, p. 133.

ears are heavy. "Settle your affairs and quit this scoundrel island, and things will be as you desire."[1]

No, they would never be that. Swift had not long to wait to be rid of her importunities, the burden she had been on his conscience and heart. For, ten months after his last letter, Vanessa lay dead, broken between:

> ". . . The two extremes of life,
> The highest happiness, the deepest woe,
> With all the sharp and bitter aggravations
> Of such a vast transition. . . ."[2]

She died on June the second, 1723.

VII

The Van Homrighs were an early-dying family and were probably consumptive. The only 18th century writer who gives any details concerning Vanessa's death attributes it to this disease, aggravated by shock. And here, as over the alleged marriage of Swift and Stella, a romantic legend has grown up, confusing fact with fancy. Yet the legend rings true: the story seems credible, if only for the reason that:

> "The people act like themselves. It was not an imaginative or romantic age. I do not think there was anyone in Dublin capable of inventing such a story."[3]

The gossip concerning Swift's marriage to Stella is said to have reached Vanessa; in great agitation she is said to have written to Stella,[4] inquiring if the rumour was true: Stella is said to have sent the letter to Swift and left Dublin precipitately without seeing him: and Swift, it is said, in a paroxysm of rage rode to Marley Abbey, stalked into Vanessa's room, fixed her with one of those "awful looks (which) struck her dumb,"[5] threw down the letter and, without uttering a single word, mounted his horse and rode away.

[1]Freeman, p. 133.
[2]Lillo's *Fatal Curiosity*.
[3]Margaret Woods.
[4]Sheridan, p. 330. Orrery says she wrote to Swift, p. 115.
[5]Her letter, 1714, supra. p. 309.

His silent fury was terrible to her, more terrible than a torrent of words. So much for her bravery, for her attempt to face the truth (better than stifling half-truths), to climb out of the limed pit into which he with his thoughtless caresses, his written endearments, his incredible blindness had snared her. She could not see that Swift would only interpret her act as an invasion of his privacy, an attack upon Stella, and an attempt to force his hand: that he struck her down in self-defence, in the same way that a wild animal, cornered and enraged at its discovery, will kill a harmless intruder: that rather than have her his vanquisher he would have her his victim.

Apparently she accepted his silence as proof of what she had dreaded, his and Stella's alliance, fatal to her happiness as she conceived it. Thus she suffered a double blow, for the thought that he had for so long deceived and deluded her was more than she could bear. It was something against which the whole of her being revolted; which crushed her like some relentless, impassive, mechanical thing, extinguishing life itself. She had mistaken him for the mask he wore, and clung still to the cherished image of him as the great, the good man she knew him at core to be, whose tenderness at times surpassed that of any other being.

The last two months of her life must have been spent in anguish of mind and body. Fever racked her,[1] bitterness poisoned her. Deceived and rejected, her intense and dependent love for Swift was now mixed with consuming hatred, a hatred which reveals itself, mingled with her love, in her disposal of her property and manuscripts.

She knew that she was going to die and when she could calm herself she made a second will, revoking a previous one which had been in Swift's favour.[2] Now she bequeathed all her goods, with the exception of small sums, to two men, almost total strangers, Swift's friend, Bishop Berkeley, and Robert Marshall, whom she made executors.[3]

She is also said to have given instructions for the immediate

[1]Sheridan, p. 285.
[2]Orrery, p. 74.
[3]Vanessa's Will, see Freeman, pp. 186-9.

publication of Swift's letters to her, and of their love-poem, *Cadenus and Vanessa*.[1] Without comment, for comment would have been heartbreakingly bitter, she showed the world the writings which had both given her life and taken it away. It was as if she said simply, "Judge for yourselves."

But with the love and hatred, painfully intermingled, there went appreciation of Swift's genius. She had felt, from the beginning, his immense significance. Everything which he wrote was of value, not only intimately for her, but for posterity. She could not endure that one jot of that neat, intellectual hand, which had aroused in her such exquisite emotions, should ever be destroyed, and she achieved the immortality which Swift sought to deny her by her final commandment.

Vanessa was buried in the old round church of St. Andrew's, which, because of its unusual shape, travellers from a distance often mistook for an oven, or bake-house. Here she lay in company with Lady Penelope Berkeley, the child from Dublin Castle whom Swift had known; with "Molkin," and her father. Here, if that "wretch of a brother" had had his way, he would also have rested.[2] Here the Irish Parliament met for public worship, and here the music which England had not yet learned to appreciate—the sacred music of Handel—was played for the benefit of charity. In 1860 the church was burnt down and Vanessa's grave was lost and forgotten.

Bishop Berkeley, mystified and embarrassed by Vanessa's legacy, gave to his religious ventures "the turn of an Atlantic quest"[3] by using it to found his missionary college in the Bermudas: and young Robert Marshall, about to be called to the Irish Bar,[4] silently set about arranging for the publication of *Cadenus and Vanessa*.[5]

[1]Delany, p. 122.
[2]Ball, II, p. 259.
[3]Rossi and Hone, p. 311.
[4]Marshall became Recorder of Clonmel, was returned as a member for that town in 1727, and was appointed Justice of the Common Pleas in 1754. He died in 1774.
[5]The letters were not published consecutively for another ninety years. For their history after Vanessa's death see Freeman, p. 89 et seq.

CHAPTER SIX

*Among men, but not of them, at war with himself, with
the world, with destiny, he set at naught the warning which
Greek wisdom was never weary of repeating—'Born into
life we are, and life must be our mould.'*

JOHN CHURTON COLLINS

I

PAST midnight of the day on which Vanessa died Swift
wrote to a friend, "I am forced to leave town sooner than I
expected."[1] Her death and the disclosures which might follow
hastened, but did not interrupt, the plans which he had
already made for his summer diversion—a "southern journey"
which he had "intended for some years."[2] In death, as in life,
he put Vanessa aside: he took no responsibility for her death
any more than he had done for the kindling or nourishing of
her love: she was incidental to his life and his main stream of
energy ran on like a subterranean river inaudibly tunnelling
out its river-bed while storms and catastrophes broke over-
head.

He was gone for four months, penetrating to the south-
western extremity of Cork, clambering dangerously near the
edge of the Schull precipices, visiting the Bishop of Clonfert
in Galway, and finally Charles Ford at Wood Park, before he
returned to Dublin. In all, he covered a distance of more
than five hundred miles on horseback.[3] As he rode, in silence
amongst total strangers, like Linnaeus travelling through
foreign England, he noted with almost scientific eyes the
poverty and desolation around him, which only accentuated
his belief in the degradation to which man comes when, dumb
and inured to misery, he loses even the hope of improvement.

Swift's behaviour is deceptive and is the result of mixed

---

[1] and [2] Letters to Knightley Chetwode and Robert Cope: Ball,
III, pp. 162 and 166.
[3] See letter to Reverend Thomas Sheridan: Ball, III, p. 173.

emotions. He appears to escape, to hide his head in shame, to seek solitude in which to recover himself, because of Vanessa's death; but this is part truth only, for his prolonged summer holiday was in reality only a repetition of his old habit of relieving the perpetual tension in which he lived by a change of scene, companions, and undertakings.[1] Formerly, he had been able to spend half the year in England and half in Ireland but, since his appointment as Dean and the succession of a Hanoverian King, England had been closed to him as an area for the dramatic release of his powers and he had to content himself with Irish scenes, or none. Continental journeys were suspect since they implied transactions with the Pretender or his supporters, and Swift, despite his restlessness, was neither a born traveller nor an explorer, hampered as he was by undependable health and tethered by his loyalties and his insecurity to the two countries which he alternately cursed.

He appears to lie fallow, and in the single letter which he wrote to anyone during those four months (with the exception of one to Thomas Sheridan) he declares that:

> "I choose my companions among those of least consequence and most compliance. I read the most trifling books I can find, and whenever I write, it is upon the most trifling subjects; but riding, walking, and sleeping take up eighteen of the twenty-four hours. I procrastinate more than I did twenty years ago, and have several things to finish which I put off to twenty years hence."[2]

Yet the bare ground visible to the naked eye is misleading, for beneath, the energy released from his preoccupation with Vanessa worked with renewed force.

If he suffered no one should know. If he was afraid no one should guess it. His pride and his strength, the belief in his own integrity, would keep his head high. Yet there were signs that the strain of witnessing so much misery, which he knew, but could not acknowledge, that he had caused both Stella and Vanessa, had told on his health. To sustain one

[1] In 1721 he was absent from Dublin from June to October, and in 1722 from April to October. See Ball, III, p. 467.
[2] Letter to Pope: Ball, III, p. 176.

continuous placid relationship of an intimate nature was for Swift always difficult enough; to sustain two conflicting ones for so long a period had been well nigh unendurable. Throughout the year of Vanessa's death, and half the following year, he had suffered from his old enemy the "vapours and vertigo,"[1] and at one time he confessed that "he was so much out of order that he could not go to church."[2] He wrote so few letters that his friends on both sides of the Channel grew alarmed for him, and Stella had to break down the barriers of loyalty enough to confide in and complain to two of Swift's friends about his increasing exactions, miserliness, and gloom of temper.

From the end of January till the first week in July, 1724, only three letters exist[3] from this plentiful letter-writer, but the gap is no less significant than the fact that all three are addressed to a single person—young Lord Carteret, of whom it was said that "no one ever combined, in a more eminent degree, the learning of a scholar with the talents of a statesman."[4] Why did Swift single Carteret out in this fashion? Was it essential for him to do so if he expected once more to launch himself in a position of prominence and power after so long a stagnation? For Swift had taken no real part in public life for nearly ten years.

Carteret was still a young man. In 1724 when he was one of the Secretaries of State, to everyone's astonishment he was suddenly named as the new Irish Viceroy, in succession to the unpopular Duke of Grafton. The subject of Swift's letters to Carteret was *Wood's Halfpence*, the debased copper coinage which Parliament had authorized an iron merchant, William Wood, to circulate in Ireland. The introduction of the coinage had aroused universal Irish opposition, and had been the engrossing political question in the country during the past year. The English government had acted without consulting Ireland, the sum to be minted was disproportionately large,

---

[1]Letter from Arbuthnot to Swift, Ball, III, p. 179.
[2]Letter to Knightley Chetwode, Ball, III, p. 189.
[3]Letters to Lord Carteret, April 28th, June 9th and July 9th, 1724; Ball, III, pp. 191, 193 and 196.
[4]Ballantyne's *Lord Carteret*; II, p. 81.

the commercial interests of the country had not been considered, and the form in which the patent was issued was regarded as insulting since it benefited private individuals, including the King's mistress, the Duchess of Kendal. Acceptance of the patent was considered likely to diminish the revenue and to ruin trade. The Commissioners of the Revenue in Dublin had taken exception to the patent, the Irish Parliament had met and appointed a Committee to consider the coinage, the House had adopted the Report of the Committee and presented it in the form of an address to the King. The King's reply had followed in December of the previous year, and an inquiry had opened in London just under three weeks before Swift approached Lord Carteret, as an old friend and at the instigation of "many of the principal persons in this kingdom." Lord Carteret replied that the matter was "under examination," and in another graceful letter assured Swift that he at least was not

> "insensible of the force of that genius, which has outshone most of this age, and, when you will display it again, can convince us that its lustre and strength are still the same."[1]

Swift had enclosed a copy of a pamphlet, which he adroitly fathered on another, concerning the detested halfpence. This was probably the first of his famous *Drapier's Letters*, and Lord Carteret neatly paid Swift the compliment of acknowledging it to be from his hand without involving him further. The six *Drapier's Letters* appeared from March to December, 1724, and were so called by Swift because in them he assumed the character of one "M.B., Drapier" (or Draper), citizen of Dublin.

Swift's reactions upon escaping from a situation which he could no longer handle into a larger, less stifling arena, followed a previous pattern. When to accept Varina entailed maintaining the Irish prebend, he returned to Temple a third time, only to hurl himself into writing *A Tale of a Tub*, which he had begun while immersed in the disturbing situation. And now the *Drapier's Letters*,[2] and, in two more years, *Gulliver's*

[1]Ball, III, p. 206.
[2]Temple Scott, Vol. VI.

Travels (already partially completed in 1724) shook the two kingdoms. The works of genius, which were in part an effort to "divert thinking" from unprofitable adventures, seem to have their roots in an emotional conflict in no way related to them.

The painter Constable once remarked that painting for him was feeling, that only in painting did he become a whole man. It was the same for Swift with writing. His actions, dramatic, dynamic and effective, brought him fame and temporary satisfaction, but the victories were always sterile, disconnected in their results, bearing neither preferment nor lasting reward. His liberation came in writing, in the expression of his urgent desire for truth and freedom: his gratification from the sense of enormous power which the effects of his writing produced, and from the feeling of righteousness at having fought a just cause and accomplished a duty. In his work alone the contrariety of his gifts, the conflicting forces which kept him on the rack in life, came together in a powerful truce of amity and concord and, united, struck home with a terrifying exactness. For in his writing, like William Penn before the Monarch, Swift need doff his hat to no one, might bear his idiosyncrasies with pride, and might in fact be himself.

The body of the world was firm and warm and demanded so imperatively, so piteously to be pressed to the heart, to be nourished and cared for. If some early tragedy had prevented Swift from moving forward simply and spontaneously into domestic happiness, he must espouse a larger cause, that of the neglected and exploited. In his writing and his labours for others he sublimated the blocked emotion and ceased to walk with circumspection, with fear forever dogging his footsteps. For to know with the intellect is a barren substitute for being able to feel; and here emotion, which in private life he refused to admit as a guest to disturb reason, happily mated with intellect: heart and mind were at one.

"A people long used to hardship, lose by degrees the very notions of liberty, they look upon themselves as creatures at mercy, and that all impositions laid on them by a stronger hand, are . . . legal and obligatory. Hence proceeds that poverty and lowness of spirit, to which a kingdom may be subject as well as a particular person. And when Esau came fainting from the field at the point to die, it is no wonder that he sold his birthright for a mess of potage.''[1]

It speaks directly to the heart with a deceptive and disarming simplicity: it admits of no argument. He who, as a boy and a young ambitious man, had sunk so often "under unreasonable fears," and been inclined so soon "to be raised by groundless hopes," now applied his experience (the experience of the abandoned, the deceived, the dependent), to that of the nation in which he had "had the misfortune to be born."

In his travels over Ireland her plight had touched his heart: it ran always, at the back of his mind, like a theme in the mind of a musician uninterruptedly pursuing its course irrespective of its author's conversation or activities.

"The people of Ireland, who are certainly the most loyal subjects in the world, cannot but conceive that most of these hardships have been the consequence of some unfortunate representations, at least, in former times; and the whole body of the gentry feels the effects in a very sensible part, being utterly destitute of all means to make provision for their younger sons, either in the Church, the law, the revenue, or, of late, in the army; and, in the desperate conditions of trade, it is equally vain to think of making them merchants. All they have left is, at the expiration of leases, to rack their tenants, which they have done to such a degree, that there is not one farmer in a hundred through the kingdom who can afford shoes or stockings to his children, or to eat flesh, or to drink anything better than sour milk or water, twice in a year: so that the whole country, except the Scottish plantation in the north, is a scene of misery and desolation, hardly to be matched on this side Lapland."[2]

So in his Fourth *Drapier's Letter* Swift went on to push rejection of the rotten coinage:

[1]The Fourth *Drapier's Letter*: Hayward, p. 484 et seq. (Capitals omitted).
[2]Letter to the Earl of Peterborough, April 1726: Ball, III, p. 310.

". . . if it once enters, it can be no more confined to a small or moderate quantity, than the plague can be confined to a few families, and that no equivalent can be given by any earthly power, any more than a dead carcase can be recovered to life by a cordial."[1]

But the rejection of the halfpence is only a symbol for a larger rejection of the Irish attitude of subservience to England.

"Those who come over hither to us from England, and some weak people among our selves, whenever in discourse we make mention of liberty and property, shake their heads, and tell us, that Ireland is a depending kingdom, as if they would seem by this phrase, to intend that the people of Ireland is in some state of slavery or dependance different from those of England . . . I have looked over all the English and Irish Statutes without finding any law that makes Ireland depend upon England, any more than England does upon Ireland. We have indeed obliged our selves to have the same king with them, and consequently they are obliged to have the same king with us."[2]

Finally he exhorts them like a prophet of old, urging them on to self-statement and self-defence:

"The remedy is wholly in your own hands, and therefore I have digressed a little in order to refresh and continue that spirit so seasonably raised amongst you, and to let you see that by the laws of God, of nature and of nations, and of your own country, you are and ought to be as free a people as your brethren in England."[3]

The pamphlet was, of course, regarded as seditious by the unsympathetic English, and the Lord Lieutenant could not allow it to pass without a stern protest. The printer was arrested and thrown into prison—(and what brave men those printers of Swift's works were, constantly endangering their trade, health, peace of mind, and even their limbs, when

[1]Hayward, p. 492.
[2]Ibid, p. 493.
[3]Ibid, p. 495.

acting as scapegoats for the great man's thunder)—and a Proclamation was issued offering a reward of £300 for discovering the author.

But on the day following the Proclamation Swift, whether acting his part in mock rage or in real sincerity, strode through the Lord Lieutenant's levee and thundered at Carteret: "Your Excellency has given us a noble specimen of what this devoted nation has to hope for from your government!" He then burst into invective.

But Carteret was a match for Swift and foiled his attack with superb finish, disarming him with instant repartee.

Res dura, et regni novitas, me talia cogunt Moliri. . . .

he parried, and Swift bowed to Virgil where ordinary English might only have inflamed him further.[1]

Swift, of course, had his way. His triumph was absolute. In the following year His Majesty's Government announced that "an entire end was put to the patent formerly granted to Mr. Wood." The Dean's *Letters*, ballads, broadsheets, epigrams and squibs had found their mark, and the victory was the more astounding since it had been achieved single-handed. A private individual, persecuted and belonging to a proscribed party, working without allies, had triumphed over the King, Parliament and people of a nation, as well as over the Government and Judges of the country in which he lived, whose cause he had advocated without hesitation. He had succeeded where Grand Juries, Corporations, and the Irish Parliament had failed.

He became the veritable idol of the people. The bells of remote villages as well as those of Dublin pealed in praise of the *Drapier*. Bonfires flamed in his honour, towns voted him their freedom, medals were struck and textiles woven with likenesses of his portrait, clubs of his name were formed, heads were uncovered to him in the street. When, in the following year, he returned from a visit to England, boats with streamers and garlands of flowers put out to meet him and he was escorted to the Deanery with a guard of honour.

[1]Sheridan, p. 214.

Lord Carteret smilingly alleged[1] that he had only succeeded as Viceroy because he had succeeded in pleasing "the Dean." Lady Carteret (who, as a young married woman in London, had plagued Swift by taking him to the window of Lady Betty Germain's house and showing him how his hat had "walked" five doors off on the railings)[2] became his devoted admirer, lacquered tea-caddies for him with her own hands, sat in his chilly Vineyard, and invited him to dine again at the Castle.

So great was the veneration in which the people held him that when a crowd collected to watch an eclipse and Swift (perhaps remembering Partridge with wry humour) sent out the bellman to inform them that the eclipse had been postponed, the crowd instantly dispersed.[3]

He had begun his work for Ireland with a pamphlet called *A Proposal for the Universal use of Irish Manufacture* in 1720. For the next twenty years he continued to work for her in papers which cover an amazing variety of subjects, economic, social, and agricultural. There are articles on banks and currency, population and education, beggars and the insane, planting, grazing and fisheries, bog-reclaiming and road-mending, the flax and linen industries—articles which exhibit his strong masculine intellect, his breadth of interests, his sound common-sense, his advanced outlook, and his intense sympathy for the people of the country which he abhorred but grew to pity and protect. In them one sees the patriot amicably walking with the divine, and their author's feminine and masculine sides happily wedded. The pamphlets stand forever as

"a bright record of the unceasing zeal with which he continued, throughout successive years, and indeed until the total decay of his mental powers, to watch over the interests of Ireland . . . and to be, in the expressive language of Scripture, 'the man set for their watchman, to blow the trumpet and warn the people.' "[4]

[1] Letter to Swift, March 24, 1736. Ball, V, pp. 428-9.
[2] Williams, p. 287.
[3] Sir Leslie Stephen, p. 161.
[4] Scott: Vol. VII, p. 94.

II

Stella regarded her relationship with Swift as quietly as emotion would allow her. Vanessa was dead. She had been, as far as Stella was concerned, nothing more than an intruder, an interloper whom Stella could not even praise, pity, or exonerate. Swift was nearing sixty: it was unlikely that he would repeat an affair which had cost him so much anxiety, humiliation, and suffering. Yet she knew when she faced it honestly, that it would never be the same again. The bloom, the lustre which gave it its eternal freshness in spite of cruel separations, contortions and effacements, was gone.[1]

She knew her power over him still, how he turned to her for that greatest of all gifts which a woman can bring—peace, and a belief in himself. She had accepted his limitations, his turbulence, his apparent faithlessness and irresponsibility, secure, as she thought, in the knowledge that no other woman would endure what she had endured, gratefully. If she had shed tears by night—the tears which Grattan's aunt shared in those midnight lamentations—she had concealed them from him by day: if he attacked her in one of his spasms of irritability she had not let him see that it had disturbed her: for she knew that the black demon in him fattened on the misery of others. So he trusted and relied on her. Vanessa, they said, had charm, intelligence, and a loving heart, spontaneity, sensibility, youth, and a fortune of five thousand pounds. But Stella knew that Swift needed something besides all this—a certain hardness in a partner if she was to combat his egotism. She had had to grow a shell with which to protect herself, to make a life of her own in spite of the limited sphere permitted her by current taste and Swift's exactions, and she was proud that she had done it.

Yet her heart ached for the past. To live even their half-life now was like living in a room whose walls have been cracked by an earthquake: walls which stood but were scarred beyond repair, and one never again had confidence in the structure.

[1]My own interpretation.

Although she rode bravely—(and how enchanting a picture Swift had drawn of the household commotion before she whisked off—

> "Well; but the horses are not come to the door; the fellow can't find the bridle; your stirrup is broken; where did you put the whips, Dingley? Marg'et, where have you laid Mrs. Johnson's ribband to tie about her? reach me my mask; sup up this before you go. So, so, a gallop, a gallop; sit fast, sirrah, and don't ride hard upon the stones."[1])—

although she walked to please him, ate frugally, again to please him (dining on "Five Nothings in Five plates of Delph"),[2] she had never been robust. She felt herself growing old and hoped the lustre of her mind would be fair exchange for the loss of her youth.[3] The mouth which had been so provocative and full had gone a trifle thin and hard, as if she had to exert especial control over its voluptuousness. And to us, looking at the portrait of the mature woman, there is something slightly spinsterish about the sitter, as if she had never known abundant love, never been warmed by physical fire.

About the time of Vanessa's death the situation between Swift and Stella grew especially difficult:

> "The Dean's disappointments . . . death of friends, and total overthrow of all his ambitious prospects, instead of calming his passions, unhappily fermented, and soured them: by a strange singularity of temper, the withdrawing of the fuel enflamed the fire. This gave *Stella* inexpressible uneasiness: and I well know a friend[4] to whom she opened herself upon that head; declaring that the Dean's temper was so altered, and his attention to money so increased: (probably by his solicitude to save for her sake); her own health at the same time gradually impaired; that she

[1]Williams, p. 301.
[2]*Poems*, II, p. 747.
[3]See her poem *To Dr. Swift on his birthday, Nov. 30, 1721* ; *Poems*, II, pp. 737-8.
[4]Sir Henry Craik thinks the friend was Sheridan.

Plate VI

Portrait of Stella, by Charles Jervas

could not take upon herself the care of his house and economy. . ."[1]

Why did Swift's uneasiness take the form of haggling over accounts? Of what was money a symbol in his mind—liberty, security, power, a means for counteracting his tendency to avarice? Or was his testiness over money merely a symptom of present dis-ease?

Whatever the cause, there remains the mystery of an order for one hundred pounds which Swift made out to Dingley at this time. His object in giving it is unknown. Was it possibly conscience money, an appeal for forgiveness for his irritability; was it intended to provide further comforts for Dingley and her mistress without Stella's knowledge? Or was it merely an earnest of the Dean's gratitude? That Dingley had some scruples in accepting it is evident from the fact that she never converted the order into money and made especial mention of both the order and its valid state in her will.[2]

The house to which Stella retired before Vanessa's death, not as legend has it, alone, but with Swift, was that of Charles Ford, the *Don Carlos* of Swift's poems, and the *Glassheel* of his letters to Vanessa. Here Stella remained for six months, returning to Dublin in October. Here, presiding over it as mistress, she queened it over Ford's servants, here Sheridan visited her and here Swift, refreshed by his westerly journey, spent a few days before renewing his decanal duties.[3] The poems which he wrote for her that autumn are lively and almost flirtatious in tone. Stella's charm worked afresh. Swift chaffs her for having to leave the rich hospitality of Ford for pinched Dublin lodgings in Ormonde Quay, where, instead of dining on partridges, venison, pigeons and quail, and wines gleaming richly in the candlelight, she must be content with:

"Small beer, a herring, and the Dean."

He ends with the endearing lines:

[1]Delany, pp. 56-7.
[2]The order bears the date October 10th, 1723. See Ball, VI, pp. 205-6.
[3]Letter to Robert Cope. Ball, III, p. 161.

"Yet granting all I said were true,
A cottage is Woodpark with you."[1]

One would like to know more of Charles Ford's intimacy
with Swift, for he had a delicate part to play since he knew
both Vanessa and Stella.   Only tact, sincerity, and genuine
affection could save him from falling foul of Swift in such an
intricate friendship.   It was at Vanessa's home in London that
Swift had met him; with Ford, Vanessa had "paddled" the
wet London streets during Swift's absence: Ford and Swift
had talked of Vanessa at Windsor, and when Swift left England
to be installed as Dean it was Ford who constantly wrote to
keep him informed of what passed amongst the Van Homrighs
and the circle of which Swift had been part.[2]   His house, Wood
Park, lay on the road to Trim, not far from Celbridge, and
Vanessa had the mortifying knowledge that Swift visited him
there without coming a few miles further to visit her, and,
when she lay dying, that he was twice there with her rival.

III

Amongst the more wretched of Irish counties was that of
Cavan.   Travellers passing through it not long after the
Union saw that the women were so poor that they worked in
the fields wearing "men's patchwork coats tied round the
middle with a thick straw, or hay-rope, and hats often without
crowns, finished with a band of the same material."[3]   On the
wild Cavan heaths Swift's school-master friend Thomas
Sheridan, father of the biographer and grandfather of the play-
wright, had built himself a house, which he called *Quilca*.

Near the house was a small lake, girdled pleasantly with
trees and sheltered by a sloping hill, which suggested to
Sheridan—the dreamer, the classical scholar living in his
world of antiquity—an amphitheatre.   Here he determined to

[1] *Stella's Distress* and *Stella at Woodpark*; *Poems*, I, pp. 744-52.
[2] For a full account of Ford see D. Nichol Smith's *Letters of
Jonathan Swift to Charles Ford*, Clarendon Press, Oxford, 1934.
[3] *Country and Town in Ireland under the Georges*: Constantia Maxwell,
p. 136.

produce open-air plays in the manner of the ancients, and Chariot races were to be held on the heaths.

Sheridan was one of Swift's dearest friends, a man who both vexed him with his unpractical nature and endeared himself to him by his humour and warmth of heart. Swift tried to encourage him, check his improvidence, smooth him down after verbal encounters with his nagging wife, who had a tongue like Xanthippe's. But Sheridan was incorrigible and had an exasperating way of cheating himself out of worldly success despite his friend's endeavours. When Swift obtained a chaplaincy for him by applying to Lord Carteret, Sheridan thoughtlessly preached a sermon on the text "Sufficient unto the day is the evil thereof." As the day was the 1st of August, the anniversary of the accession of George I, Sheridan was suspected of Jacobite leanings, which his family were known to have had, and was struck off the list of chaplains.

To Sheridan's home, "falling down before it is finished," came Swift, Stella and patient Dingley, in December of the year of Vanessa's death. In *The Blunders, Deficiencies, Distresses and Misfortunes of Quilca* Swift draws an amusing picture of their daily life, which Sir Walter Scott remarks might well stand as "no bad supplement to Swift's account of Ireland."[1] Dilapidations of the Dean's bed, "threatening every night to fall under him," take up a prominent place in the list which Swift humorously proposes to extend to "one-and-twenty volumes in quarto and to continue weekly if due encouragement is given." Stella's and Dingley's rooms are in an equally parlous state—"The grate in the ladies' bed-chamber broke, and forced to be removed . . . the chimney smoking intolerably: the Dean's greatcoat employed to stop the wind from coming down the chimney."[2]

With that penetrating eye which, as Lady Gregory observes, seemed to probe into the wainscoats "to round up the very mice" and inquire "into their scurrying thefts of back-pantry crumbs,"[3] Swift noticed that locks and hinges

[1]Scott: Vol. VII., p. 104.
[2]Temple Scott: Vol. VII, pp. 75-7.
[3]*Stella, Vanessa, and Swift,* 19th Century and After, June, 1933.

were rusting away, and that keys were lost; that there were insufficient plates, pots and pans—

"A messenger sent a mile to borrow an old broken tun dish"; that the furniture is loose in the joints; that there is a dearth of pokers and tongs, there being only one pair of the latter "which travels through the house, and is likewise employed to take the meat out of the pot, for want of a flesh fork. . . . The spit blunted with poking into bogs for timber, and tears the meat to pieces."

There is a perpetual going and coming of "arrant thieves" and "savages," friends of the servants and hangers-on, who steal like dogs round a gypsy fire, hoping not to be seen and to escape being kicked. There is a constant battle of tongues —the "battle of the women" who disagree on cleanliness in the kitchen, the "battle of the milk" between the Dean and his "savage crew" who insist that milking at eleven is time enough, who temporarily succumb to his verbal bludgeonings but, as soon as they think he has forgotten, revert to their old ways.

"The ladies' and Dean's servants growing fast into the manners and thieveries of the natives: the ladies themselves very much corrupted; the Dean perpetually storming, and in danger of either losing all his flesh, or sinking into barbarity for the sake of peace."[1]

Even the household cats steal from the larder, for which demeanour one "was tried, condemned and executed by the sword." Above all, there is never sufficient fuel.

"Not a bit of turf in this cold weather: Mrs. Johnson and the Dean in person, with all their servants, forced to assist at the bog in gathering up the wet bottoms of old clumps."[2]

This is Swift at his lightest and best, for the satire is harmless and tinged with love. He frets for his own deafness, for Stella's poor health, for the stupidity of Dingley, now growing old, full of "blunders and negligencies for her friends."

[1] and [2]op. cit., p. 76.

No doubt the Cavan servants, the "rascally knaves" of the Quilca kitchens, were more flagrant in their acts of "borrowed hospitality" than those of more prosperous Irish counties, but the picture is alive and sets one laughing. It is all there in those few pages, the native "Irishry", the dirt, the slovenliness, thriftlessness and quarrelsomeness of a people who go to law if their neighbour's horse looks over the hedge. There are the hot tempers and quick tongues, the humour and warm-heartedness: the lack of any sense of time—for the day is endless and night succeeds, as good for drinking, gambling, story-telling, dancing, fiddling and making love as any of the whiter hours. For is there not, in every field, in every stone or earthen-floored kitchen, a fiddle?—

"and the lasses footing it till they are all a-foam, growing infinitely proud with the blear eye of affection their sweet-hearts cast on their feet as they dance to a tune played on an instrument that makes a worse noise than a key upon a gridiron."[1]

To be translated to Cavan meant being carried into another world. Swift's letters begin to show signs of an increasing estrangement from reality, interspersed with his pre-occupations with real and present problems. Their language adopts here and there the images of *Gulliver*:

"I have often reflected in how few hours, with a swift horse or a strong gale, a man may come among a people as unknown to him as the antipodes."[2]

And to dear, feckless Sheridan he wrote: "You will everyday find my description of Yahoos more resembling."[3] In 1725 he had retired to Quilca and revised the *Travels,* destined to "wonderfully mend the world."[4] He shared them in manu-script with Sheridan and other intimate friends, as he had done with Vanessa, and surely Stella.

[1] *The Western Wonder*, Richard Head, 1674.
[2] Letter to Pope: Ball, III, p. 334.
[3] Letter to Sheridan: Ball, III, p. 267.
[4] Letter to Ford, 14 Aug., 1725. *Letters of Jonathan Swift to Charles Ford,* ed. by D. Nichol Smith, p. 120.

In the spring of 1726 and in April, 1727, Swift made his last two visits to England. He stayed with Pope at Twickenham, he met Bolingbroke returned from exile, he was introduced to the Prime Minister, Walpole, whom he endeavoured to interest in Irish reforms, he spoke with Mrs. Howard, mistress of the Prince of Wales, and with the Princess, soon to become Queen Caroline. Once again the influence and promises of princes appeared to hold out hopes that at long last Swift's genius and ability would be suitably rewarded. But the introductions, the conversations, the easy civilities blew like wind over the grass bearing nothing with them. He returned to Ireland in a mood of black resentment.

IV

Gulliver's Travels was published in the autumn of 1726. Within a year it won the hearts of both English and French readers as well as the admiration of Voltaire, who confessed that "he owed to Swift's writings the love he bore to the English language."[1] But if Stella had the gratification of seeing Swift famous once again she had in the same year the shock of reading his long published poem *Cadenus and Vanessa* which celebrated his love for her namesake.

Swift's reactions to its publication were to own but to disparage it. When a friend wrote to him to warn him that copies were being circulated and it might be as well to forestall publication until Swift could attend to an authentic version he replied:

"As to the poem you mention, I know several copies of it have been given about, and (the) Lord Lieutenant told me he had one. It was written at Windsor near fourteen years ago, and dated. It was a task performed on a frolic among some ladies, and she it was addressed to died some time ago in Dublin, and on her death a copy (was) shown by her executor. I am very indifferent what is done with it, for printing cannot make it more common than it is; and for my own part, I forget what is in it, but believe it to be

[1] Letter to Swift: Ball, III, p. 438.

only a cavalier business, and they who will not give allowances may choose, and if they intend it maliciously, they will be disappointed, for it was what I expected, long before I left Ireland.

"Therefore what you advise me, about printing it myself is impossible, for I never saw it since I writ it. Neither if I had, would I use shifts or arts, let people think of me as they please. Neither do I believe the gravest character is answerable for a private humoursome thing, which, by an accident inevitable, and the baseness of particular malice, is made public. I have borne a great deal more; and those who will like me less, upon seeing me capable of having writ such a trifle so many years ago, may think as they please, neither is it agreeable to me to be troubled with such accounts, when there is no remedy, and only gives me the ungrateful task of reflecting on the baseness of mankind which I knew sufficiently before."[1]

To another friend he wrote three months later:

"The thing you mention, which no friend would publish . . . shows how indiscreet it is to leave anyone master of what cannot without the least consequence be shown to the world. Folly, malice, negligence, and the incontinence in keeping secrets, for which we want a word, ought to caution men to keep the key of their cabinets."[2]

The inability of women to keep secrets was one of Swift's chief quarrels with them,[3] and Vanessa is dismissed as a malicious tell-tale wretch.

Robert Marshall, the executor to whom Swift refers above, and whose action in publishing the poem he attributed to antagonistic motives, had made arrangements to print it and been interrupted by Sheridan, jealous of Swift's reputation. But admiration rather than malice was probably the motive; everything goes to show that Marshall was one of Swift's admirers and not a detractor. When Swift's fame had increased with his participation in the coinage battle, and

[1] Letter to Knightley Chetwode : Ball, III, pp. 305-6.
[2] Letter to Thomas Tickell : Ball, III, pp. 313-4.
[3] See Laetitia Pilkington, *Memoirs*, p. 87.

Vanessa's death was distant, Marshall probably thought that publication might occur without scandal. Why, though, did he not first ask Swift's permission? Probably he suspected it would not be granted and that Swift, if his conscience troubled him over the contents of the poem which he said he had not seen since the day he wrote it, would thereafter regard him as an enemy. The poem was published in 1726 in separate editions in London, Edinburgh and Dublin, so that Stella, even if she had not yet seen one of the manuscript copies in circulation (and probably her friends tried to shield her from this), now received its full blast. In it Stella might recognize familiar precepts. The very words were akin to those which Swift had used to her, and if she could but know it, in letters to her predecessor in his affections, Varina.

There was his usual veneration of the classical concepts of virtue and honour, which she had lately heard him repeat from the pulpit in a Sermon called *On Doing Good*[1]: the typical presentation of Venus, Goddess of Love, and Juno, Goddess of Matrimony, in disagreement: the familiar emphasis upon the necessity for feminine cleanliness of person, and decency of mind: the old belittling of feminine character, coupled with the assertion that women would as soon throw themselves away upon a dancing, fiddling, or singing-master as upon a proper subject for respect: there was the winning humour. Even Stella, reading with avid eyes, must have smiled at the picture of Venus banished from the Courts of Love to her birthplace, the sea, being forced to

> "... *live with daggl'd mermaids pent,*
> *And keep on fish perpetual Lent.*"

But more bitter still, she now found him celebrating in another the very qualities for which he had been wont to praise her.

> "*A modest youth said something new,*
> *She placed it in the strongest view.*
> *All humble worth she strove to raise;*
> *Wouldn't be prais'd, yet lov'd to praise.*

[1]Compare with Vanessa's reflection of Swift's concept, supra. p. 150.

The learned met with free approach,
Although they came not in a coach.
Some Clergy too she wou'd allow
Nor quarrell'd at their awkward bow. . . ."[1]

But how explain Stella's confusion when she read Swift's tributes to Vanessa's mind and body—the pricking jealousy, the ache of pain?

"When, lo! Vanessa *in her bloom,*
Advanced like Atalanta's *star,*
But rarely seen, and seen from far;
In a new world with caution stept. . . ."

She "shone with native beauty" and was endowed with every virtue of character which Stella knew Swift to admire, as well as with an "open heart and bounteous mind." She was "neither coquette nor prude."

It must have been some satisfaction to read that Vanessa, so Swift alleged, had made the first advances. And when he spoke of

"That innocent delight he took
To see the Virgin mind her book. . . ."

what a flood of memories of his tender tutelage of her at Moor Park must have invaded her, and how well she understood Vanessa's longing—

"She wished her tutor were her lover."

For an instant, reading those lines on virtue—(lines which she could not know Vanessa in her bewilderment and anguish had quoted back to him in prose)—

"That virtue, pleas'd by being shown,
Knows nothing which it dare not own;
Can make us without fear disclose
Our inmost secrets to our foes. . . ."

[1]*Poems*, II, p. 697, et seq. (Capitals ommitted). Compare with his tributes to Stella in *On the Death of Mrs. Johnson*, Hayward, p. 732, ll. 9-14.

her heart leapt up, remembering her own early sensations of reverence for the young secretary-chaplain who had devoted so much time and care to her early studies.

She recognized only too well the stern, perplexed figure who claimed that he had in every scene "kept his heart," and "understood not what was love."

> *"Love, hitherto a transient Guest*
> *N'er held Possession of his Breast."*[1]

If, in this sophisticated, yet dramatic, poem he confessed to feeling

> *"Shame, Disappointment, Guilt, Surprise. . . ."*

at his second pupil's declaration of love, *Stella* was not surprised. She knew heartbreakingly well his obtuseness to the emotional reactions of others, and always sensed his dread of too close an intimacy, had known his dislike of sentiment, had felt his deep aversions, and been wise in restraining herself. Vanessa's weakness lay in her impetuosity, her artlessness, her lack of control. Stella had been wiser. Yet how torturingly difficult it had been not to be natural.

Thus she could believe Swift when he declared that:

> *"His thoughts had wholly been confin'd*
> *To form and cultivate her mind:*
> *He hardly knew, 'till he was told,*
> *Whether the nymph were young, or old;*
> *Had met her in a public place,*
> *Without distinguishing her face. . . ."*

for his irresponsiveness to feminine charm and appearance was not merely affectation, but a studied policy of concentration upon attributes of the mind and character, which sprang from his repulsion to physical habits and physical contacts.

And when, on reading further, Stella found:

[1]Compare with *To Stella: Poems*, II, p. 728, l. 14: "I n'er admitted love a guest," and Letter to Reverend John Kendall: Ball, I, pp. 3-6.

"She thought he had himself describ'd,
His doctrines when she first imbib'd;
What he had planted, now was grown;
His virtues she might call her own;
As he approves, as he dislikes,
Love or contempt her fancy strikes. . . .
While every passion of her mind
In him is centr'd and confin'd. . . ."

how well she knew that feeling of having been both annexed by and incorporated in him. How had he the right to treat another as he had treated her? The repetition was humiliating, and the fact that Vanessa had also mistaken Swift's doctrines for the man himself and believed them to be an integral part of his character, the fact that they had both been betrayed in the very search for knowledge, did not mollify her anger.

Yet despite her anger and disillusion something forced her to read on:

"Cadenus, who cou'd ne'er suspect
His Lessons would have such Effect,
Or be so artfully apply'd,
Insensibly came on her Side;
It was an unforseen Event,
Things took a Turn he never meant

. . . .
. . . . . .

Cadenus, to his Grief and Shame,
Cou'd scarce oppose Vanessa's Flame."

Finally there were those tantalizing lines which no one, least of all, Swift, would ever be able, or deign, to elucidate:

"But what success Vanessa met,
Is to the world a secret yet:
Whether the nymph, to please her swain;
Talks in a high romantic strain;
Or whether he at last descends
To like,[1] with less seraphick ends;

[1] *Poems,* II, p. 712. Freeman, p. 175, reads "act" instead of "like."

Or, to compound the business, whether
They temper love and books together;
Must never to mankind be told,
Nor dare the conscious muse unfold."

She saw sadly that it was the poem of a man seduced by
his pride, who played with sexual thoughts while avoiding
sexual intimacy; delighting in his chastity while at the same
time drawn to explore the forbidden experience mentally; of
a man who could not resist basking in the love and admiration
of others while claiming the right to withhold himself. It
was polished and lucid, aesthetic and analytical, dispassionate
and egotistical, dramatic and complex, and yet strangely simple
in its statements. It placed all the responsibility for Vanessa's
ardour upon *her*, which was unchivalrous of him, possibly
untrue; but true, Stella knew, in this sense, that that was how
Swift saw it.

Stella need not have been distressed by the poem, which
was really a recital of intellectual love. Her rival in Swift's
affections was dead. Swift was still attached to her by deep
ties of affection, and she saw that he acknowledged their
relationship with increasing openness. Nevertheless it was
a shock, a profound disillusion to her to find that her idol, too,
had feet of clay, had deceived her for so long, had written this
effusion at the very time that he had been binding her with
statements of intense affection in her *Journal*. The long
strain of their unnatural situation with its daily evasions and
explanations, her protection of the man who should have
protected her, and the confrontation of the world's thoughts
and tongue which *she* must face and not he, had worn down her
health. The publication of the poem embittered a mind already
overladen. It was the proverbial straw, too heavy for the back
of the bearer, and Stella's reactions to it are given by Delany,
the hospitable host of Delville, whom Carteret was shortly to
make Chancellor of Christ Church Cathedral.

One day, he says, when she was staying at Wood Park,

". . . some gentlemen dropped in to dinner, who were
strangers to *Stella's* situation. And as the poem of *Cadenus
and Vanessa* was then the general topic of conversation, one

of them said, surely that *Vanessa* must be an extraordinary woman that could inspire the Dean to write so finely upon her. Mrs. Johnson smiled, and answered that she thought that point not quite so clear; for it was well known, the Dean could write finely upon a broomstick."[1]

Delany, in charitable fashion, excuses Stella for this gibe by emphasizing her chagrin and the "sickness which followed soon, and sensibly increased after this event."

Stella's retort is that of a wounded person, a feline animal who strikes back when she is hurt. Her long years of selfless service are blotted out for an instant by the wit of the repartee, so much easier to record. It is neither gracious nor generous, and Stella could afford to be both, since she had had so much more of Swift than Vanessa could ever have—her letters, the faithful *Journal*, her birthday poems, those exciting gifts from London into which he infused so much thought and tenderness —three little volumes of Lucian in French, six pounds of chocolate in a little wooden box, a silk green apron, the little microscope with all its "equipage in a little trunk that you may carry in your pocket,"[2] always everything diminutive, which fitted the childish language which he invented for her and shared with no one else. She had had the privilege of nursing him when he was ill; her position, although equivocal, was acknowledged and respected by those to whom Swift cared to reveal it: and there had been the interchange of ideas with his hospitable and distinguished friends which gave a richness, tone, and direction, to her mental life.

Vanessa, one feels, would not have been so spiteful. All that we know of her indicates that she was gentle, pliant, and hence more defenceless. If, as some allege, she bequeathed her property to total strangers or at best mere acquaintances, in order to wound Swift, the act was dignified by an absence of written comment.

[1] *Observations*, p. 58.
[2] Williams, p. 97.

V

During Swift's last two visits to England he had been distressed by accounts of Stella's declining health. He trembled when the letters of his friends came, lest they should bear him news that he had lost the most "perfect friend" he had ever had. He was constantly on the rack, fearing "the worst that is possible." He is alternately torn by the desire to see Stella again and a longing to escape from anything so painful as the sight of death. In order to avoid it in imagination he already thinks and speaks of Stella as if she were dead: he renounces her in advance.

> "What you tell me . . . I have long expected, with great oppression and heaviness of heart. We have been perfect friends these thirty-five years. Upon my advice they both came to Ireland, and have been ever since my constant companions; and the remainder of my life will be a very melancholy scene, when one of them is gone, whom I most esteemed, upon the score of every good quality that can possibly recommend a human creature. I have these two months seen through Mrs. Dingley's disguises. And indeed, ever since I left you, my heart has been so sunk, that I have not been the same man, nor ever shall be again; but drag on a wretched life, till it shall please God to call me away."[1]

If Stella cannot "hold out till his return" he will not "think of crossing over." He will go to Wales, to Derbyshire, or to France. To another friend Swift bemoans the very strength of the affection which has brought him so much joy in life, because it now brings him such intense suffering.

> ". . . I think there is not a greater folly than that of entering into too strict and particular a friendship, with the loss of which a man must be absolutely miserable, but especially at an age when it is too late to engage in a new friendship. Besides, this was a person of my own rearing and instructing, from childhood, who excelled in every good quality that can possibly accomplish a human creature.

[1]Letter to Reverend John Worrall: Ball, III, p. 317.

They have hitherto writ me deceiving letters, but Mr.
Worrall has been so just and prudent as to tell me the
truth; which, however racking, is better than to be struck
on the sudden. Dear Jim, pardon me, I know not what I
am saying; but believe me that violent friendship is much
more lasting, and as much engaging, as violent love.
Adieu."[1]

Writing to Sheridan, and it is to the lovable school-
master that he turns most often for consolation, again Swift
declares that:

> "I look upon this to be the greatest event that can ever
> happen to me; but all my preparations will not suffice to
> make me bear it like a philosopher, nor altogether like a
> Christian. . . . Nay, if I were now near her, I would not see
> her; I could not behave myself tolerably, and should re-
> double her sorrow. Judge in what a temper of mind I write
> this . . . I have been long weary of the world, and shall for
> my small remainder of years be weary of life, having for-
> ever lost that conversation, which could only make it
> tolerable."[2]

Swift's emphasis on an exchange of ideas as the supreme
pleasure of life has not altered since he was twenty-four years
old. At the moment in which he visualizes the soul of the
person dearest to him on earth to be leaving her body he
speaks of her conversation as her most precious gift to him—
that product of a mind shaped by him to solace, invigorate and
delight him. Once again the inhibition which prevents him
from giving himself wholly to her, even at the gates of death,
overpowers him, keeps him from going to her as fast as land,
sea, and wind will permit, and makes him morbidly estimate
his own distress rather than submerge it in Stella's need. He
is even thankful that he is ill, "for it would have been a reproach to me to be in perfect health, when such a friend is
desperate."[3]

But he returned and upon his return Stella revived. Al-

[1]Letter to Reverend James Stopford: Ball, III, pp. 320-3.
[2]Ball, III, p. 324.
[3]Letter to Sheridan: Ball, III, p. 417.

though "still very lean and low," she lingered for another eighteen months. Bolingbroke sent her an invitation to come on a visit with Swift to them: Lady Bolingbroke sent her some fans "just arrived from Lilliput." She copied out Swift's verses in her neat, circular hand, modelled on his, rejoicing that *Gulliver* was "the conversation of the whole town . . . from the cabinet council to the nursery it is universally read."[1]

Once more Swift, with his old restlessness and that sense of impending disaster which he might avert by flight or action, crossed to England on a final visit, and the news of Stella's recurrent illness dogged him afresh. Once more he is distracted:

"What have I to do in the world? I never was in such agonies as when I received your letter, and had it in my pocket. I am able to hold up my sorry head no longer."[2]

He is torn in half, trying to maintain his own equilibrium, to appease the various voices which clamour within him, among them, his thought for his cloth, his reputation as a clergyman. *Stella must not die in the Deanery.* He writes it most carefully in Latin in a letter of directions; and there is something pitifully mean in this stipulation, which epitomizes Swift's fears and neuroses. (As if it mattered where she died. Her dying was what he could not face, for it meant submission to a law of life, and throughout his own he had fought not to accept life as it is.) Even in death he tries to exclude Stella, from his heart, from under his very roof. He had never taken her to him, or given her a proper home. He repudiates her to the very end, squeezing her into lodgings as he had pressed her out of his heart.

As if in revenge upon him, fate plays one of her abominable tricks; for to add to his distress, which already amounts to frenzy, Swift is misguided enough to turn down the offer of the Captain of the government yacht which crossed to Dublin, thinking that to sail from Holyhead will get him there more quickly. But he has misjudged the weather and is held prisoner for nearly ten days.

[1]Letter from Pope and Gay: Ball, III, pp. 358-60.
[2]Letter to Sheridan: Ball, III, p. 417.

At four in the morning he is on horseback, riding from Chester to Holyhead. Even in his state of acute apprehension he is careful for the horses of his guide and himself; he walks rather than cause one animal suffering from the loss of a foreshoe. On the following day he tries to distract himself by going to look at ancient tombs, and craggy rocks. Three days later, the Captain of the ship which Swift hopes will finally carry him is still delaying, declaring the wind to be too fierce. He has no books to read and no tolerable companion. He is debarred from talking with the common people since neither the farmers nor the shopkeepers speak English. A dog would be better company than the Vicar, whom he remembers of old. The rain streams down, the chimneys smoke, and Swift, always meticulous about the cleanliness of his own person, is forced to wear dirty linen owing to the blunders of his servant, Wat. The food consists of tough mutton, the wine is raw and the ale vile. His eyes ache from smoke and candle-light. There is nothing to do but write, and sleep. Yet too much sleeping makes him sick: he counts the hours before he must take himself off to bed. He scribbles and scribbles to dispel the awful suspense and his "listless wretchedness,"

"I will write close, and do as the Devil did at Mass— pull the paper with my teeth to make it hold out."[1]

He fears an attack of vertigo. He fears that the wind will either prolong the gale or drop so suddenly that he will be becalmed, and with horrible irony remarks that he has half a mind to "take a house and garden here." But always, gnawing at his heart, are his fears of losing Stella.

Could any situation be more agonizing? Even when he gets to sea the fierce and inconsiderate wind turns the ship back. Swift is forced to lie on board all night "to avoid broken bones," and then to go back on to land again, "to get in a new stock of patience."[2] It infuriates him to think that had he taken Captain Lawson's offer he would have been at home over a week ago.

[1]*Holyhead Journal*, Temple Scott, XI, p. 402. Churton Collins, p. 218, compares this diary to that of Byron at Ravenna.
[2]Ibid, XI, p. 396.

When he reaches Dublin at last, after a racking journey from Carlingford with poor horses, bad roads, and wretched inns, Swift looks at Stella. It is as he feared. He cannot see, as he had done when she had been a child at Moor Park, desperately ill, "the seeds of life—which seldom fail."[1]

In three months she was dead. Vanessa had been only thirty-six and Stella was forty-seven. But the mental sicknesses of those we love and who are near to us, unless we are strong, infect mind and body and wear both away.

"Do not the corruption and villainies of men (in power) eat your flesh and consume your spirits?"[2], Swift had once asked Sheridan. Stella had shared those black torments, the fears, evasions, reticences; embarrassments, elations and despondencies, of one stronger than herself, more fully than any other being, and now that illusion, too, had received its death-blow, she succumbed like Vanessa.

For once, Swift had not been able to escape. He could not disavow the hand of death as easily as he had always denied responsibility. In the prayers which he had written for Stella in her illness,[3] the cry over and over again is for pity in his own sufferings, for strength and consolation.

And in a measure they came. For while the grave-diggers threw up the earth in the Cathedral aisle, while her funeral service was being read, he moved into another room in order not to see the Cathedral lights, bowed himself mutely over his paper, and wrote out his sorrow as he had always written out his rage or despair, when life with its relentlessness had racked and torn him. Yet with a lucidity frightening in its cold, analytical intensity, he still tried to shut out suffering as he had tried to exclude love, life, and now death.

"January 28th. . . . She expired about six in the evening of this day; and, as soon as I am left alone, which is about eleven at night, I resolve, for my own satisfaction, to say something of her life and character. . . .

"January 29th. My head aches, and I can write no more.

[1] Williams, p. 143.
[2] Delany, p. 148.
[3] *Three Prayers for Stella*: Hayward, pp. 735 et seq.

"January 30th. This is the night of the funeral, which my sickness will not suffer me to attend. . . ."[1]

The recital is like some terrible stony route-march which truth, remorse, his unacknowledged love of Stella, and the need to torture himself, force him to make, almost in expiation. But sorrow will not let him escape her, and it is only after a few days, when he has utterly renounced Stella, and when he has calmed himself, that the sentences flow with ease. Then at last Swift is released and he gives himself to Stella with a simplicity which he had never achieved while she was alive.

VI

In looking at the lives of these three people in retrospect one does not know whom to pity most—Vanessa, taken unawares and drawn closer and closer into the orbit of two older, stronger characters, whose sphere of action she collides with but cannot interrupt; finally living wretched and alone, "reasoning and forming teasing conclusions from mistaken thoughts";[2] waiting, perpetually waiting, for a few scant hours with the man she loves, to whom she is susceptible with every fibre of her being: Stella, living a fettered life, ostensibly so free, but really irrevocably bound to a man whose mental images obliterate her character; who finds at the end of her years of devotion that she has seemingly been cheated of even her half-measure of fidelity: or Swift, suffering as only a strong man stretched taut by opposing forces can suffer; in continual conflict, morbidly dreading pain, or to be the cause of pain, and yet daily hurting himself and mortally wounding others; watching himself do so relentlessly, like a surgeon killing the patients he has sworn to heal; unable to stop revolving in this dreadful circle, binding himself with a misuse of his own strengths, blinded with pride and intellect.

When Hamlet's uncle asked his mother concerning his condition she answered that her son was:

[1]*On the Death of Mrs. Johnson*: Hayward, pp. 725-7.
[2]Freeman, p. 144.

*"Mad as the sea and wind, when both contend
Which is the mightier. . . ."*

and this was Swift's condition. His immobility under a net-work of inhibitions is frightening to observe. It was not for nothing that while he struggled with the problem of his devotion to Stella and Vanessa he wrote *Gulliver's Travels,* and drew the strong man, a giant compared to his adversaries, tethered by maddening, invisible packthreads which, for all his strength, he could not break. For if he studied his predicament it made him frenzied and ashamed, without enabling him to remedy it. To retreat was impossible, to persevere was culpable, to capitulate was fearful, to temporize was the only solution. Anything to gain time, to avoid committing himself, to escape without facing the issue, to remain passive, to yield to circumstance, to force one or another of the actors in this tragedy to release him by making the first move. If he waited long enough, if he endured and did nothing, time, caprice, or accident, would be merciful and cut the strangling threads. Stella's affection, or Vanessa's passion, might wane, or be transferred to another, and so divert this torrent which threatened to submerge but not to support him. And at the worst, death, endured but not encouraged, whether the death of another or himself, would set him free.

Meanwhile, he watched himself running furtively, like some nocturnal animal who winds its dark and tortuous way down hedge or rank alley, dreading the step of pursuers. The spiteful tongues and prying eyes were always around him.

"I ever feared the tattle of this nasty town. . . . It is not a place for any freedom, but where everything is known in a week, and magnified a hundred degrees."[1]

In his flayed condition he was distressed if some old woman of the Dublin streets, one of his begging parishioners, failed to curtsey to him.[2]

Yet he knew himself to be, like Temple, "an exact admirer and observer of truth," who hated hypocrisy, who lived

[1]Freeman, p. 99.
[2]Ball, II, p. 234.

dangerously without thought for his own safety when serving others.   Had he not taught both Stella and Vanessa the principles of honour, virtue, and candour?   But there was the rub, for his former pupils turned on him, taunting him with his own precepts, disclosing the gap between ideals and behaviour which he could not mend.

"You once had a maxim which was to act what was right and not mind what the world said. I wish you would keep to it now."[1]

He was cornered by his own words and he could not answer, for to face Vanessa with her reminder meant facing himself, and that Swift could not do.   His sermon *On the Difficulty of Knowing One's Self*[2] elaborates his stubborn perplexity.

We are left with an enigma.   How are we to reconcile the man who wrote that he hated "anything that looks like a secret,"[3] and whom Bolingbroke described as "a hypocrite reversed," with the man who behaved with such duplicity?

"Those who know anything of Swift know with what loathing he always shrank from anything bearing the remotest resemblance to duplicity and falsehood.   As a political pamphleteer he might, like his brother penmen, allow himself licence, but in the ordinary intercourse of life it was his habit to exact and assume absolute sincerity. It was the virtue by which he ostentatiously prided himself: it was the virtue by which, in the opinion of those who were intimate with him, he was most distinguished. . . . He was never known to tell an untruth."[4]

If this is the whole portrait, do we recognize the man who involved himself so long, and so culpably, with two women simultaneously?   For his intimacy with Vanessa was not a matter of months, or even a few years; it covered nearly a dozen, overlapping those with Stella.

How can one explain his predicament without condemning,

---

[1]Freeman, pp. 103-4.
[2]Temple Scott, IV, p. 148.
[3]Freeman, p. 106.
[4]Collins, p. 147.

or condoning? How estimate the strengths and counter-strengths which interlocked and held Swift pinned? We are ignorant of so much in the past and can only make surmises. Yet something in Swift's infancy suggests a solution which we may adopt without imagining too wildly, or stating too didactically.

Laetitia Pilkington, writing three years after Swift's death, says:

> "The account I have frequently heard the Dean give of himself was that he was . . . a posthumous son . . . but, as he said, came time enough to save his mother's credit. He was given to an Irish woman to nurse, whose husband being in England and writing to her to come to him; as she could not bear the thoughts of parting with the child, she very fairly took him with her, unknown to his mother or any of his relations, who could learn no tidings either of him or her for three years; at the end of which time she returned to Ireland, and restored the child to his mother, from whom she easily obtained a pardon, both on account of the joy she conceived at seeing her only son again, when she had in a manner lost all hope of it, as also that it was plain the Nurse had no other motive for stealing him but pure affection, which the women of Ireland generally have in as eminent degree for the children they nurse as for their own offspring."[1]

The author of this paragraph, who had an extraordinary memory, has been criticized for her "reckless indifference to truth."[2] But her story differs in only two respects from Swift's own[3]—she speaks of the nurse as being married and crossing to her husband (instead of a "relation") in England, and says that Mrs. Swift was ignorant of the child's whereabouts throughout his absence, whereas Swift says that she eventually learned them, though not how soon. But these are trifling differences which in no way influence the main facts—that the child was stolen from his mother when very young, and

[1] *Memoirs* of Laetitia Pilkington. The English Library. J. Isaacs: pp. 57-8.
[2] Collins, p. 4.
[3] *Fragment of Autobiography*: Scott, I, p. 477.

returned to her at three years old. We know from a writer of the next century[1] that when children sent out to wet-nurse returned to their homes and rightful parents, they sometimes regarded themselves as changelings and felt unsettled, more especially if they did not resemble their brothers and sisters or their parents in physical appearance. Such a circumstance alone is sufficient to set up a doubt in a child's mind as to its origins, to create a feeling of insecurity and of not belonging to its parents, or surroundings. If further grave emotional disturbance occurred, such as the quarrelling[2] of nurse and mother over the child—violent temper, words, tears, threats and recriminations—further damage would ensue. Thirdly, if the child, as in Swift's case, was remarkable for his precocity, sensitivity, and retentive memory, he would soak up an atmosphere of strangeness, secrecy, and hostility, more readily than a placid, insensitive child. The probable result of all these conspiring factors is that the growing child, and later the man, would feel an overpowering and unconscious need to escape from the dangerous complications of feminine affection, and, if not to escape, then perpetually to charm and placate women in order to prevent their anger, or their desertion of him.

As a helpless child he cannot dismiss women, for his existence depends on them. In Swift's case, weaned by violent and unnatural methods first from his mother, then from his nurse, and then from his mother again, he gives every sign of having carried forward into mature years the idea that women were the all-powerful sex, whose disapproval and rejection he feared more than anything else in life. This attitude made him dependent on them to an abnormal degree, with the result that, in turn, he feared their dependence on him. Thus the circle completed itself: the damaging conflict was set up— the healthy forces of life drawing him forward, the unhealthy (whose origins he could not understand, since they were so deeply embedded and occurred so early that the conscious mind could not recover them) drawing him backwards.

[1]Susan Sibbald's *Memoirs*, edited by Francis Paget Hett, p. 21.
[2]For Swift's dislike of feminine quarrels see Williams, pp. 276 and 285.

He could not go forward even though he wished, for, amongst other things, he became ignorant of the very fact that he desired a normal relationship, since to him it seemed too dangerous to contemplate. His fears were reinforced by aversions which provided the unavowed reason for his withdrawal, until finally he hated his fellow-creatures for being able to act in a manner distasteful to him.[1]

Swift's love of his mother, which is attested and well-known, and his nausea for the human body, imply that both his fears and his disgust sprang from an association with his nurse. His mother does not appear ever to have treated him possessively: she urged the nurse not to risk returning him to her until he might be older and stronger, she left him at six years old in order that he might benefit from better circumstances than she could provide, she let him go and come as he pleased to her home in Leicestershire. His fear of a "tyrant sex" is therefore much more likely to have originated from his experiences with his ignorant, possessive abductress. This theory becomes more plausible when one finds no mention of the nurse in after years. If she lived, and Mrs. Swift or her son had been devoted to her, it is likely that Swift, with his passionate protectiveness for the old and defenceless, would have befriended and succoured her if she was in need.

When Swift as a child, scarcely out of the nursery, was sent away to school, something else occurred to divert his natural growth, and again we do not know what the actual causes were; we can only read the results and make surmises. But something tyrannical, whether his uncle's disposition, or the despotism of masters and older boys, oppressed the naturally resilient lad, making him resentful, unable to defend himself, divided by his own thwarted powers which, finding no outlet, turned inward to do their work of disintegration.

Lermontov describes this process:

"Such was the fate allotted to me from my very early childhood. Everyone read on my face the signs of bad

[1] See Swift's ferocity concerning the fiddler to be hanged for rape, whose pardon he prevented. Williams, p. 320. And *Poems*, II, p. 516: "An Excellent New Ballad, or the True English Dean to be Hanged for a Rape."

qualities which were not there: but they suspected them
and so they were born in me. I was modest, so I was
accused of cunning: I became secretive. I felt deeply good
and evil, no one caressed me but all offended me instead: I
became resentful. I was sullen while the other children
were happy: I felt I was superior to them, but they put me
lower than they: I became envious. I was ready to love the
whole world but no one understood me: I learned to hate.
My colourless youth was wasted on a struggle with myself
and the world: my best feelings, fearing ridicule, I buried in
the depths of my heart and there they perished. I spoke the
truth, I was not believed: I began to simulate.

"Having got to know the world and the springs of society,
I became experienced in the science of life and saw how
others were happy, making use without effort of those very
advantages which I fought for so relentlessly. And then a
despair was born in my breast: not that despair which is
cured by the barrel of a pistol, but a cold powerless despair
concealed by affability, and a good-natured smile. I became
a moral cripple. One half of my innermost side dried up,
ceased to exist, evaporated and died. I cut it off and threw
it away."[1]

This is a terrible picture, an indictment of society, of man's
tyranny over man, of the subjection of growing natures by
their ignorant and more powerful elders. Swift came near to
being crippled in the same way, but not so completely. Part
of him had mortified, so that by the time he was of age and
was philandering in Leicestershire he already called himself
"cold."

Yet how could such a man be cold? Everything in his
actions, behaviour and writing bespeaks passion, strength, and
ardour; but ardour repressed. If he was cold it was the
coldness of a scalded character, burnt and shocked into
paralysis, with muscles and fibres—not shot away—but
seared and hardened into numbness.

"His careful assertions of the coldness of his nature
could have been but protections against the world. How
could a man so easily shaken, as proud as a palace cat, as
subtle as a gipsy, have had one drop of cold blood in his

[1] *A Hero of Our Time.*

veins? No, there is some explanation that eludes us. . . . His endearments are sexual, protective, but never passionate."[1]

His affective life had suffered a blight and all tenderness must be repressed. Thus the violence of his aberrations showed the measure of his illness: his deep disgust, which is at such variance with flowering life, was the measure of his seared desires. Shame, disgust, and fear, were only the masks of love —desire negatively expressed—and one senses in lines of the early Odes what a sublime poet, instead of a writer of polished verses or scarifying satire, Swift might have been, just as one senses in the *Journal* what an ardent lover he would have made if only he had released his love. What Taine calls his "cruel, positive mind" with its passion for dissection, understatement of beauty and overstatement of the unattractive, might, if early influences had been kinder, have given us some of the loveliest of lyrics, the most imaginative and impassioned prose. For a satirist is after all only a despairing idealist and the greater the diverted emotional force, the more vicious the satire.

But the degradation of spirit to which Swift had been forced to sink as a child found its compensation in adult inflation, and made him a man of extremes. There was always either too little or too much of everything—thought, passion, force, art. A see-saw of complementary trends was set up: he suffered excruciatingly, so he inflicted pain on others: he was conscious of being too submissive, so he determined to dominate: he loved to display himself publicly, walking like a king of men, yet simultaneously he cloaked himself with mystery: he ruthlessly attacked acquaintances when he first met them and then suddenly shut himself away, or fled, like a timid, wild creature: he was so modest that he never sought fame from any of his writings, nor cared if they were published, once they had driven home the nail on which he had concentrated the power of his hammer, yet his vanity was excessive: he was meticulously clean, yet obsessed with images of filth: he appears to have suffered from gnawing feelings of inadequacy and

[1]Lady Gregory.

peculiarity which he counterbalanced with fantasies of heroic birth, and heroic behaviour. In short, the dwarf and the giant of *Gulliver's Travels* typify these nightmare states between which Swift was perpetually suspended, maintaining his precarious balance like one of his own tightrope-walkers at the Lilliputian court.

The effect of these mental states on his conduct was that, living as he did with one foot in the realm of reality and the other in that of unreality, he was bound to be inconsistent. When he "slipped his person", escaping from the more solid world to the imagined one, he vexed and baffled people who looked for reliability, consistency, and integration. He was consistent to his divided nature, to his shell of egotism, but that they could not understand. Irrationally inclined to behave like two people, and claiming merits for each, he was surprised and angered if others failed to accept both, or to trust either.

This tendency to double tightrope-walking is revealed in his behaviour when he wrote the *Discourse*: he expected preferment both from the Tory churchmen whose institution he had defended, and from his former associates the Whigs, whom he had covertly attacked. It is apparent in his treatment of Varina whom he ardently wooed, despised for hesitation, and then virtually rejected, by tendering proposals for their union which no woman with dignity could accept. It is obvious in his relations with Sir William Temple, under whose suspected patronage he reared and smarted while at the same time expecting affectionate trust and appreciation. It is plainer still with Vanessa, whom he alternately encouraged and discouraged—and then was annoyed if she complained; and with Stella, whom he placed in an impossible position and defied not to be loyal. If either had ceased to love, or had abandoned him, he would probably have been the first to complain of ingratitude.

The shocks of early, unpleasant physical encounter, the bitter disappointments and emotional starvation of childhood and adolescence, were followed by discouragement and by rising hatred and, since real love and support were denied, by a turning inward upon the self of unhappy self-love and admiration. The theft of Stella and Vanessa's hearts followed "as the night the day"—just restitution for what he un-consciously felt had been stolen from him earlier. In his own mind he became a hero; none should be loved or worshipped like him.

Yet the substitution of false love, the inversion of emotions which should have been directed outward, and the preference for a world of fantasy, brought with it unhappy results—a lack of interest in, or understanding of, the thoughts and feelings of others; a failure to appreciate objectivity, so that reality became provisional; and an over-estimation of the value of the intellect—thoughts and ideas being considered superior to feeling. The real self was lost: the capacity to love was terribly impaired: confusion as to what he was, or what love might be, abounded: and positive emotional ties with others, even those dear to him, were, in some incalculable, and for them painful, way made thin and discontinuous. Thus not only Vanessa, but Swift's male friends as well constantly complained of his disappearing, of his failure to write and to keep them informed of his position and welfare.[1]

One wonders, in the circumstances, what made him attrac-tive to women; for if Swift remained in part prisoner to Stella and Vanessa, they were his prisoners for life. Despite his protestations of friendship, and friendship only, despite his guarded and outwardly correct behaviour, something deeper held them both. I think the answer lies in this: that there was for each the promise, the implication of something, always in the future, which had already blossomed and would bear fruit for her, and her alone. There was the hint of passion about to be fulfilled, for in reading Vanessa's letters one sees that she writes like a woman who has known something more than mere verbal protestations. Something vital had passed between them, some gesture or look of affection, signifying warmth and abundance to come: her response speaks from those tragic letters which are not entirely the fabrication of a

---

[1] "The conclusion that Swift was not a frequent correspondent . . . is sustained by the repeated and prolonged complaints in the letters of his friends as to his slowness in sending a reply, and by his lists of letters which show that his letter writing was spasmodic in character." Ball, III, p. 453, II.

morbidly imaginative mind. Swift must, as Thackeray says, have given some love to have received so much in return.[1]

He held both Stella and Vanessa with such tenacity and with such sincerity. These, his two salient virtues, intensified, bound them to him with belief and devotion. And then, his fascination of them was so complete: it is almost as if he rendered them powerless by a look, or merely by his presence. His force was a compelling one, without apparent mercy, or real tenderness, since it never had their ultimate welfare at heart. A "bundle of paradoxes,"[2] he charmed and held them by those very contradictions so often found in the highly-strung, but particularly marked in Swift.

He was male and female compounded, ferociously male and tenderly female: compassionate yet cruel: he was strong with the strength of Samson, yet surprisingly, suddenly, weak, appealing to their pity: he was sensitive yet harsh, full of delicacies, yet coarse to a degree: proud as Lucifer, yet often humble in their presence, deferring to their judgment:[3] generous and parsimonious: remarkable for his common sense yet unaccountably superstitious:[4] unassailable, yet painfully vulnerable: guiltless, yet guilty: professedly religious, yet fundamentally atheistical, determinedly clinging to his religion to counteract that bleak, cerebral pessimism bred by his disgust with humanity: reckless, yet apprehensive: gifted with intuitive insight,[5] yet perversely blind: eloquently per-suasive and banefully silent: eminently sane, yet fearfully mad, as if some demon gadfly forever pursued him: the protector of the poor, insane, and needy, yet at heart the hater of the human race.

[1]*English Humourists.*

[2]Sir Edmund Gosse: *Short History of Modern English Literature*, p. 220.

[3]See Williams, p. 62. "I want your judgment of things."

[4]"I have lain in thirty beds since I left the town; I always drew up the clothes with my left hand, which is a superstition I have learn't these ten years"; Freeman, p. 140. See also the *Journal to Stella* for his belief in the sovereign's ability to cure scrofula: and, elsewhere, his references to the devil and his power.

[5]"Mr. Harley complained he could keep nothing from me, I had the way so much of getting in to him." Williams, p. 92.

"*Damn'd* Poets, *Damn'd* Criticks, *Damn'd* Block-Heads,
   Damn'd Knaves,
Damn'd Senators *brib'd*, *Damn'd prostitute* Slaves:
Damn'd Lawyers *and* Judges, *Damn'd* Lords *and Damn'd*
   Squires,
Damn'd Spies *and* Informers, *Damn'd* Friends *and Damn'd*
   Lyars;
Damn'd Villins. *corrupted in every* Station
Damn'd Time-Serving Priests *all over the* Nation;"[1]

Above all, he tangled the wits and emotions of his women
by making them worship the very thing which ensnared them
—his intellect, which with its involutions and convolutions
made him the conjured spirit that he was. Neither of them
could understand the terrible need to love which had become
divided and poisoned at its source, and each hoped to heal the
wound which neither had caused.

After the death of Stella, Swift's disgust with human beings
who so inconveniently, so indecently had bodies—that disgust
which made him portray the Yahoos pelting the traveller
with faecal filth from the trees of the island—became intensified.
He had felt himself to be the despised animal, smeared with
filth, and so had portrayed the Yahoo.[2] He could not be
lenient with himself, or forgive himself for being what he
was, and so he was harsh on others. This inability to accept
the human body and its animal functions arose from an inability to accept life itself, and this rejection produced further
confusion.

For since the male and female sides of his nature were so
pronounced, and intermingled so completely, they bred in him
an outer confusion and lack of discrimination. He responded
readily to the demands made upon him by both men and
women, and he identified himself profoundly with the demands
of each in turn: yet in some extraordinary way he did not distinguish between the sexes fundamentally, but laid down laws
and axioms for their behaviour irrespective of their structural

---

[1] *The Place of the Damn'd.* 1731. *Poems*, II, pp. 575-6.
[2] In disagreement with Lord Orrery who says "In painting
Yahoos Swift becomes one himself," p. 120.

Plate VII

Dublin May ye 25st 1723.

Sr

I receiv'd yours to day, with two Bills enclosed, one to Mrs Dingley, of one hundred and eight pounds; and the other to me, of foure hundred and thirty two; I am extreamly obliged to you for the favour you have done me, and return you my most hearty thanks for it, I got them accepted this morning so I think all that bussiness is over; to be sure you did extreamly right to give a receipt in full of all demands. Be-pleased to give my most humble service to Mrs Dingley

I am Sr
    your most obliged
    humble Servant
    Esther Johnson.

Facsimile of the handwriting of Stella (her only extant letter)

and emotional divergencies. Although he wrote in a vein of sound common sense to Sheridan smarting under reproof,

> ". . . expect no more from man than such an animal is capable of. . . . You should think and deal with every man as a villain, without calling him so, or flying from him, or valuing him the less. . . ."[1]

although he wrote to Vanessa "For Nature will be Nature still,"[2] he did not really accept the weaknesses and meannesses of mankind, the basic humanity of man, or the inevitable course of nature, with clear mind and emotions. His advice to Sheridan—

> "Sit down and be quiet, and mind your business as you should do,"[3]

resembles that to Vanessa—"Grow less romantic and talk and act like a man of this world."[4] The tone to the woman is the same as that to the man, with no shade of difference.

Swift would not have understood the attitude of Thomas Hardy, who held that women are fundamentally different from men; that they do not react in the same way as men to the same stimuli; virtues and vices for them have different consequences; and their very language differs from that of men in essence, though their words may be the same. He would have laughed at Bathsheba who says that "It is difficult for a woman to define her feelings in a language made by men to express theirs." The result of this unconscious confusion on the part of Swift, coupled with his compelling power, was that he caused bewilderment and suffering to the women with whom he came in closest contact. Minds tended to become warped, one heart at least was broken, lives were shortened, and life for Swift himself was unendurably difficult.

During his latter years he made no secret of cursing the day on which he had been born. Yet it was neither affectation nor morbid self-pity which caused him to read out the Third

[1]Ball, III, pp. 266-7.
[2]*Cadenus and Vanessa.*
[3]Ball, III, pp. 266-7.
[4]Freeman, p. 135.

Chapter of the Book of Job, with its insistent questionings, its savage anathemas, its plea for the obliteration of darkness as well as light, its longings for freedom from servitude, and for the dreamless tranquillity of the grave. "Why is light given to a man whose way is hid, and whom God hath hedged in?"

Naturally, if one looks upon the body as vile and its functions as unnatural, if one believes life to be evil, one rails against intercourse and marriage, one has a horror of begetting children to clutter the world with further sorrow. "I hope it will die the day after the christening"[1], is Swift's uncharitable exclamation when he hears that a friend is about to bear a child, and when, as if in answer to that withering wish, the babe only ekes out two breathless days, he imagines that the mother is "not very sorry."

Furthermore, granted a mind like Swift's, which argues relentlessly along logical lines even when handling absurd propositions, if that mind gets its premises wrong and does not observe its error, like some inhuman clockwork thing, it will inevitably wind itself up and run down along a course fatal to its own content. It will deceive and victimize its owner by the seeming veracity of its original blunders. Truth and reality will, like the broomstick, and like the inverted world of Swift's early *Ode*, appear topsy-turvy, standing on their heads:

> "*For this inferior world is but Heaven's dusky shade,*
> *By dark reverted rays from its reflection made;*
> *Whence the weak shapes wild and imperfect pass,*
> *Like sun-beams shot at too far distance from a glass;*
> *Which all the mimic forms express,*
> *Tho' in strange uncouth postures, and uncomely dress;*
> *So when Cartesian artists try*
> *To solve appearances of sight*
> *In its reception to the eye,*
> *And catch the living landscape thro' a scanty light,*
> *The figures all inverted show,*
> *And colours of a faded hue;*

[1]Williams, p. 129.

Here a pale shape with upward footstep treads,
And men seem walking on their heads;
There whole herds suspended lie
Ready to tumble down into the sky;
Such are the ways ill guided mortals go
To judge of things above by things below.
Disjointing shapes as in the fairy-land of dreams,
Or images that sink in streams;
No wonder, then, we talk amiss
Of Truth, and what, or where it is. . . ."[1]

The tragedy lies here, that, being human, he cannot escape the need to love or to be loved and so, in writing the *Journal to Stella*, Swift recreates the childhood and the world of affection which he never had. It is not *only*, as many critics have insisted, that for the sake of safety he tries to prolong Stella's childhood, but rather that he invents for her and for *himself* the nursery-world of play and prattle which he had never known. He, a grown man, the severe Doctor of Divinity in his black flowing clothes, and she the mature woman, hide away in a world of "naughty boys and naughty girls," and he must, even while he is undressing, be "speaking monkey things in air" to her, "just as if MD had been by."[2] Her presence is so near to him, so essential to his starved heart, whose hunger and immaturity no one but she must ever know, that he thinks himself bewitched by her.

"Let me go, will you? and I'll come again to-night. . . but I can, nor will, stay no longer now; no, I won't for all your wheedling; no, no, look off, don't smile at me, and say 'Pray, Pray, Presto, write a little more!' Ah! you're a wheedling slut, you be so. Nay, but prithee, turn about, and let me go, do; 'tis a good girl, and do. . . ."[3]

Had he not taught this enchanting child as she grew older to appreciate crusty Hobbes? And why was Swift so drawn to Hobbes? Was it that he recognized a familiar voice calling

[1]*Ode to Dr. William Sancroft*, 1692. *Poems*, I, p. 35.
[2]Williams, p. 155.
[3]Ibid.

from a generation earlier—"Fear and I were born twins"?
For Hobbes like Swift had had a clouded birth, precarious and
premature, and had twice known what it was to be a fugitive.
Man, he says, is a creature driven by fear and emotions
derived from fear, which urge him to a "perpetual and restless
desire of power after power, that ceaseth only in death."[1]

Could there be a better description of Swift himself, searching, searching to destroy that haunting fear of inadequacy,
of being different from other men, by repressing tenderness
and affection, by refusing to surrender to love lest he lose
virility, by pursuing power, for ever power, and so being
cheated of his ambitions and becoming impotent?

Very early in life this conception of power as a substitute
for all that he had lacked in life must have occurred to Swift.
The anecdote of the fish which he nearly caught but which
eluded him, which became for him the symbol "of all his future
disappointments,"[2] illustrates this early ambition and the
furious, vexatious frustration of the older man always cheated,
as he says, by Fate, of all his prizes. The rewards from
Temple and the King, the lost prebend of Canterbury or
Westminster, the promised chaplaincy to Lord Berkeley, the
Deanery of Derry, the Bishopric of Hereford or Dromore, the
recognition by Whigs, Tories, or the Queen of his whole-
hearted and apparently disinterested services, had likewise
been drawn up "almost on the ground" when they "had
dropped in" and vanished. Again and again the lesson had
been set him to learn, again and again he refused it. His early
misfortunes had forced him to envisage the attainment of
certain pinnacles of worldly eminence as compensation for his
early emotional losses. By such a substitution and such a
restitution he had determined to balance, or square life. But
the very intensity of his pursuit, the insistence upon this
remedy and this alone, precluded capture and solace. His
Maker had determined otherwise for him and he could not
submit: the angel of life and mercy brought him other books
wherein to record his name, but like Temple's friend, the
young Countess of Essex who, losing one child, neglected

[1]*Leviathan*, ed. by A. D. Lindsay, J. M. Dent, 1924, p. 49.
[2]*Supra*, p. 18.

another, Swift grieved for the lost delights; or, stooping to accept a substitute as a sop to his injured pride, he did so with ingratitude.

"As *Prometheus* (which interpreted, is, the prudent man), was bound to the hill *Caucasus*, a place of large prospect, where, an Eagle, feeding on his liver, devoured in the day, as much as was repaired in the night; so that man, which looks too far before him, in the care of future time, hath his heart all the day long, gnawed on by fear of death, poverty, or other calamity; and has no repose, nor pause of his anxiety, but in sleep."[1]

Was not Swift similarly obsessed, and is not this the clue to his need to seize and consider only the moments as they fly? There is much in the temper of Hobbes and Swift which is akin—their disposition to original and unconventional thought, their inclination to disbelief, and their defiance of opinion; but the real bond between them was the bond of fear, which Hobbes had the courage to state but Swift whispered only to Stella.

And if so distracted by perpetual fears, tormented by conflicting forces, obsessed by the filth, stupidity and cruelty of mankind, what more natural than to long for death, to curse one's father for begetting one, and one's Maker for prolonging senseless life? Christian consolation and the willingness to pay life's arrears joyfully are swallowed up in a howl of defiant misery, reminiscent of the despair of Job, the agony of Oedipus, and the vilification of life by the mediaeval philosophers.

> *"Call no man fortunate that is not dead,*
> *The dead are free from pain."*

VII

If, before the death of Stella, Swift had never been known to laugh, now he never smiled, only "sucked in his cheeks, as folks do when they have a plug of tobacco in their mouths."[2]

[1]*Leviathan*, p. 55.
[2]Laetitia Pilkington, *Memoirs*, p. 69.

And if he thought or dreamt of Stella—(and in London in the breakneck days he was always dreaming of her, sometimes "grieving and crying for her all night"[1] like a lost child)—now he never mentioned her. The reserve which prevented him from telling Pope of his distress when he had been staying with him and she was rumoured to be dying, forcing him to make his, or Pope's, maladies the sole excuse for his uneasiness, sealed his lips with regard to her for ever. In his anguish he had called her "The fairest soul in the world"[2] (an unusually poetical phrase for Swift), and had confessed that "for her sake only life was worth preserving."[3] At times his physical and mental distress was so acute that he thought he had not long to live and devoutly hoped he might not. But the strength of body which he had always been at such pains to build would not let him fall away so easily. He lived another seventeen years, years remarkable for his activity on behalf of the nation and for public and private charity, and for something in contrast to that activity which pulled at him always like a dead weight. He wrote some of his finest verse—(*Verses on the Death of Doctor Swift*, *The Legion Club*, *The Day of Judgment*, and *On Poetry: A Rhapsody*): some of his most savage and ironic prose—(the *Modest Proposal for Preventing the Children of Poor People being a Burden to their Parents*,[4] and *A Serious and Useful Scheme to Make an Hospital for Incurables*): some of his filthiest work—(*The Ladies' Dressing Room*, *Strephon and Chloe*, and *A Beautiful Young Nymph Going to Bed*): some of his most wrathful and despairing pamphlets (*A Short View of the State of Ireland*; *Judas*, and *The Irish Bishops*); and some of his most observant comments on human nature—(the *Directions to Servants* and the *Complete Collection of Genteel and Ingenious Conversation*). He jested and punned with Sheridan and other friends, exchanging trifles, riddles, anglo-latin jargon, and worthless sentences whose purpose was a play upon words. He grew phrenetically proud—("Covetous as

---

[1]Williams, p. 111.
[2]Letter to Sheridan: Ball, III, p. 324.
[3]Ibid, p. 417.
[4]Compare the theme of this work with Shaw's remark that the English rear their game with more thought than their children.

Hell, and ambitious as the Prince of it,"[1] had been his description of Marlborough)—and battled with his episcopal superiors like Christian with Apollyon. He likened these gentlemen to highwaymen in clerical clothing which they had stripped from their victims, the proper clergy, whom they had murdered on Hounslow Heath! His animosity to individuals was such that often he appeared to go out of his way to invent causes for pugnacious behaviour: for example, he argued with the descendants of the Duke of Schomberg about a monument to that hero which they refused to erect, partly because of his dislike of the Hanoverian King and Queen who had neglected Gay. He took the cause of the Dublin beggars and the starving vagrants who slept under dripping hedges to his heart and went to endless trouble for their sakes. He concerned himself with personal dependants—his sister who had married a man of whom he had not approved; his housekeeper's daughter; Dingley (who lived on fifteen years after Stella although she was fifteen years older), upon whose behalf he approached Temple's descendants, and to whom he paid a disguised annuity which he pretended was drawn from investments. He was tireless in his efforts to straighten out the life of lovable, blundering, gifted Sheridan: took young people who were unhappy at home under his protection and tactfully appealed to their parents: bullied his friends into letting him direct their household and garden management: pressed the claims of deserving curates, and even women writers: corresponded with Gay, Pope, Bolingbroke and other old friends until death snatched them away from him and he regretted that he ever had a friend since losing them was such pain.

But despite all this activity, one is conscious of Swift living out his life, as Vanessa had lived out hers for him. At least once, if only for a fleeting second, he must have remembered that telling phrase of hers—"to live a life like a languishing death" (a simile I believe she learnt from him)[2]—for it was his turn to experience loneliness, despair, and a sense of the utter futility of life. He was killing time in the most bitter,

[1]Williams, p. 145.
[2]Swift used it nine years earlier in the *Journal*. See Williams: p. 442.

the most ironic fashion, for he who had always advocated
seizing the moments as they fly no longer wished to use them.
Like a "prisoner for life" trying "to relieve himself of the
intolerable burden of solitary confinement"[1] by scratching
words on stony walls, he wasted his powerful intellect, which
hitherto had thrown off his excess of febrile energy in puns
with the Viceroys or nonsense rhymes for Stella, upon
trifling ingenuities, whole manuscript books of which are still
in existence. His mind was, as Sir Leslie Stephen wisely
says, "preying on itself." The conjured spirit, like a devilish
jinn bottled inside him, who would never leave him in peace
until soul parted from body, still worked against him.

Stella had been his protection against this familiar; and so
in their pathetic transitory way had Betty Jones, the girl in
Leicester, and Varina; so had the great court ladies, the
King's mistresses, the Queen's favourites, with whom he
corresponded, and his "white witch," Vanessa. The mysterious and oracular quality of their women's minds had
intervened between him and the evil spirit, lessening its power.
Talking to Stella, even on paper, had relieved him so profoundly—("I have got a foolish trick, I must say something
to MD when I wake . . . fresh and fasting,"[2] and in the evening,
"Let us sit up a little longer, and talk. No, 'tis a lie, I an't
sleepy yet.")[3] Her conversation had been the very elixir of
life to him. The intellectual harmony which existed between
them had, in spite of his stern determination to value her only
for her more masculine qualities of mind, charmed him with a
magic more subtle than he had known. It had been a "conspiracy of alien essences, and a kissing, as it were, in the
dark,"[4] for the passion which he dare not express with his
body was therein distilled and exhaled.

And now to this strange being, several beings paradoxically
compounded in one, came the most terrible of all fates, to go
mad and to know that he was going mad.[5] The merciless

[1]Sir Leslie Stephen, p. 198.
[2]Williams, p. 47.
[3]Ibid, p. 112.
[4]Santayana: *Little Essays.*
[5]Although in 1742 a Commission was appointed to inquire into

goddess who seemed to preside over his life so much more faithfully and minutely than the Christian God whom he elected to serve—(perhaps to constrain his instinctive atheism)—decreed that he should finally resemble his own creations, the Struldbrugs. His memory was gone, and his reason: paroxysms of rage sometimes shook him like the storms breaking over *Lear*, or over some old defiant royal oak which will not crack though nothing but the shell remains. So great were the strengths which bound him, so long, so hard, so painful the disintegration, that thinking of him at the end is, as Thackeray says, "like thinking of an empire falling."

Yet before he sank into the torpor of final imbecility some pale reflection of reason returned sufficient for him to study and comment on his image in a pier-glass, to which he muttered piteously "Poor old man," over and over again. At another time he was heard to say as if talking to himself, "I am what I am: I am what I am."[1]

In the same way a more tender poet of the next century, John Clare, broken with madness, strove in lucid intervals to record his existence and identity:

> "... *I was a being created in the race*
> *Of men, disdaining bounds of place and time,*
> *A spirit that could travel o'er the space*
> *Of earth and heaven, like a thought sublime*
> *Tracing creation, like my Maker, free!*
> *A soul unshackled, like eternity!*
> *Spurning earth's vain and soul debasing thrall:*
> *But now I only know I am. That's all."*

But for Swift these simple words were the ultimate pellet of undigestible matter, spewed forth as the tiercel rejects the

the lunacy of Swift, medical opinion now holds that he was not insane in the modern meaning of the word. His mental state was in no way the result of progressive mental disease, but of senility, and a lesion of the brain, "weakened by senile decay." See the studies of Wilde, Menière, Bucknill; and the French specialists given in Rossi and Hone, p. 392.

[1] Delany, quoted by Sheridan, p. 406.

hard, round morsels from which he has extracted all nourishment.

He could go no further. He had fought like Pilgrim in the Valley of Humiliation. His whole life had been nothing but a battle, not only for others—for Ireland, for his friends, for the downtrodden and dejected, the defenceless, the enslaved— but for an affirming and accepting of himself, for the peace within which never came. How could such a nature know peace —succouring, seeking to protect, daring to love on the one hand; fearing, fleeing, despising and castigating mankind with all the volcanic fury of a madman on the other? But soon, justification to the world, to oneself, to one's Maker, would no longer be necessary. 'I am what I am.' These words, together with his epitaph, were the final statement, the final plea.

HIC DEPOSITUM EST CORPUS
IONATHAN SWIFT, S.T.D.
HUIUS ECCLESIAE CATHEDRALIS
DECANI,
UBI SAEVA INDIGNATIO ULTERIUS
COR LACERARE NEQUIT.
ABI, VIATOR,
ET IMITARE, SI POTERIS,
STRENUUM PRO VIRILI
LIBERTATIS VINDICATOREM.
OBIIT 19 DIE MENSIS OCTOBRIS
A.D. 1745.   ANNO AETATIS 78

The Epitaph on Swift's Tomb
in St. Patrick's Cathedral,
Dublin.
Written by Himself.

NOTE ON THE ANCESTRY OF DEAN SWIFT

After writing *The Conjured Spirit* I received a letter from Mr. William Welply of Greenisland, Co. Antrim, in which he made the following statements:

"1.   Godwin Swift's first wife, Elizabeth Wheeler, was dead before he became Attorney General for the Palatinate County of Tipperary in 1662. She is said to have been a relative of Elizabeth Preston, 1st Duchess of Ormonde, but although I believe this to have some foundation no one has offered any proof of it.

2.   Jonathan, father of the Dean, had gone over to Ireland by 1658, if we can believe his own statement.

3.   The celebrated historian of Leicestershire, John Nichols, did not believe in the Wiston (sic) Magna theory of Abigail Erick's humble origins.

4.   The Marriage Licence between Jonathan Swift, the father, and Abigail Erick was issued by the Prerogative Court of Dublin in 1664 or 1665. This Jonathan was baptized at Goodrich church in Herefordshire on the 24th of May, 1640.

5.   There is no proof that Swift's forbears came from Yorkshire. They came from Kent where the Swifts had been since about the year 1300, the name of Swift being found in twenty-five English counties. Nor was Philpot a Yorkshire gentleman. He was also of a Kentish family."

I would point out that I was quoting from what Swift himself wrote about his ancestry in the fragment of autobiography included in *The Prose Works of Jonathan Swift*, edited by Temple Scott, Vol. XI, Bell & Sons, London, 1913.

BIBLIOGRAPHY

SWIFT'S PROSE, LETTERS AND VERSE

The Prose Works of Jonathan Swift,
Edited by Temple Scott. 12 Vols. G. Bell and Sons, Ltd.,
London, 1913.

The Poems of Jonathan Swift,
Edited by Harold Williams. 3 Vols. Clarendon Press,
Oxford, 1937.

The Correspondence of Jonathan Swift, D.D.,
Edited by F. Elrington Ball. 6 Vols. G. Bell and Sons,
Ltd., London, 1914.

Letters of Jonathan Swift to Charles Ford,
Edited by Dr. David Nichol Smith. Clarendon Press,
Oxford, 1934.

Vanessa and her Correspondence with Jonathan Swift,
Edited by A. Martin Freeman. Selwyn and Blount,
London, 1921.

Swift (Gulliver's Travels and Selected Writings in Prose
and Verse),
Edited by John Hayward. Nonesuch Press, London, 1934.

Gulliver's Travels, Introduction by Harold Williams, Everyman Edition. J. M. Dent and Sons, Ltd., London, 1941.

Journal to Stella,
Edited by Harold Williams. Clarendon Press, Oxford,
1948.

18TH CENTURY BOOKS ON SWIFT, BY THOSE ACQUAINTED WITH
HIM OR HIS CIRCLE

Memoirs of Mrs. Laetitia Pilkington (1748),
Edited by J. Isaacs. George Routledge and Sons, London,
1928.

Remarks on the Life and Writings of Dr. Jonathan Swift,
John, Earl of Orrery. London, 1751.

Observations upon Lord Orrery's Remarks,
Dr. Delany. London, 1754.

Essay upon the Life, Writings and Character of Dr. Swift,
Deane Swift, 1755.

Life of the Rev. Dr. Jonathan Swift,
Thomas Sheridan. 2nd edition, London, 1787.

Enquiry into the Life of Dean Swift,
Monck Berkeley, London, 1789.
Swift, in *Lives of the Poets,*
Samuel Johnson, Vol. III. London, 1779.

19TH CENTURY BOOKS ON SWIFT

Life of Swift, Vol. I, *Works of Jonathan Swift,*
Sir Walter Scott, 19 Vols. 2nd Edition. Bickers and
Son, London, 1883.
Swiftiana,
C. H. Wilson. 2 Vols., London, 1804.
Essay on the Earlier Part of the Life of Swift,
Dr. John Barrett, London, 1808.
History and Antiquities of the Collegiate Church of St. Patrick,
W. Monck Mason, 1820.
The Closing Years of Dean Swift's Life,
Sir W. R. Wilde, F.R.C.S., Dublin, 1849.
Life of Jonathan Swift (unfinished),
John Forster, 1875.
Life of Jonathan Swift,
Sir Henry Craik, 1882.
Jonathan Swift, a Biographical and Critical Study,
John Churton Collins, Chatto and Windus, London, 1893.
Swift, (in The English Men of Letters series)
Sir Leslie Stephen. Macmillan and Company, London,
1889.
Swift, in *The English Humourists of the 18th Century,*
William Makepeace Thackeray. Smith Elder and Com-
pany, London, 1874. (2nd Edition.)
Swift, in *The History of English Literature,*
H. A. Taine, Translated by H. Van Laun. Chatto and
Windus, London, 1890.
Recollections of The Table Talk of Samuel Rogers,
Edited by A. Dyce, 1856.

BOOKS ON SWIFT IN THE 20TH CENTURY

Swift and Defoe,
J. F. Ross, University of California Press, 1941.
The Mind and Art of Swift,
R. Quintana, Oxford, 1936.

Dean Swift's Library,
Harold Williams. Cambridge University Press, 1932.
Swift's Verse,
F. Elrington Ball. John Murray, London, 1929.
The Skull of Swift,
Sir Shane Leslie. Chatto and Windus, London, 1928.
The Script of Jonathan Swift, and other Essays,
Sir Shane Leslie. Oxford University Press, 1935.
Swift, or The Egoist,
Mario Rossi and Joseph Hone. Victor Gollancz, London, 1934.
Swift,
Carl Van Doren. Martin Secker, London, 1931.
Swift, in *A Short History of Modern English Literature.*
Sir Edmund Gosse. William Heinemann, London, 1923.
Swift. Les Années de Jeunesse et Le "Conte du Tonneau,"
Émile Pons, Vol. I. Oxford University Press, 1925.

ESSAYS ON SWIFT IN THE 20TH CENTURY

Stella, Vanessa and Swift,
Lady Gregory. 19th Century and After, June, 1933. Vol. CXIII.
Swift, Stella and Vanessa,
Margaret Woods, 19th Century and After, July-December, 1913. Vol. LXXIV.
The Alleged Marriage of Swift and Stella,
Stanley Lane-Poole. Fortnightly Review, LXXXVII, 1910.
New Light on the Evidence of Swift's Marriage,
Marguerite Hearsey. Modern Language Society of America, Vol. XLII, 1927.
The Irony of Swift,
F. R. Leavis, Scrutiny, Vol. II. March, 1934.
Dean Swift in Dublin,
J. H. Bernard. Blackwoods Magazine, November, 1908.
The Deaneries of St. Patrick's,
The Very Rev. H. J. Lawlor. Journal of the Royal Society of Antiquaries of Ireland, 1932. LXII.
Jonathan Swift,
C. Whibley. Leslie Stephen Lecture, 1917.

Jonathan Swift, in *From Anne to Victoria*,
    John Hayward, London, 1937.
Swift, in *Do What You will*,
    Aldous Huxley. Chatto and Windus, London, 1929.
Essay on the Character of Swift,
    Mario Rossi. Life and Letters, VIII, March-December,
    1932.
Mrs. Dingley, The Spirit of Place and other Essays,
    Alice Meynell. John Lane, London, 1899.
The Little Language, Essays,
    Alice Meynell. Burns and Oates, London, 1914.
Swift and Thomas Brown,
    W. A. Eddy, Modern Philology, XXVIII (1931), pp.
    163-8: Studies in Philology, XXIX (1932), pp. 29-40.
The Mysterious Origin of Dean Swift,
    Denis Johnston, Dublin Historical Record, Vol. III, No. 4.

BOOKS ON 18TH CENTURY IRELAND AND ENGLAND

Dublin, Historical and Topographical Account,
    S. A. Ossory Fitzpatrick, London, 1907.
History of the City of Dublin,
    F. Elrington Ball, 4 Vols. Dublin, 1902-6.
History of the City of Dublin,
    Sir J. T. Gilbert, 3 Vols. Dublin, 1854-9.
Country and Town in Ireland under the Georges,
    Constantia Maxwell, Harrap & Co., Ltd., London, 1940.
Dublin under the Georges, 1714-1830.
    Constantia Maxwell, Harrap & Co., Ltd., London, 1936.
Irish Life in the 17th Century, After Cromwell,
    Edward MacLysaght, London, 1939.
Dublin Old and New,
    Stephen Gwynn, London, 1938.
Ireland in the Days of Swift,
    J. B. Daly, London, 1887.
*History of the University of Dublin, to the End of the 18th
    Century*,
    J. W. Stubbs, Dublin, 1889.
An Epoch in Irish History, Trinity College, Dublin, 1591-1600,
    Dr. J. P. Mahaffy, Dublin, 1903.
The Diary of Mrs. Evans-Freke, 1641-1714,
    Edited by Edward Carbery, Cork, 1913.

The English Child in the 18th *Century,*
   Rosamond Bayne-Powell, London, 1939.
History of English Thought in the 18th *Century,*
   Sir Leslie Stephen, London, 1876.
Dr. Johnson's England,
   2 Vols. Edited by A. S. Turberville, Oxford, 1933.
Memoirs of Susan Sibbald, 1783-1812,
   Edited by Francis Paget Hett, London, 1926.

EDUCATION OF WOMEN

The Education of Women (in The Essay upon Projects),
   Daniel Defoe, London, 1697.
*A Serious Proposal to the Ladies for the Advancement of their
   True and Great Interest,*
   Mary Astell, London, 1694.
Advice to a Daughter (1700),
   George Savile, Marquis of Halifax. Edited by Sir
   Walter Raleigh, Oxford, 1912.
Education of Girls and Women in Great Britain,
   Christina Bremner, London, 1897.
Women in English Life (2 Vols.),
   Georgiana Hill, London, 1896.

THE TEMPLES.

The Works of Sir William Temple
   London, 1770.
Early Essays and Romances of Sir William Temple,
   Edited by G. C. Moore Smith, Clarendon Press, Oxford,
   1930.
Martha, Lady Giffard, Life and Letters,
   Julia Longe, George Allen, London, 1911.
The Letters of Dorothy Osborne to Sir William Temple,
   Edited by E. A. Parry, London, 1888.
Dorothy Osborne's 'Letters:' and *Swift's 'Journal to Stella,'*
   Virginia Woolf, in The Common Reader, 2nd Series,
   The Hogarth Press, London, 1935.

INDEX

H

Hague, The, 34, 35, 39
Halifax, 1st Marquess of, 46
——, Earl of, 86, 89
Hamlet, 180, 233
Handel, George Frederick, 203
Hanoverian succession, 159, 205
Hardy, Thomas, 245
Harley, Robert, 1st Earl of Oxford, xii, 110, 111, 120, 122, 124, 126, 143, 145, 150, 155, 156, 159–63, 164–5–6, 167
Harrison, William, 115, 154
Héloise, 193, 197
Herbert, George, 81
Hereford, Bishopric of, 248
Herefordshire, 9, 161
Herrick, Robert, 12, 61
Hill, General, 146
Historiographer Royal, the, 121
Hobbes, Thomas, 247–9
Hogarth, William, xi.
Holland, 34, 70, 123–4, 133, 143
Holyhead, 148–9, 230 et seq.
Hosea, 117
Hounslow Heath, 251
Houses of Lords and Commons: see Parliament
Howard, Mrs., 220
Huntingdon, William, 2

I

Ireland, xi, 1, 9, 11, 13, 15, 20, 24, 31, 34, 39, 40, 43, 51, 55, 63–4–5, 74, 79, 81, 85, 87, 89, 90, 91–2, 110, 114, 117, 141, 158, 161–2, 167, 205, 207–12, 220
Isham, Sir Justinian, 38

J

Jamaica, 176
James II, 24, 122
Jervas, Charles, xi, xii
Jews, the, 70, 84
Job, Book of, 246
Johnson, Hester, or Esther, xi, xii, 2, 3 4, 5, 15, 26, 30, 31, 43 et seq., 57, 61 et seq., 63, 64, 84, 85, 90 et seq. 110–1, 114, 115, 120, 121, 122, 127, 128, 129, 139, 140, 142, 144–5, 147–8–9, 152, 153, 156, 158, 162, 166, 172, 183 et seq., 205–6, 213 et seq., 217 et seq., 220 et seq., 233–4, 241, 252

alleged marriage to Swift, 173–83, 201–2
her will, 174; her death, 232
——, Mrs. (Stella's mother), 31, 44, 92–3, 104–5–6
——, Mr. (Stella's father), 44, 133
—— Dr. Samuel, 21, 33, 116
Johnston, Rev. John, 81
Jones, Betty, 26, 29, 252

K

Kells, 80
Kendall, Duchess of, 207
Kensington, 127, 196
—— Palace, 49
Kildare, Bishop of, 88
Kilkenny, 13, 15, 17, 18, 19, 31
Killaloe, Bishop of, 122
Kilroot, 51, 52, 61, 65, 71, 83, 88
King, Archbishop, 118, 125, 127, 133, 164, 166
King's Inns, see Dublin
King's Lynn, 130

L

Lamb, Charles, 33
Lapland, 209
Laracor, 2, 36, 69, 75, 79, 80 et seq., 89, 91, 121, 162, 166
Lawson, Capt., 230–1
Lear, King, 1, 54, 253
Leeper, Dr. R. R., xi
Leicester Fields, 127
Leicestershire, 11, 13, 25, 26, 31, 32, 42 65, 80, 238–9, 252
Lely, Sir Peter, xi
Lent, 130, 222
Lermontov, 238–9
Letcombe, see Upper Letcombe
Lewis, Erasmus, 143, 150, 151, 159
Liffey, the, 167, 191
Lilliput, 230
Linen Trade, the, 17
Linnaeus, 204
Lisbon, 23
Little Rider Street, 127, 153–4
Locke, John, 63
London, 1, 32, 34, 39, 42, 43, 62, 65, 83, 86, 87, 89, 103, 119, 122, 130, 142, 158, 159, 160–1–3–6, 192, 216, 222
Long, Anne, 130, 133, 134, 142
Lord Privy Seal, the, 143
Louis XIV, 34, 144
Lucian, 227